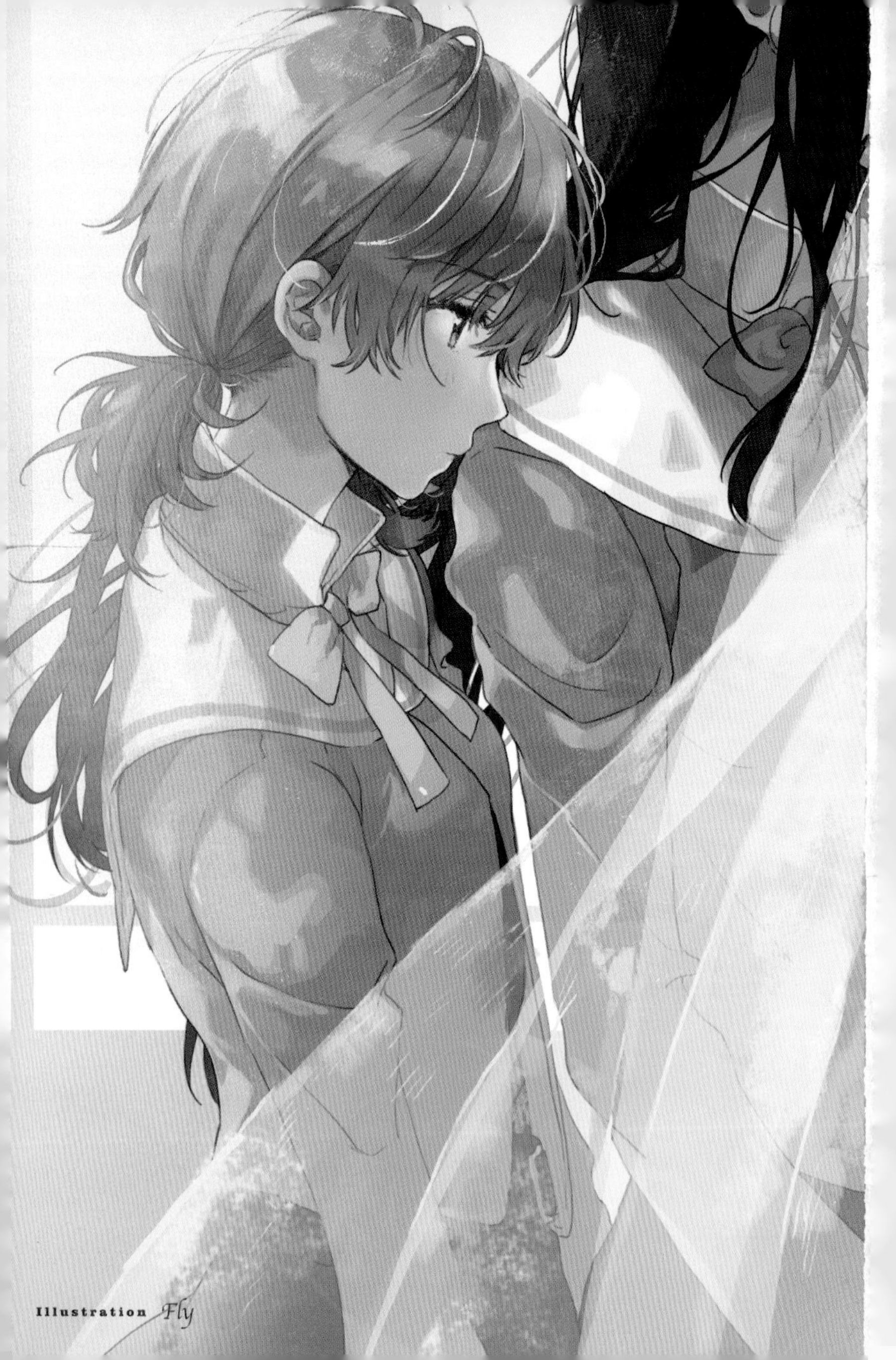

Illustration *Fly*

(**Table of contents**)

Illustration

Manga

Special Comments

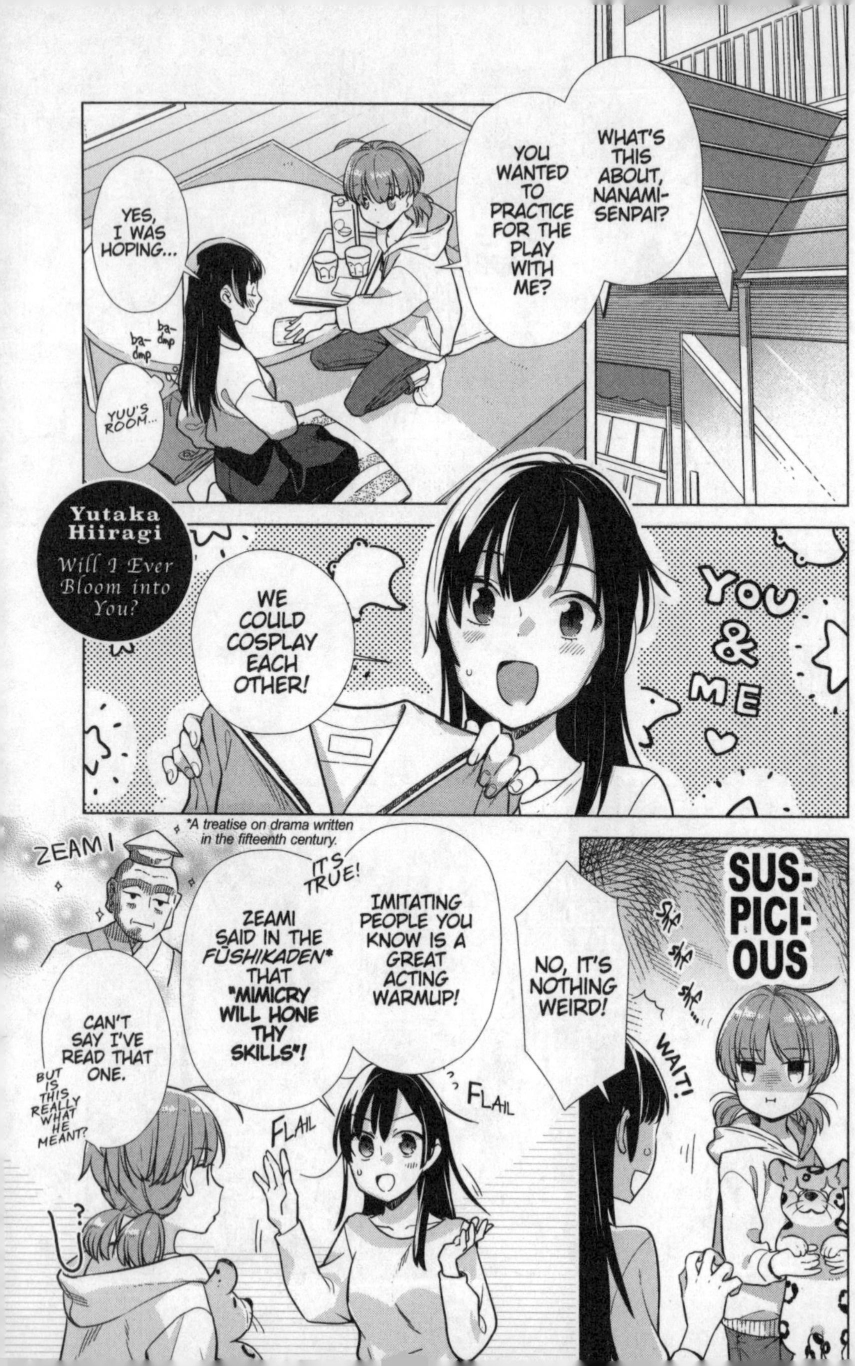
WHAT'S THIS ABOUT, NANAMI-SENPAI?
YOU WANTED TO PRACTICE FOR THE PLAY WITH ME?
YES, I WAS HOPING...
ba-dmp ba-dmp
YUU'S ROOM...
Yutaka Hiiragi
Will I Ever Bloom into You?
YOU & ME
WE COULD COSPLAY EACH OTHER!
SUS-PICI-OUS
shf shf shf...
WAIT!
NO, IT'S NOTHING WEIRD!
IT'S TRUE!
IMITATING PEOPLE YOU KNOW IS A GREAT ACTING WARMUP!
ZEAMI SAID IN THE FŪSHIKADEN* THAT "MIMICRY WILL HONE THY SKILLS"!
FLAIL
FLAIL
ZEAMI
CAN'T SAY I'VE READ THAT ONE.
BUT IS THIS REALLY WHAT HE MEANT?
?

*A treatise on drama written in the fifteenth century.

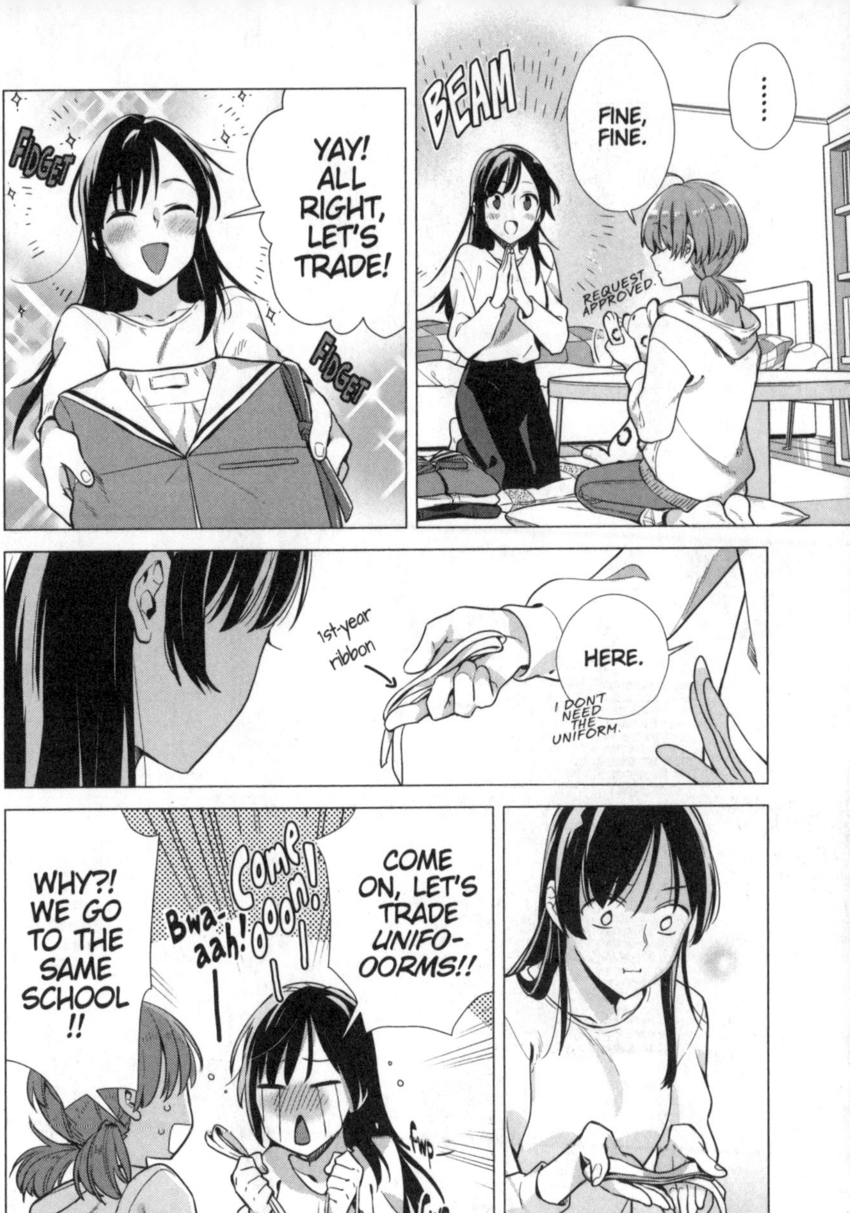
......
FINE, FINE.
BEAM
REQUEST APPROVED.
YAY! ALL RIGHT, LET'S TRADE!
FIDGET
FIDGET
HERE.
I DON'T NEED THE UNIFORM.
1st-year ribbon
COME ON, LET'S TRADE UNIFO-OORMS!!
Come ooon!
Bwa-aah!
WHY?! WE GO TO THE SAME SCHOOL !!
fwp
fwp

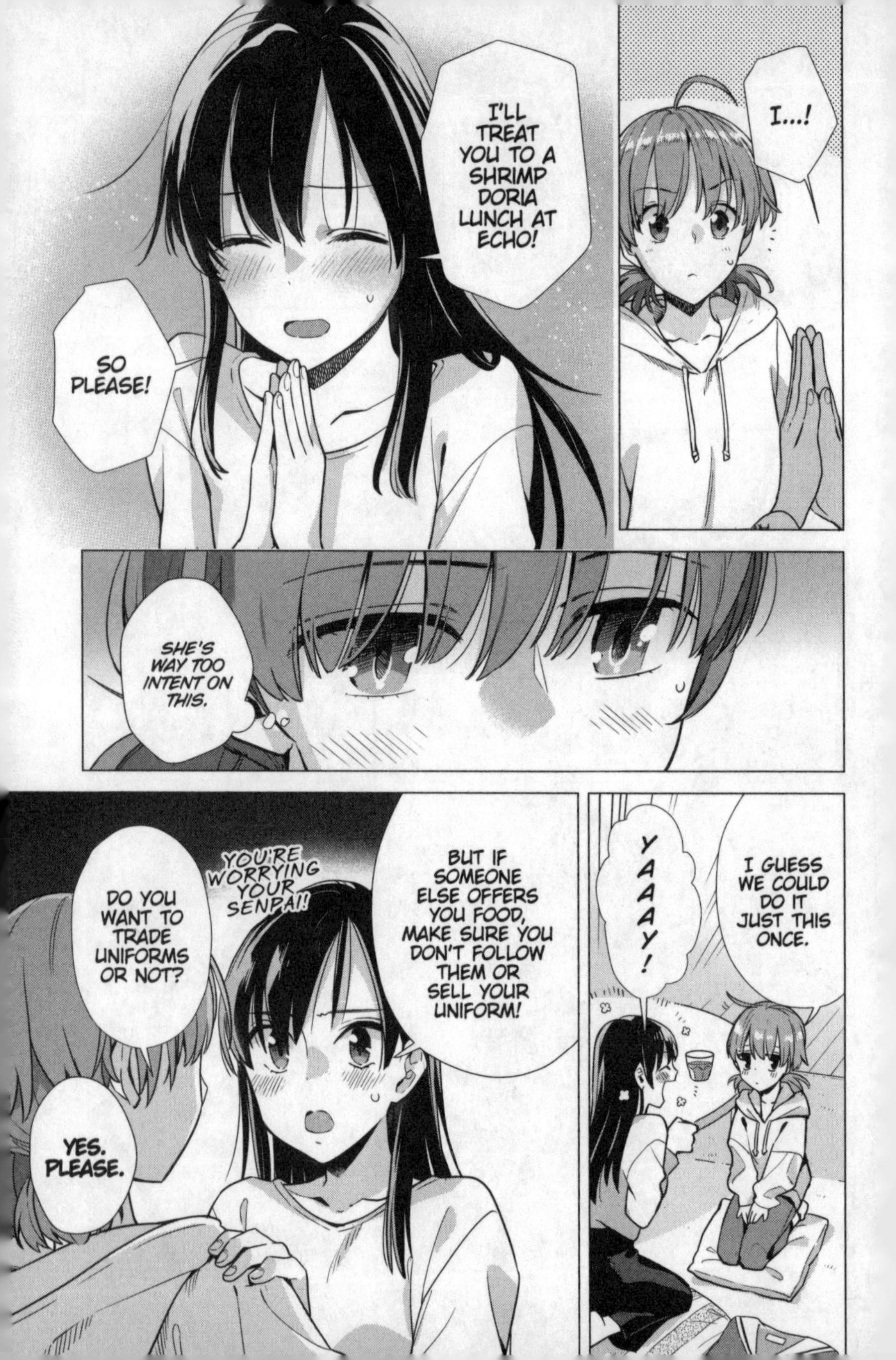
I...!
I'LL TREAT YOU TO A SHRIMP DORIA LUNCH AT ECHO!
SO PLEASE!
SHE'S WAY TOO INTENT ON THIS.
I GUESS WE COULD DO IT JUST THIS ONCE.
YAAAAY!
BUT IF SOMEONE ELSE OFFERS YOU FOOD, MAKE SURE YOU DON'T FOLLOW THEM OR SELL YOUR UNIFORM!
YOU'RE WORRYING YOUR SENPAI!
DO YOU WANT TO TRADE UNIFORMS OR NOT?
YES. PLEASE.

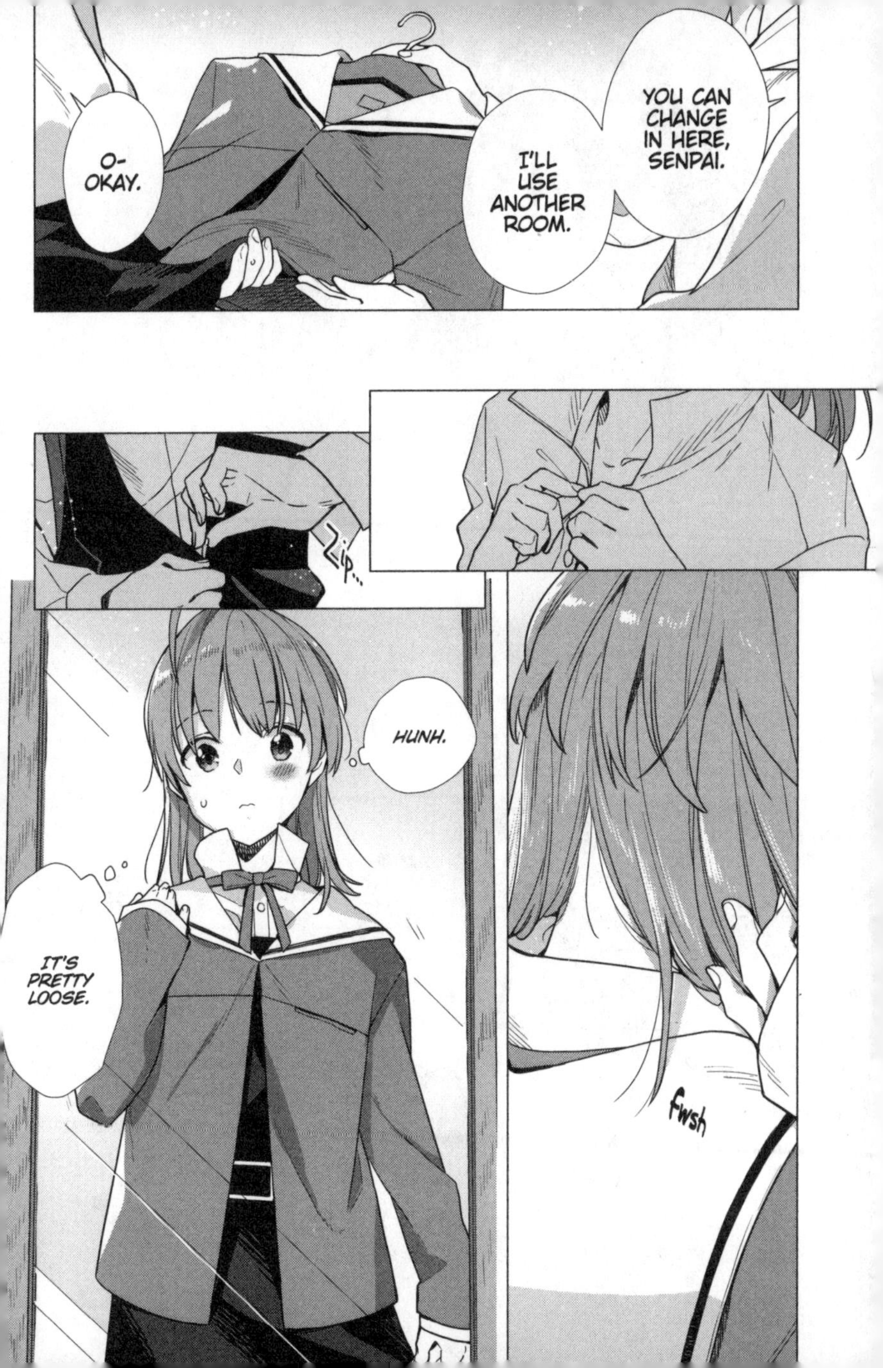
YOU CAN CHANGE IN HERE, SENPAI.
I'LL USE ANOTHER ROOM.
O-OKAY.
Zip...
fwsh
HUNH.
IT'S PRETTY LOOSE.

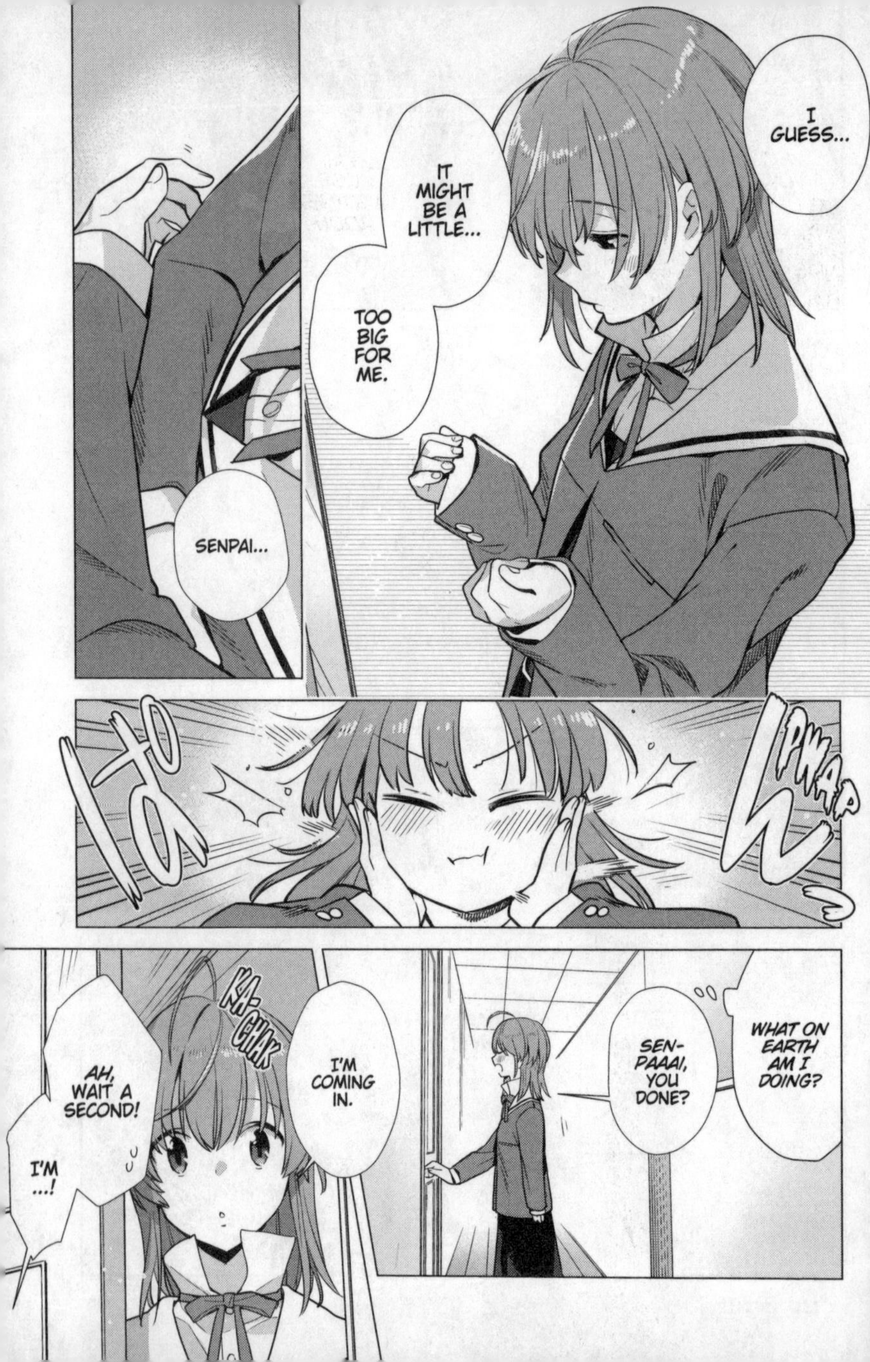
I GUESS...
IT MIGHT BE A LITTLE...
TOO BIG FOR ME.
SENPAI...
PWAP
WHAT ON EARTH AM I DOING?
SEN-PAAAI, YOU DONE?
I'M COMING IN.
KA-CHAK
AH, WAIT A SECOND!
I'M ...!

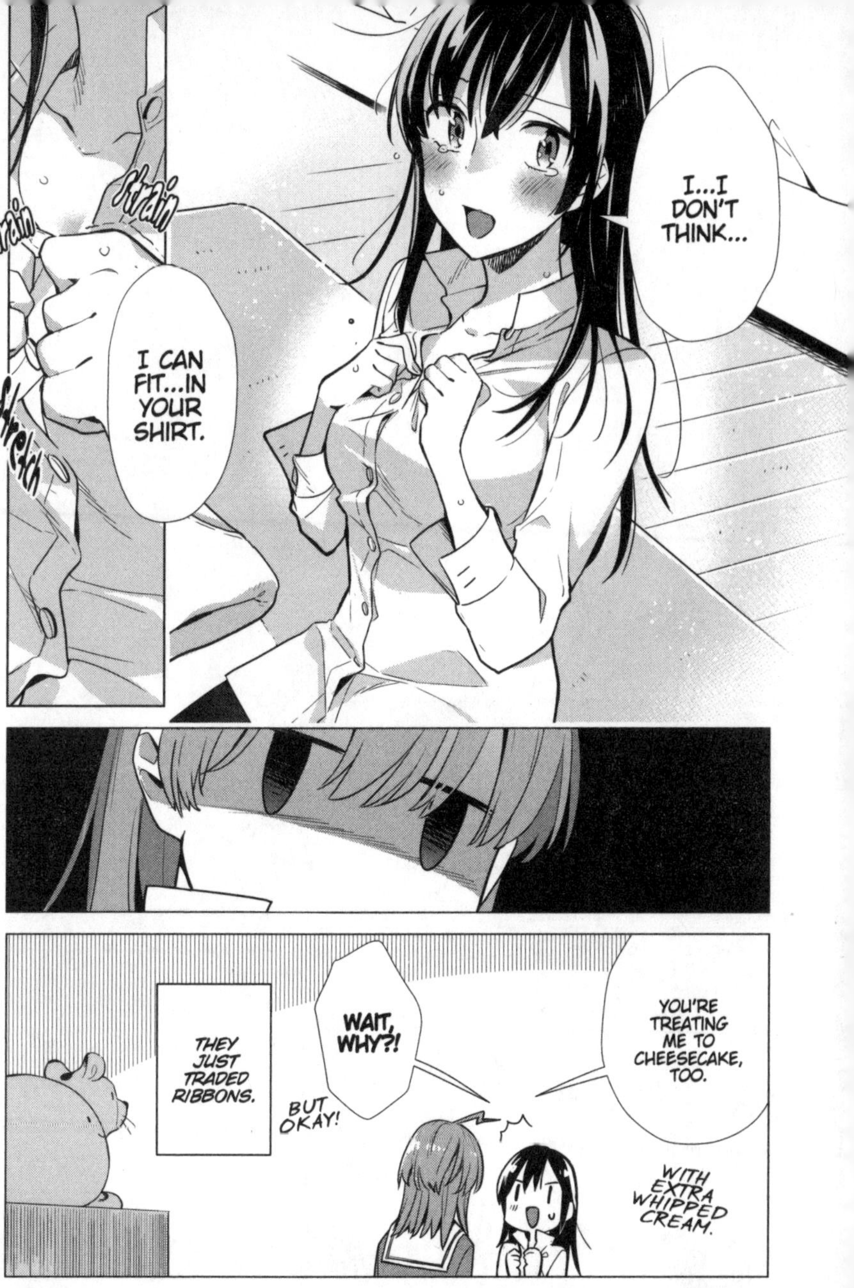
I...I DON'T THINK...
I CAN FIT...IN YOUR SHIRT.
strain
strain
stretch
YOU'RE TREATING ME TO CHEESECAKE, TOO.
WITH EXTRA WHIPPED CREAM.
WAIT, WHY?!
BUT OKAY!
THEY JUST TRADED RIBBONS.

The End

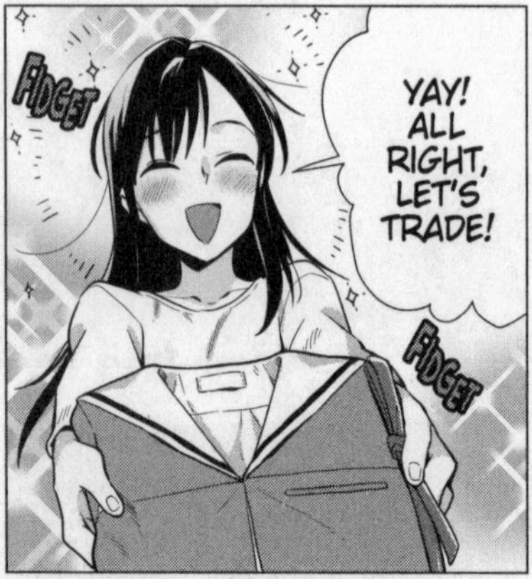
FIDGET
YAY! ALL RIGHT, LET'S TRADE!
FIDGET

Yutaka Hiiragi

Best known for *Shinmai Shimai no Futari Gohan (Let's Have a Meal Together)* (KADOKAWA).

(**Bloom Into You**)

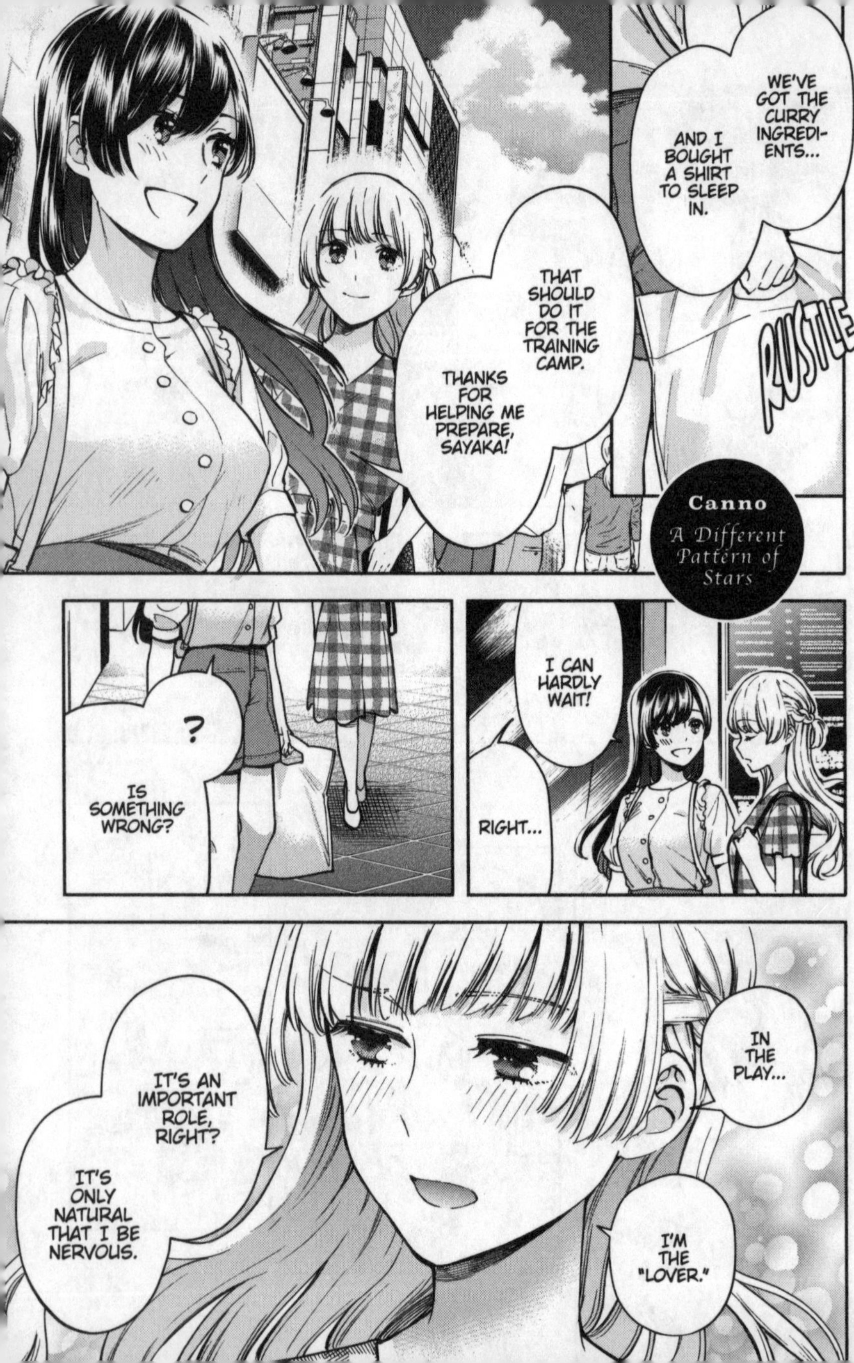
WE'VE GOT THE CURRY INGREDIENTS...
AND I BOUGHT A SHIRT TO SLEEP IN.
RUSTLE
Canno
A Different Pattern of Stars
THAT SHOULD DO IT FOR THE TRAINING CAMP.
THANKS FOR HELPING ME PREPARE, SAYAKA!
I CAN HARDLY WAIT!
RIGHT...
?
IS SOMETHING WRONG?
IN THE PLAY...
I'M THE "LOVER."
IT'S AN IMPORTANT ROLE, RIGHT?
IT'S ONLY NATURAL THAT I BE NERVOUS.

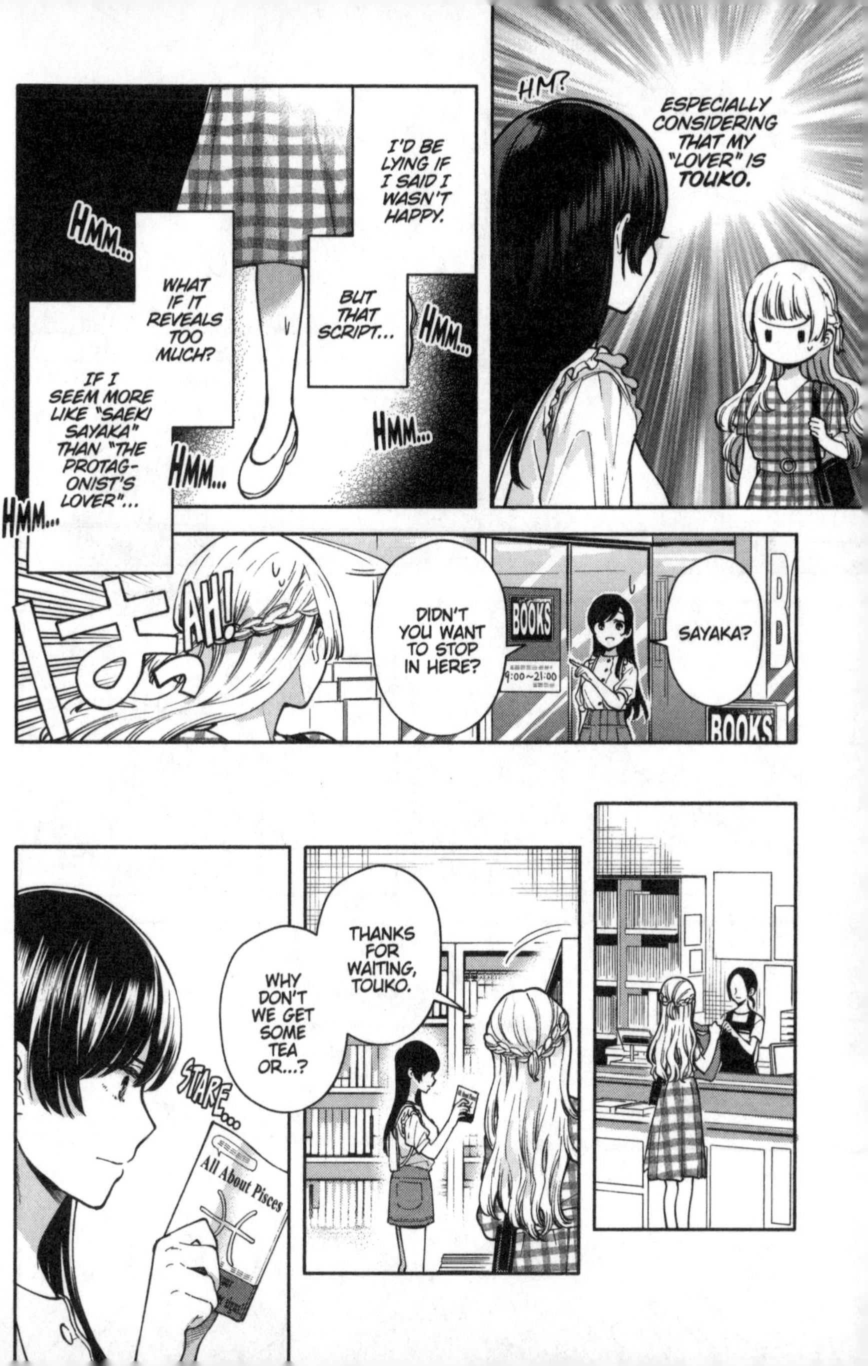
HM?
ESPECIALLY CONSIDERING THAT MY "LOVER" IS TOUKO.
I'D BE LYING IF I SAID I WASN'T HAPPY.
BUT THAT SCRIPT...
HMM...
HMM...
HMM...
WHAT IF IT REVEALS TOO MUCH?
IF I SEEM MORE LIKE "SAEKI SAYAKA" THAN "THE PROTAGONIST'S LOVER"...
HMM...
HMM...
SAYAKA?
BOOKS
BOOKS
9:00~21:00
DIDN'T YOU WANT TO STOP IN HERE?
AH!
THANKS FOR WAITING, TOUKO.
WHY DON'T WE GET SOME TEA OR...?
STARE...
All About Pisces

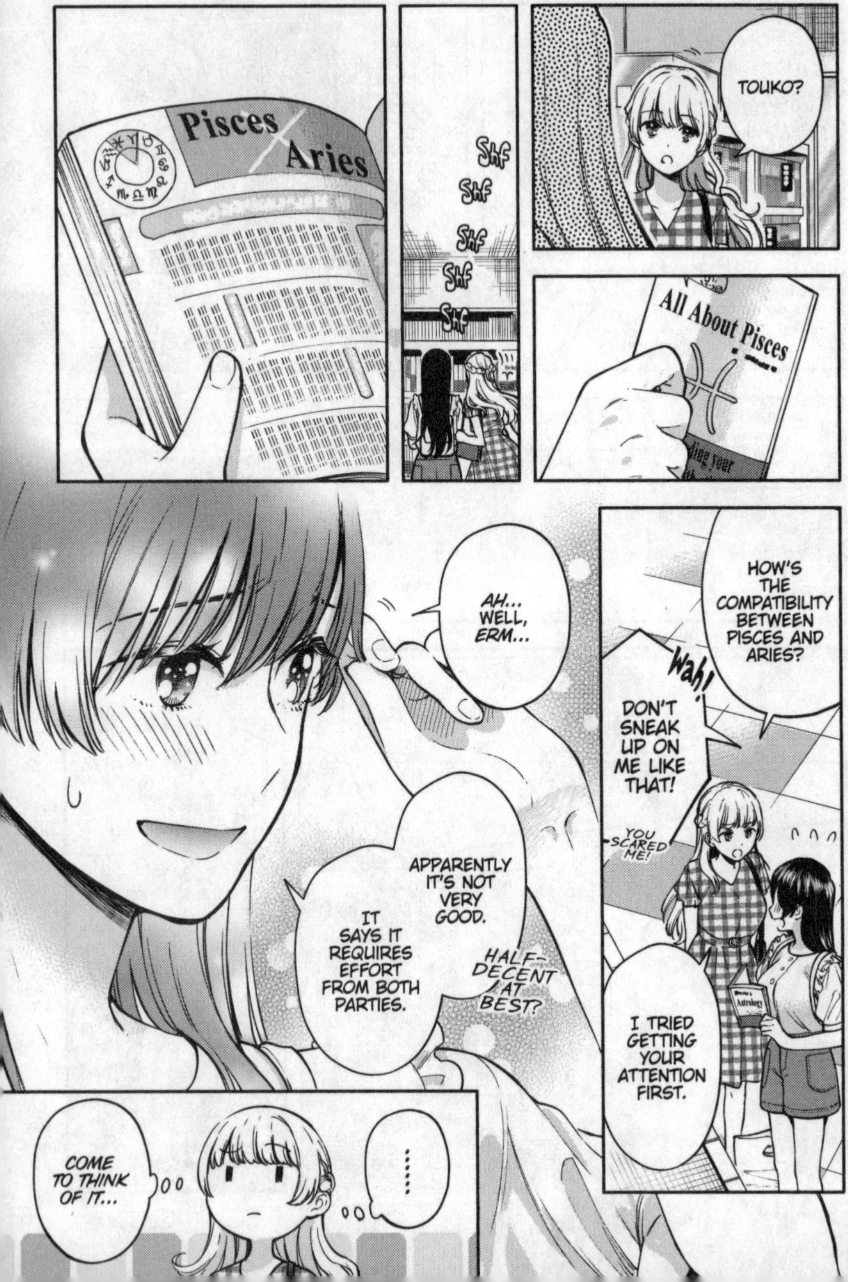
TOUKO?
All About Pisces
Shf
Shf
Shf
Shf
Shf
Pisces
Aries
HOW'S THE COMPATIBILITY BETWEEN PISCES AND ARIES?
Wah!
DON'T SNEAK UP ON ME LIKE THAT!
YOU SCARED ME!
I TRIED GETTING YOUR ATTENTION FIRST.
Astrology
AH... WELL, ERM...
APPARENTLY IT'S NOT VERY GOOD.
IT SAYS IT REQUIRES EFFORT FROM BOTH PARTIES.
HALF-DECENT AT BEST?
......
COME TO THINK OF IT...

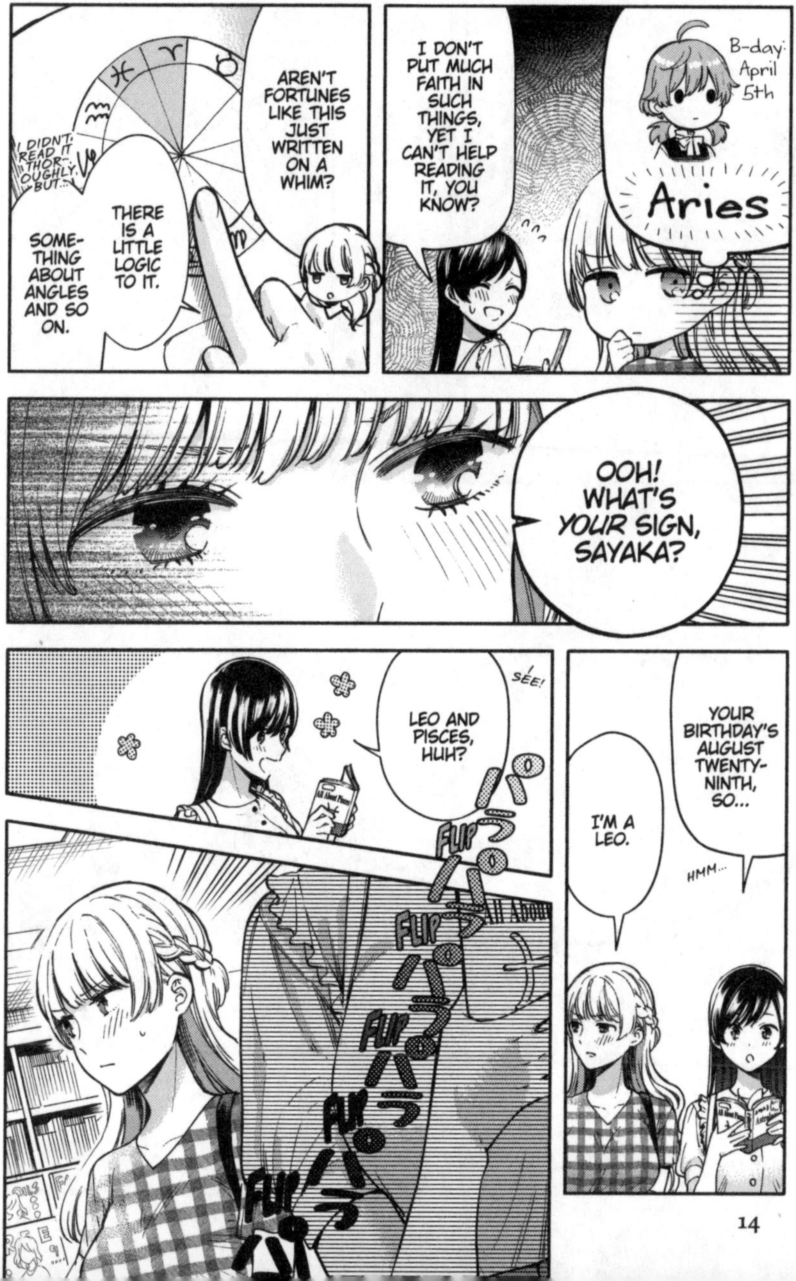
B-day: April 5th
Aries
I DON'T PUT MUCH FAITH IN SUCH THINGS, YET I CAN'T HELP READING IT, YOU KNOW?
AREN'T FORTUNES LIKE THIS JUST WRITTEN ON A WHIM?
I DIDN'T READ IT THOR-OUGHLY, BUT...
THERE IS A LITTLE LOGIC TO IT.
SOME-THING ABOUT ANGLES AND SO ON.
OOH! WHAT'S YOUR SIGN, SAYAKA?
YOUR BIRTHDAY'S AUGUST TWENTY-NINTH, SO...
HMM...
I'M A LEO.
I SEE!
LEO AND PISCES, HUH?
All About Pisces
パラ
FLIP
パラ
FLIP
パラ
FLIP
パラ
FLIP
パラ
FLIP
パラ

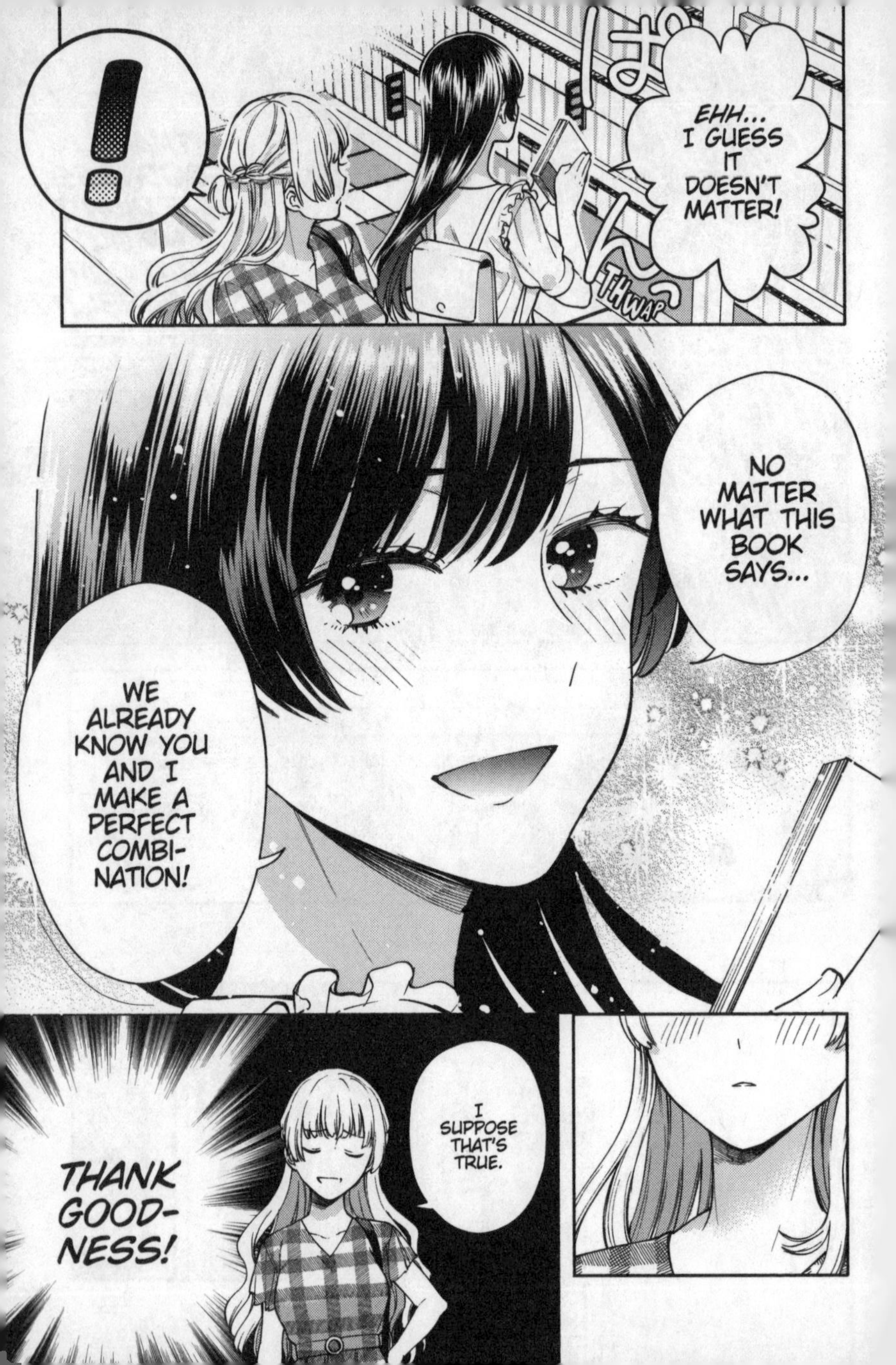
EHH... I GUESS IT DOESN'T MATTER!
THWAP
!
NO MATTER WHAT THIS BOOK SAYS...
WE ALREADY KNOW YOU AND I MAKE A PERFECT COMBI-NATION!
I SUPPOSE THAT'S TRUE.
THANK GOOD-NESS!

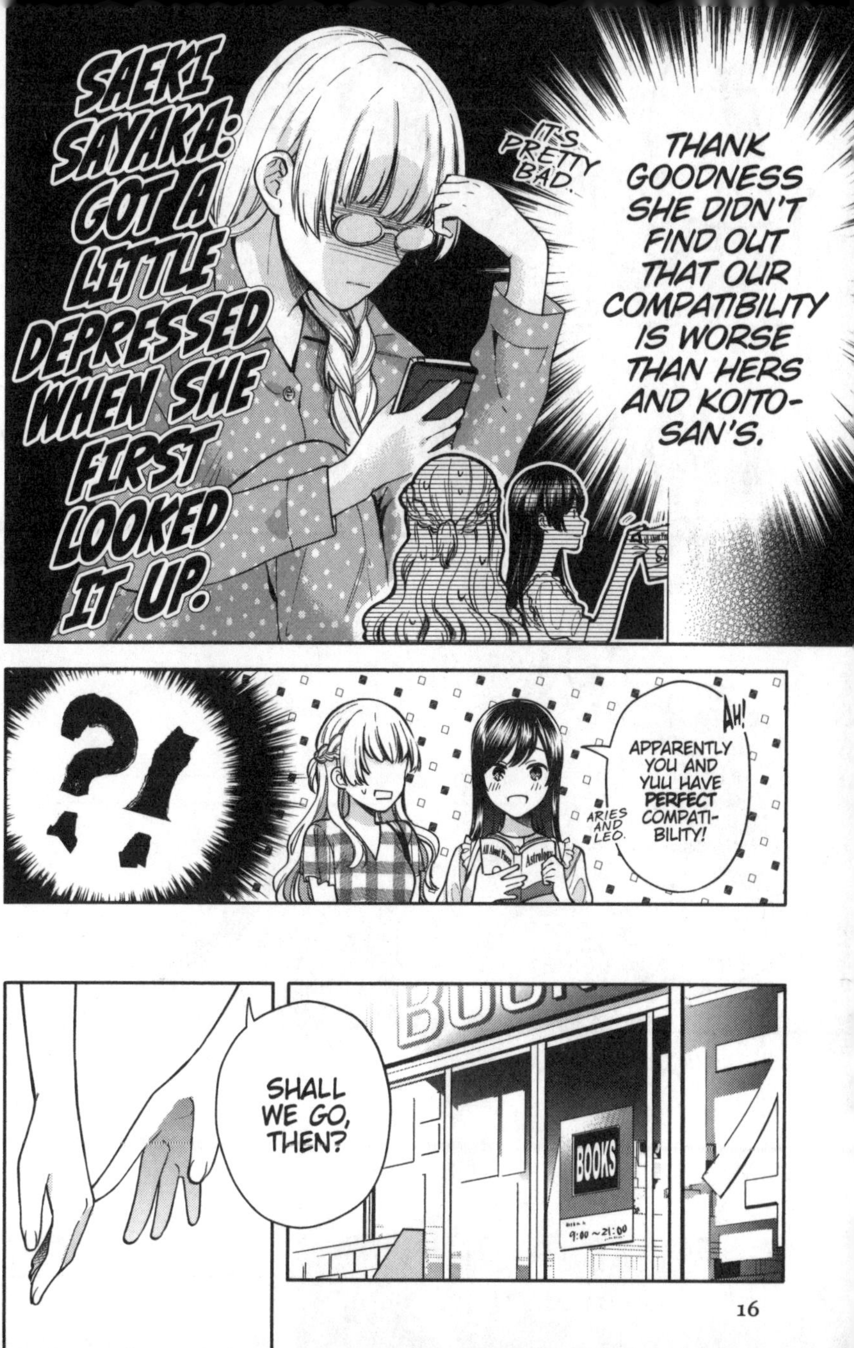
THANK GOODNESS SHE DIDN'T FIND OUT THAT OUR COMPATIBILITY IS WORSE THAN HERS AND KOITO-SAN'S.
IT'S PRETTY BAD.
SAEKI SAYAKA: GOT A LITTLE DEPRESSED WHEN SHE FIRST LOOKED IT UP.
AH!
APPARENTLY YOU AND YUU HAVE PERFECT COMPATIBILITY!
ARIES AND LEO.
?!
BOOKS
9:00~21:00
SHALL WE GO, THEN?

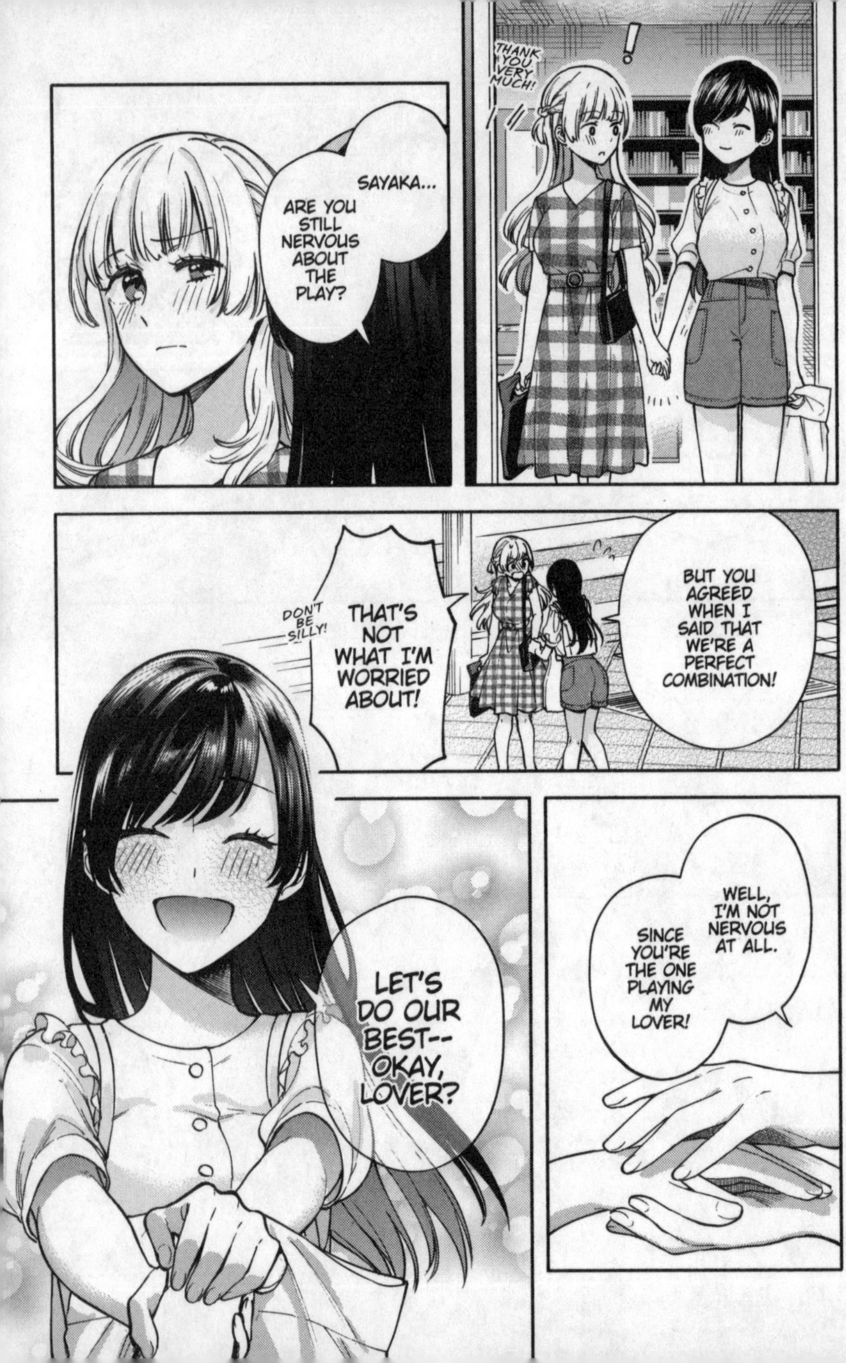
THANK YOU VERY MUCH!
!
SAYAKA...
ARE YOU STILL NERVOUS ABOUT THE PLAY?
BUT YOU AGREED WHEN I SAID THAT WE'RE A PERFECT COMBINATION!
DON'T BE SILLY!
THAT'S NOT WHAT I'M WORRIED ABOUT!
WELL, I'M NOT NERVOUS AT ALL.
SINCE YOU'RE THE ONE PLAYING MY LOVER!
LET'S DO OUR BEST--OKAY, LOVER?

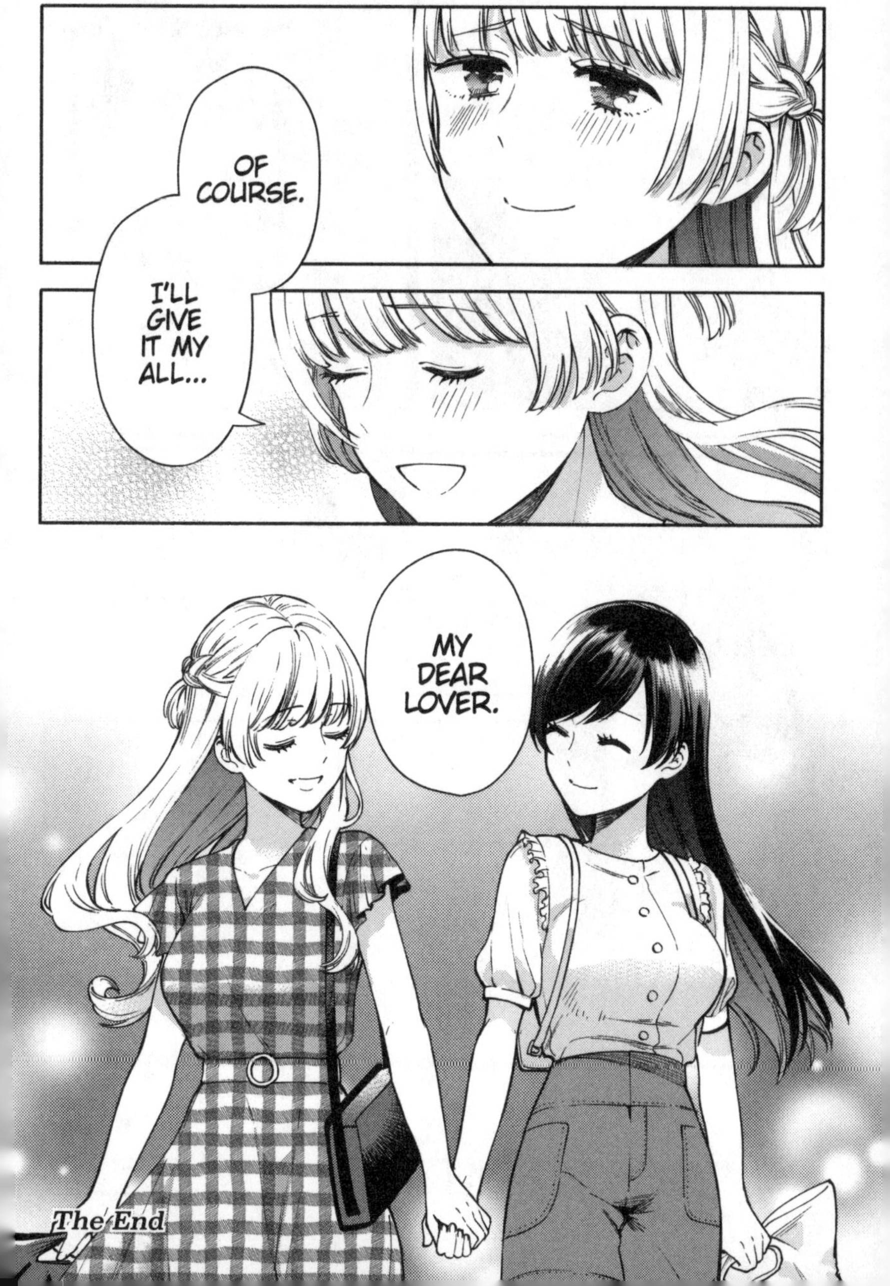
OF COURSE.
I'LL GIVE IT MY ALL...
MY DEAR LOVER.
The End

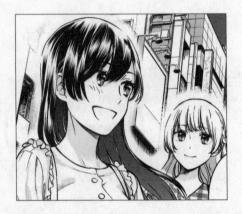

Canno

Best known for *Kiss and White Lily for My Dearest Girl* (KADOKAWA).

(**Bloom Into You**)

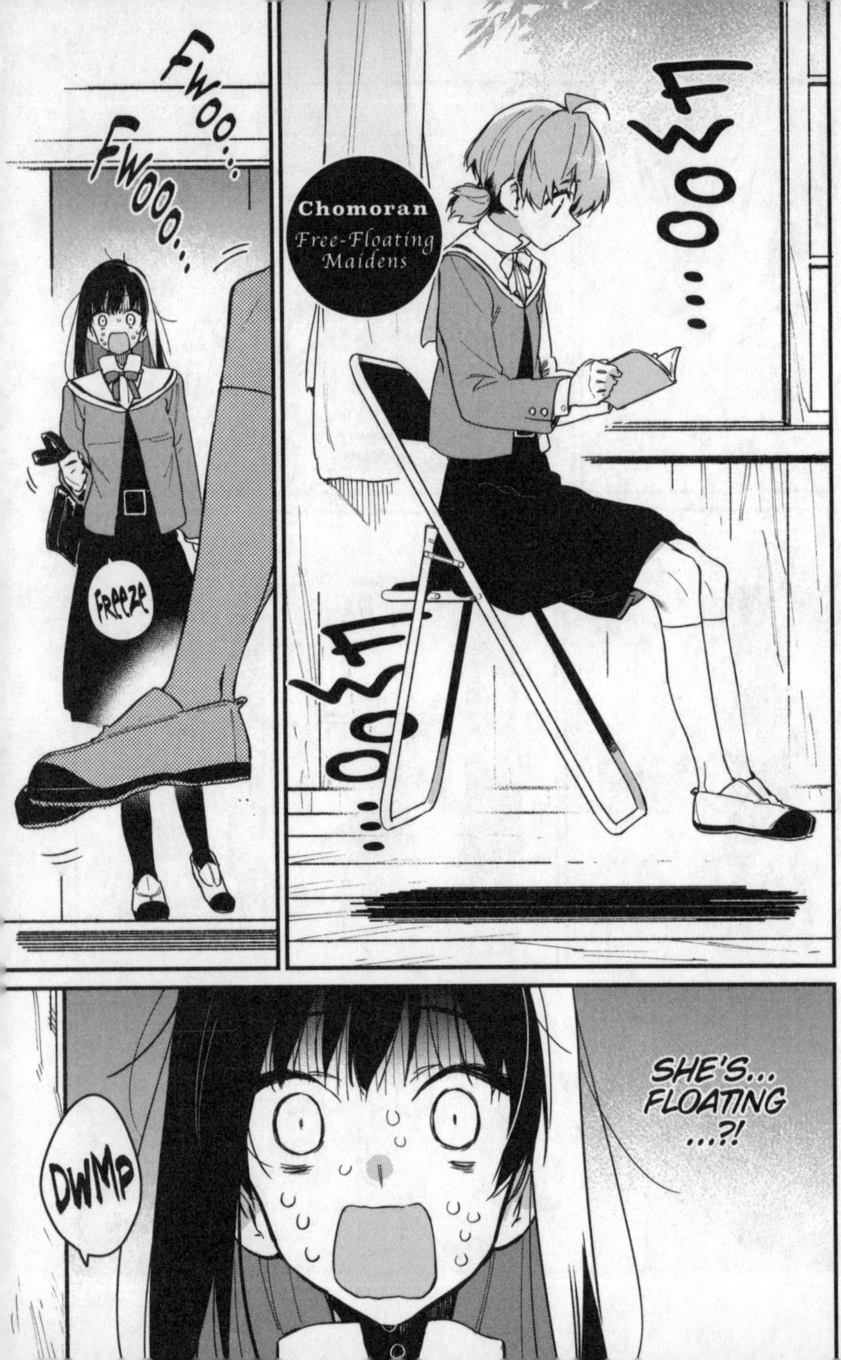
FWOO...
Chomoran
Free-Floating Maidens
FWOO...
FWOO...
FWOOO...
Freeze
SHE'S... FLOATING ...?!
DWMP

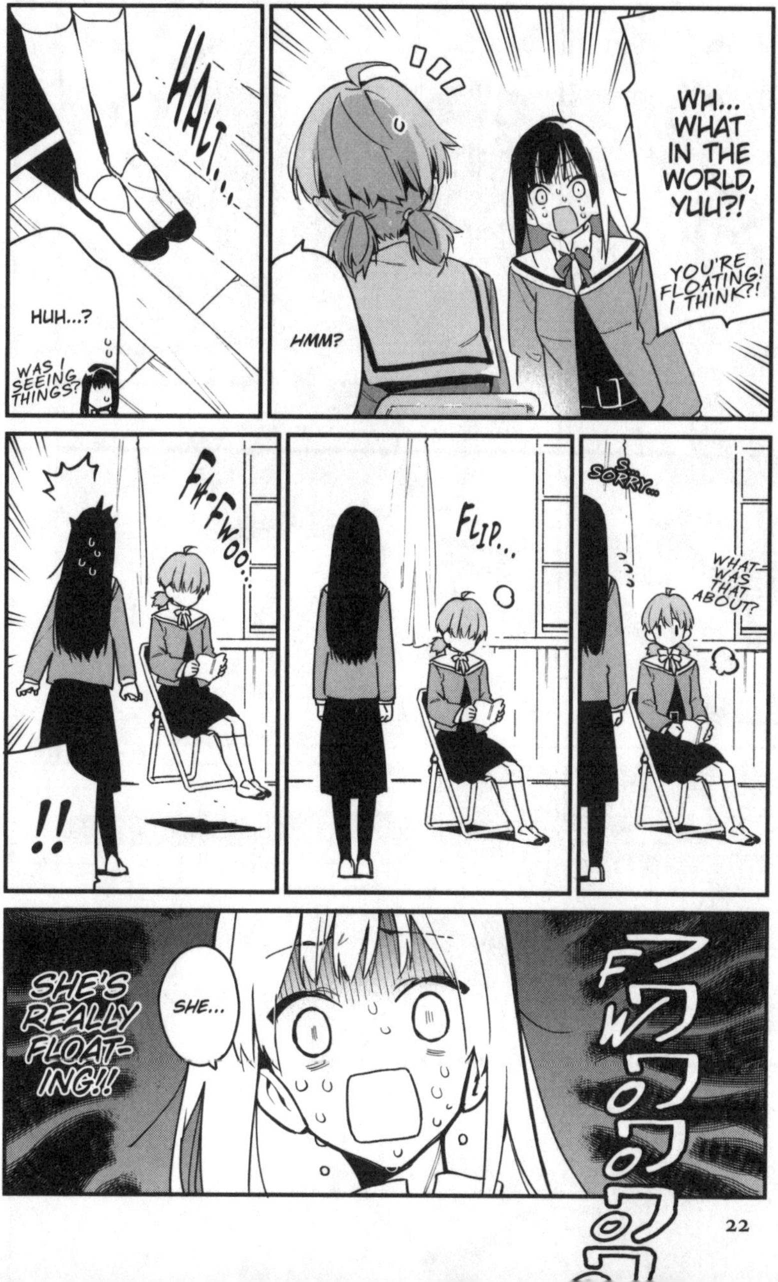
WH... WHAT IN THE WORLD, YUU?!
YOU'RE FLOATING! I THINK?!
HMM?
HALT...
HUH...?
WAS I SEEING THINGS?
S... SORRY...
WHAT— WAS THAT ABOUT?
FLIP...
FW-FWOO...
!!
SHE...
SHE'S REALLY FLOAT-ING!!

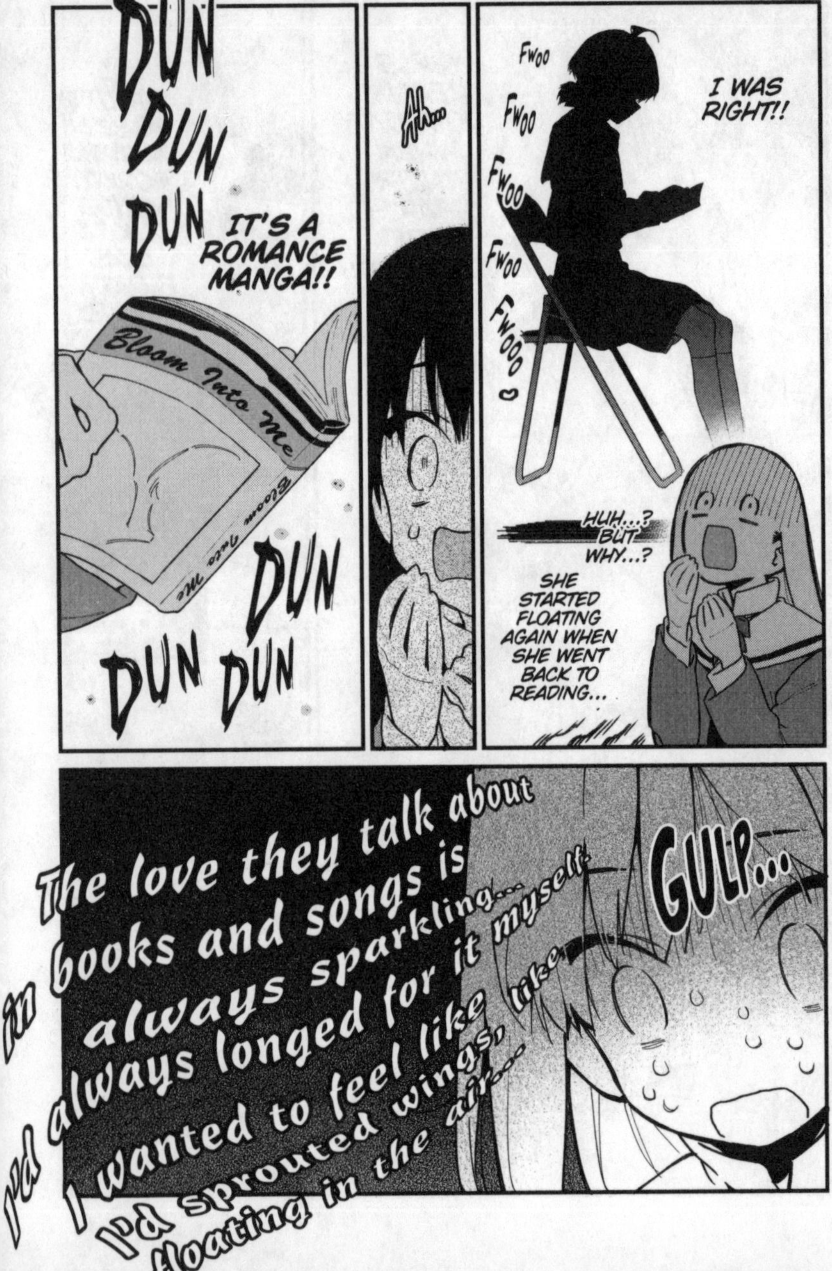
Fwoo
Fwoo
Fwoo
Fwoo
Fwooo
I WAS RIGHT!!
HUH...? BUT WHY...?
SHE STARTED FLOATING AGAIN WHEN SHE WENT BACK TO READING...
Ah...
DUN
DUN
DUN
IT'S A ROMANCE MANGA!!
Bloom Into Me
Bloom Into Me
DUN
DUN
DUN
The love they talk about
in books and songs is
always sparkling...
I'd always longed for it myself.
I wanted to feel like
I'd sprouted wings, like
floating in the air...
GULP...

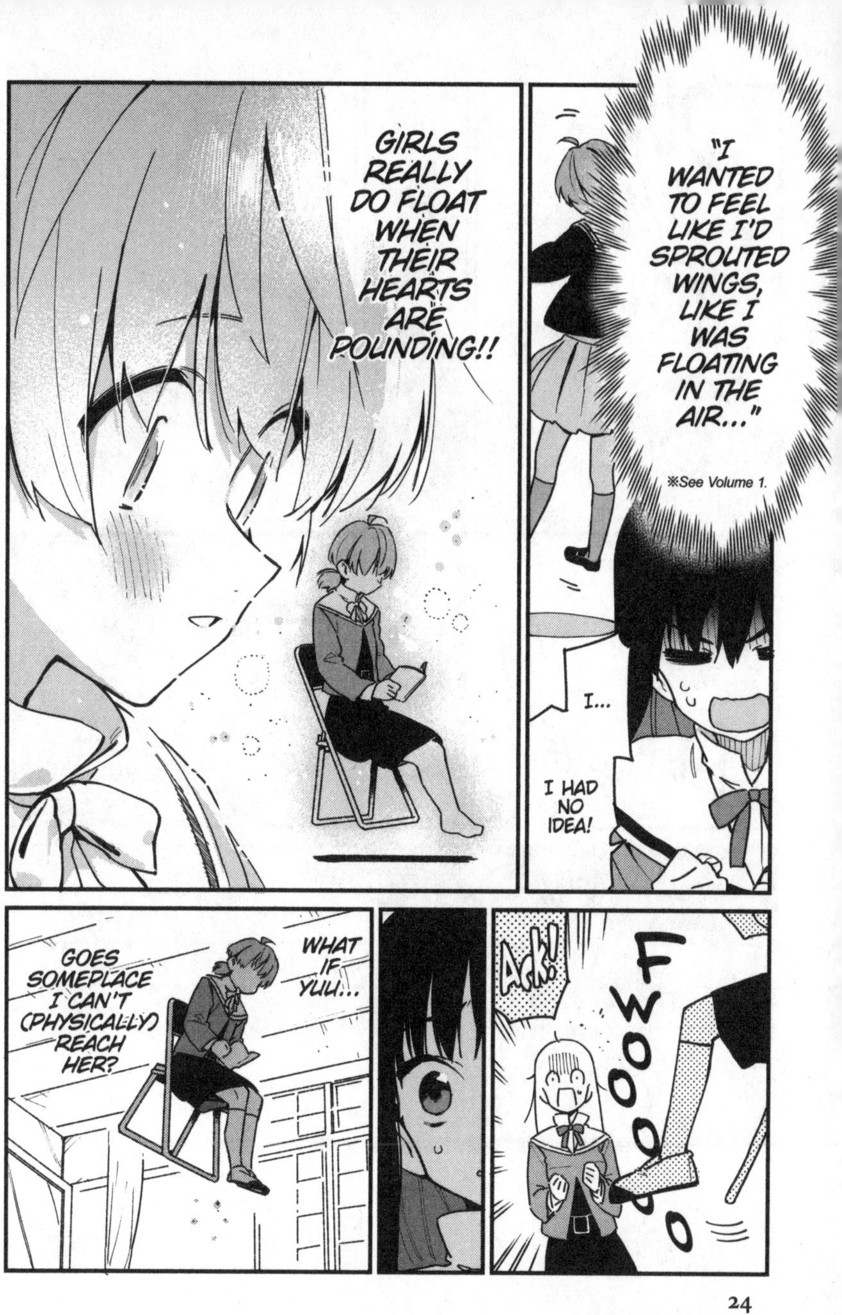
"I WANTED TO FEEL LIKE I'D SPROUTED WINGS, LIKE I WAS FLOATING IN THE AIR..."
※See Volume 1.
I...
I HAD NO IDEA!
GIRLS REALLY DO FLOAT WHEN THEIR HEARTS ARE POUNDING!!
Ack!
FWOOOOOO
WHAT IF YUU...
GOES SOMEPLACE I CAN'T (PHYSICALLY) REACH HER?

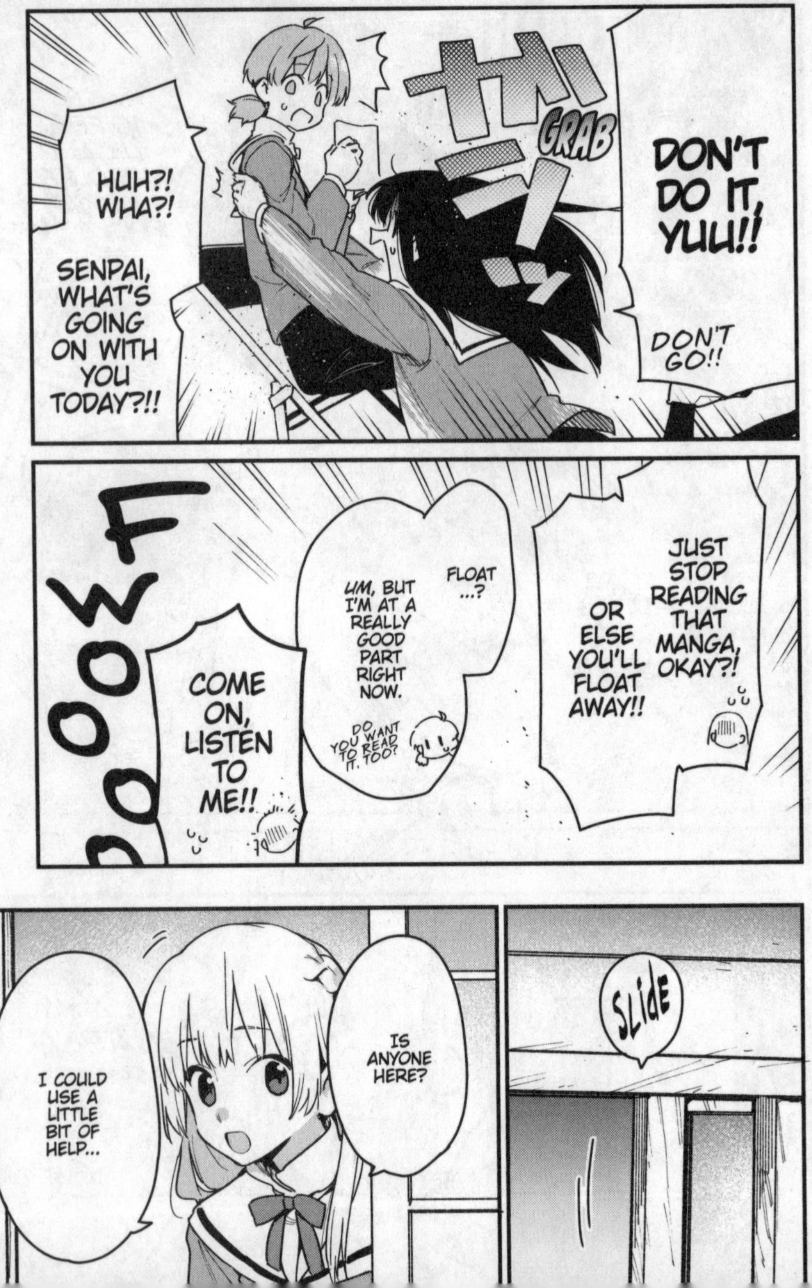
DON'T DO IT, YUU!!
DON'T GO!!
GRAB
HUH?! WHA?!
SENPAI, WHAT'S GOING ON WITH YOU TODAY?!!
JUST STOP READING THAT MANGA, OKAY?!
OR ELSE YOU'LL FLOAT AWAY!!
FLOAT ...?
UM, BUT I'M AT A REALLY GOOD PART RIGHT NOW.
DO YOU WANT TO READ IT, TOO?
COME ON, LISTEN TO ME!!
FWOO
Slide
IS ANYONE HERE?
I COULD USE A LITTLE BIT OF HELP...

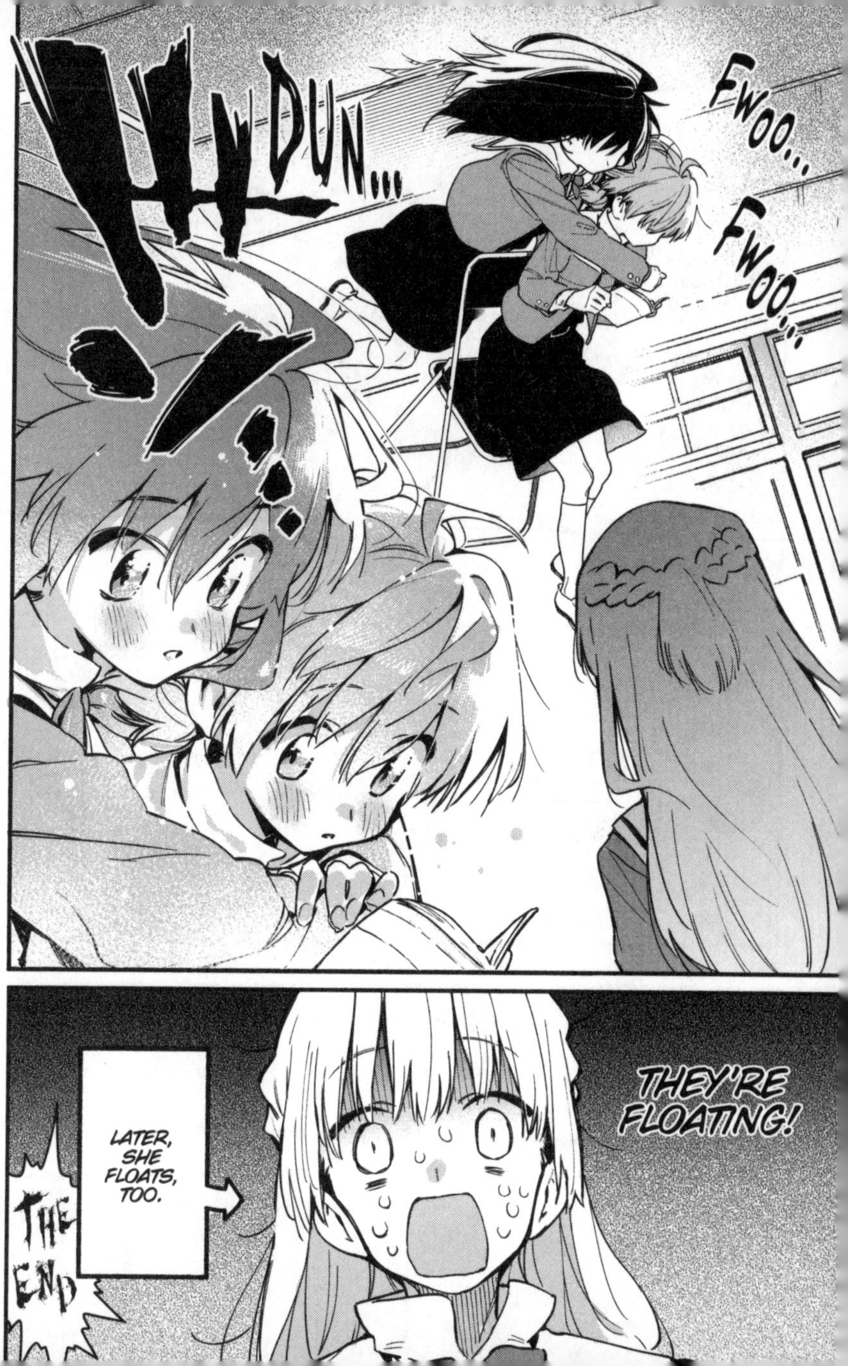
FWOO... FWOO...
DUN...
THEY'RE FLOATING!
LATER, SHE FLOATS, TOO.
THE END

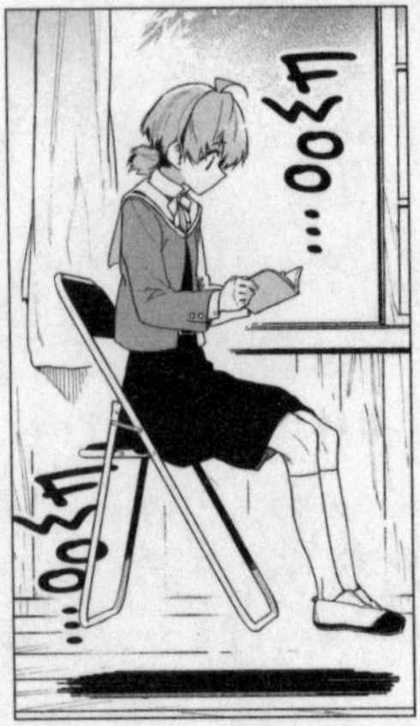
FWOO...
FWOO...

Chomoran

Best known for *Sachi's Monstrous Appetite* (Kodansha).

(Bloom Into You)

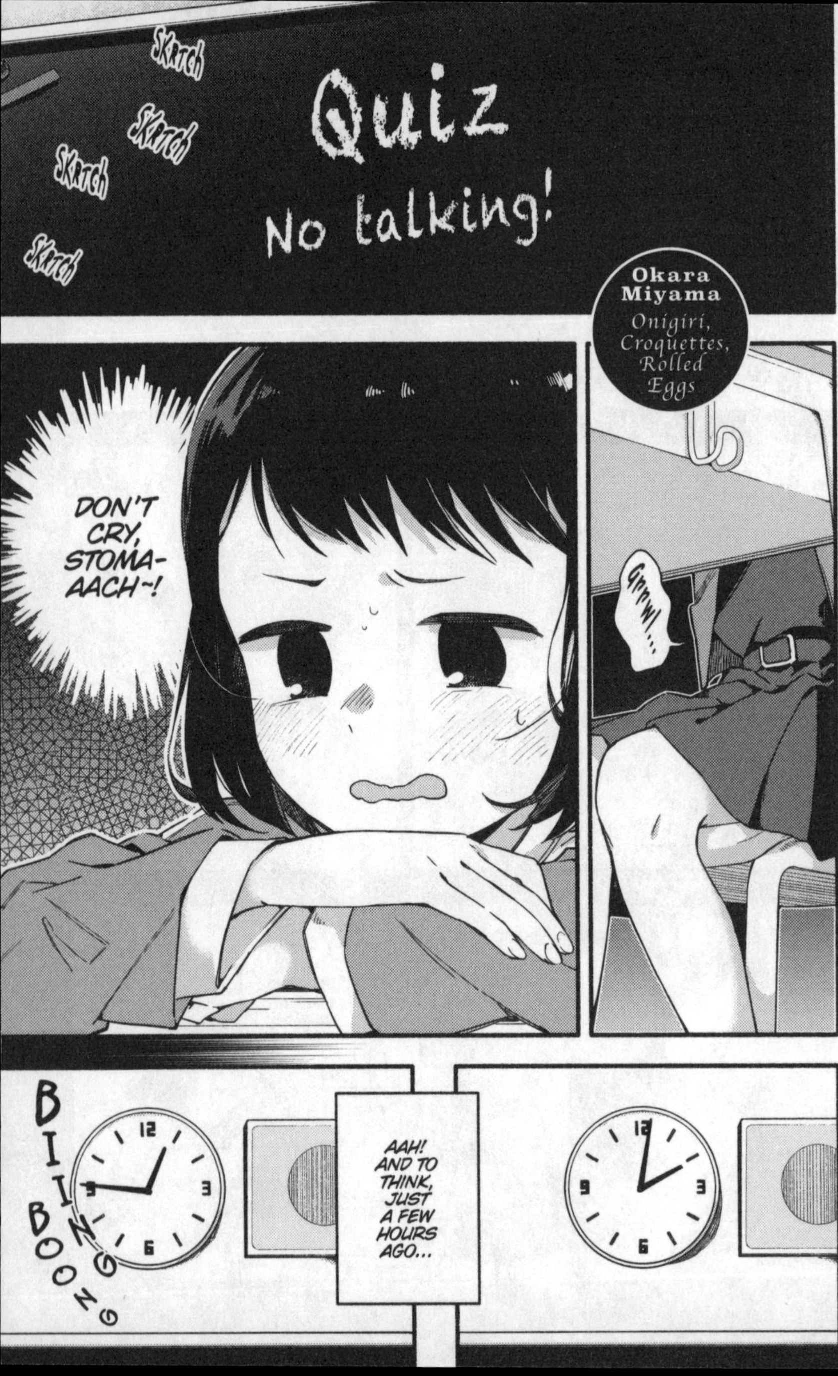
Quiz
No talking!
SKRTCH
SKRTCH
SKRTCH
SKRTCH
Okara Miyama
Onigiri, Croquettes, Rolled Eggs
Grrowl...
DON'T CRY, STOMA-AACH~!
AAH! AND TO THINK, JUST A FEW HOURS AGO...
BIING BOONG

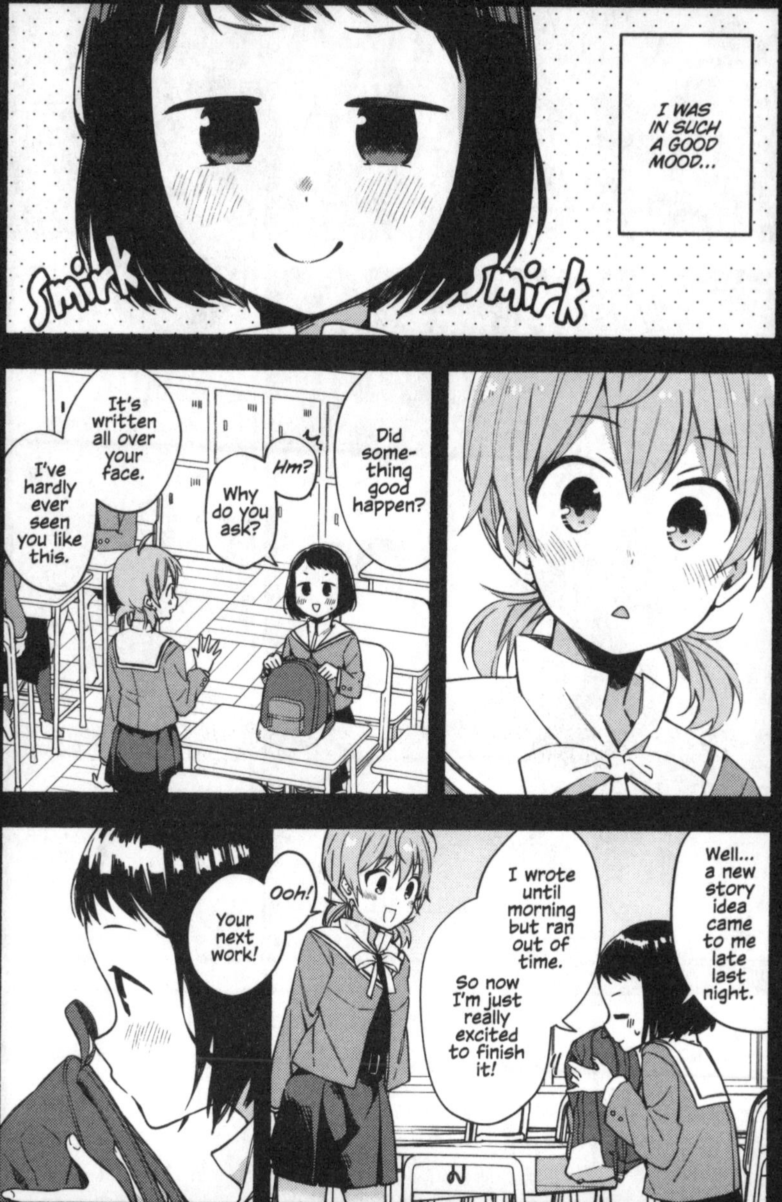
I WAS IN SUCH A GOOD MOOD...
Smirk
Smirk
Did something good happen?
Hm?
Why do you ask?
It's written all over your face.
I've hardly ever seen you like this.
Well... a new story idea came to me late last night.
I wrote until morning but ran out of time.
So now I'm just really excited to finish it!
Ooh!
Your next work!

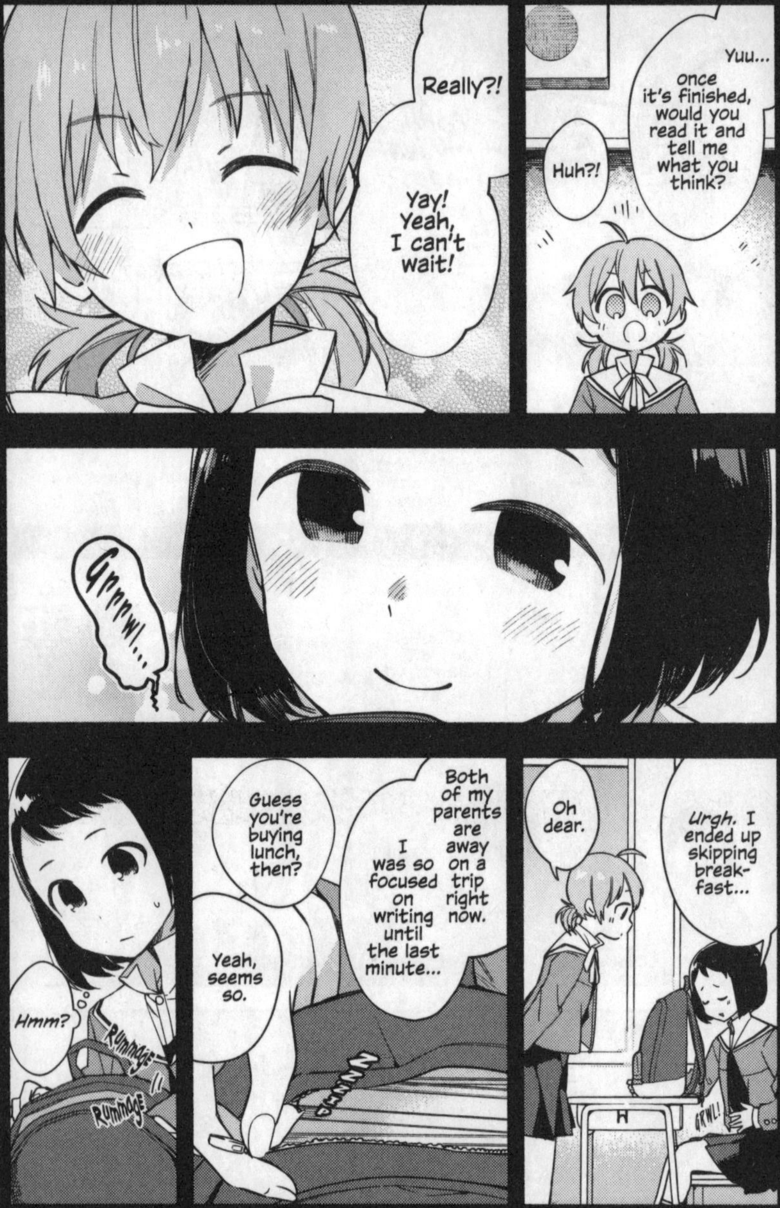
Yuu... once it's finished, would you read it and tell me what you think?
Huh?!
Really?!
Yay! Yeah, I can't wait!
Grrrw!...
Urgh. I ended up skipping breakfast...
Oh dear.
GRWL!
Both of my parents are away on a trip right now.
I was so focused on writing until the last minute...
Guess you're buying lunch, then?
Yeah, seems so.
Hmm?
Rummage
Rummage

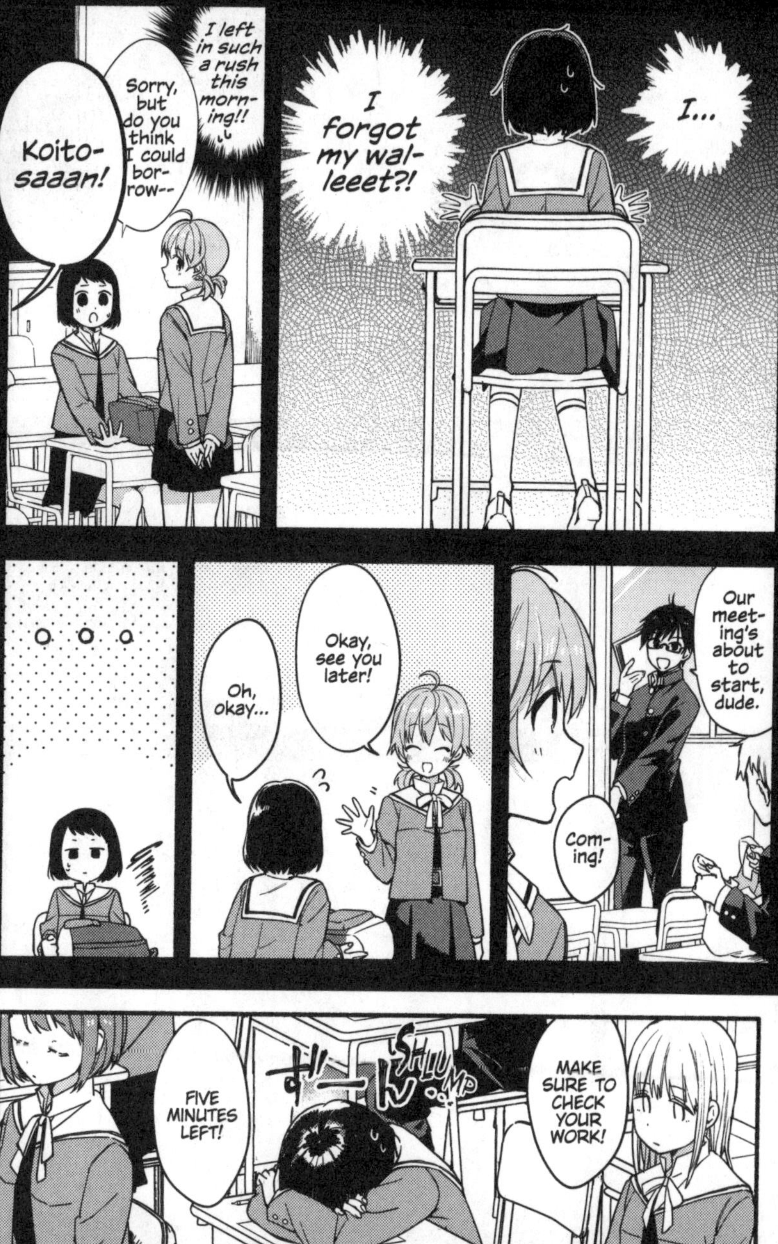
I...
I forgot my wal-leeet?!
I left in such a rush this morning!!
Sorry, but do you think I could borrow--
Koito-saaan!
Our meeting's about to start, dude.
Coming!
Okay, see you later!
Oh, okay...
...
MAKE SURE TO CHECK YOUR WORK!
SHLUMP
ずーん
FIVE MINUTES LEFT!

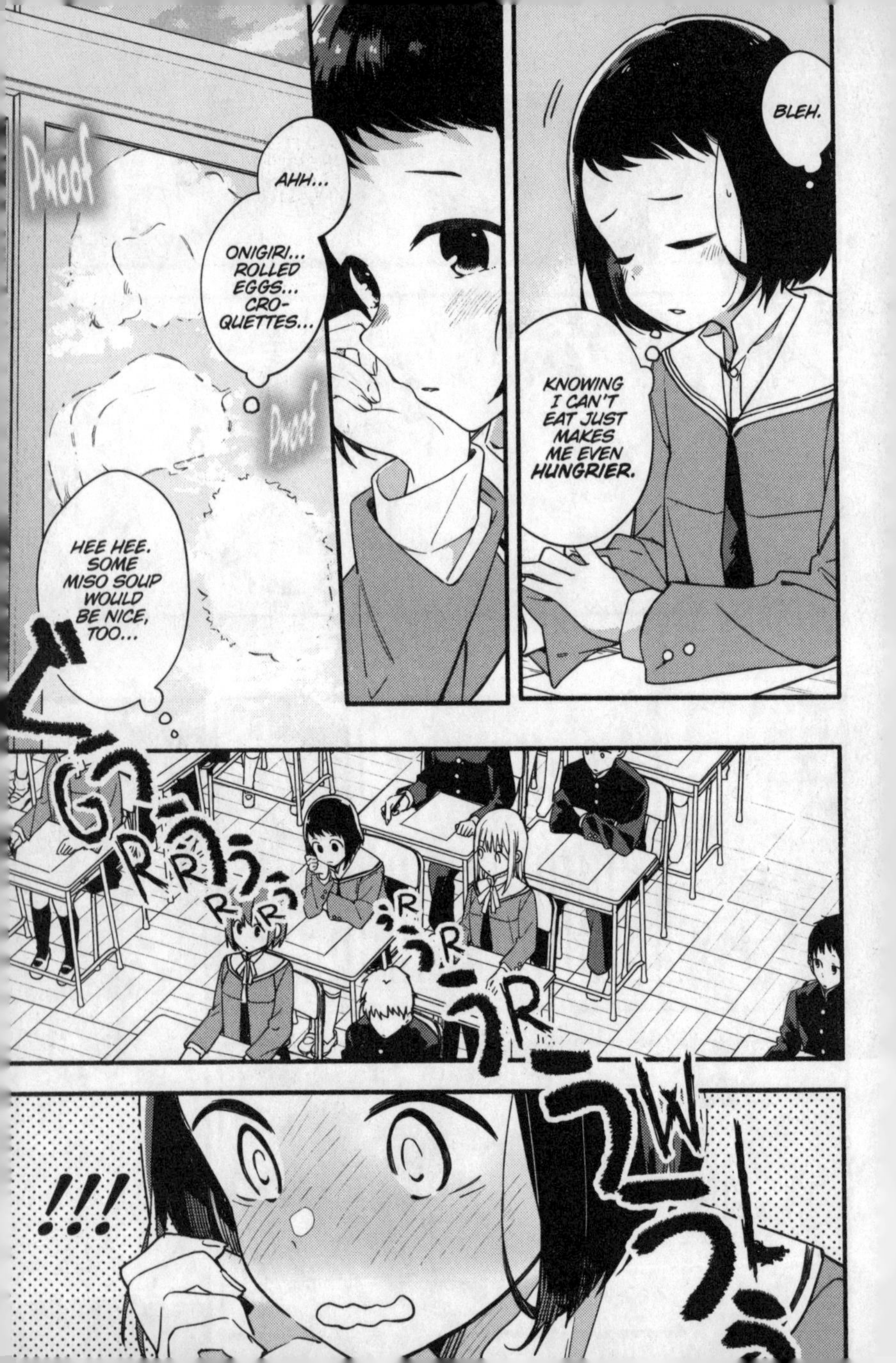
BLEH.
KNOWING I CAN'T EAT JUST MAKES ME EVEN HUNGRIER.
AHH...
ONIGIRI... ROLLED EGGS... CRO-QUETTES...
Phoof
Phoof
HEE HEE. SOME MISO SOUP WOULD BE NICE, TOO...
!!!

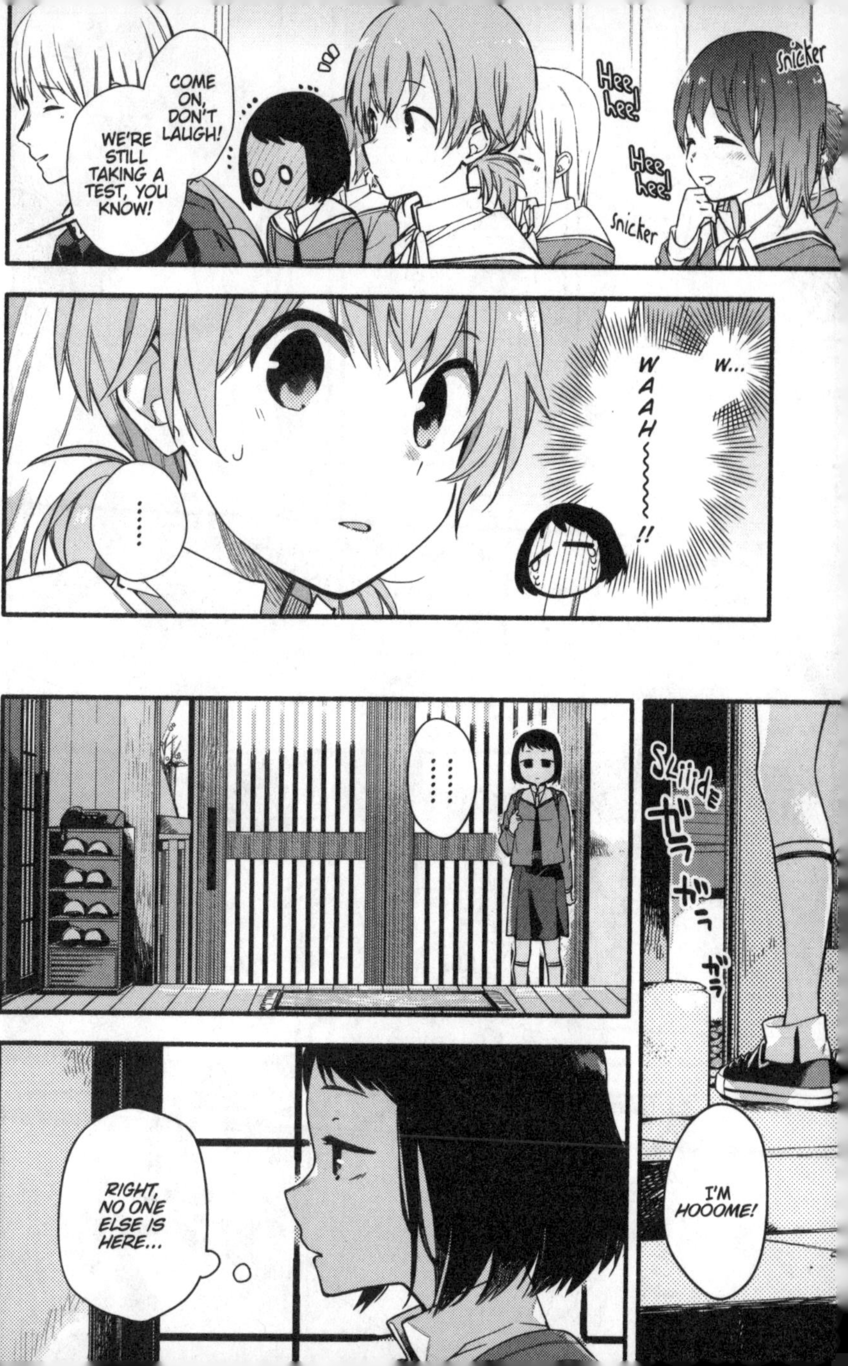
Snicker
Hee hee!
Hee hee!
Snicker
COME ON, DON'T LAUGH! WE'RE STILL TAKING A TEST, YOU KNOW!
W...
WAAAH~~~!!
......
Sliiide
I'M HOOOME!
......
RIGHT, NO ONE ELSE IS HERE...

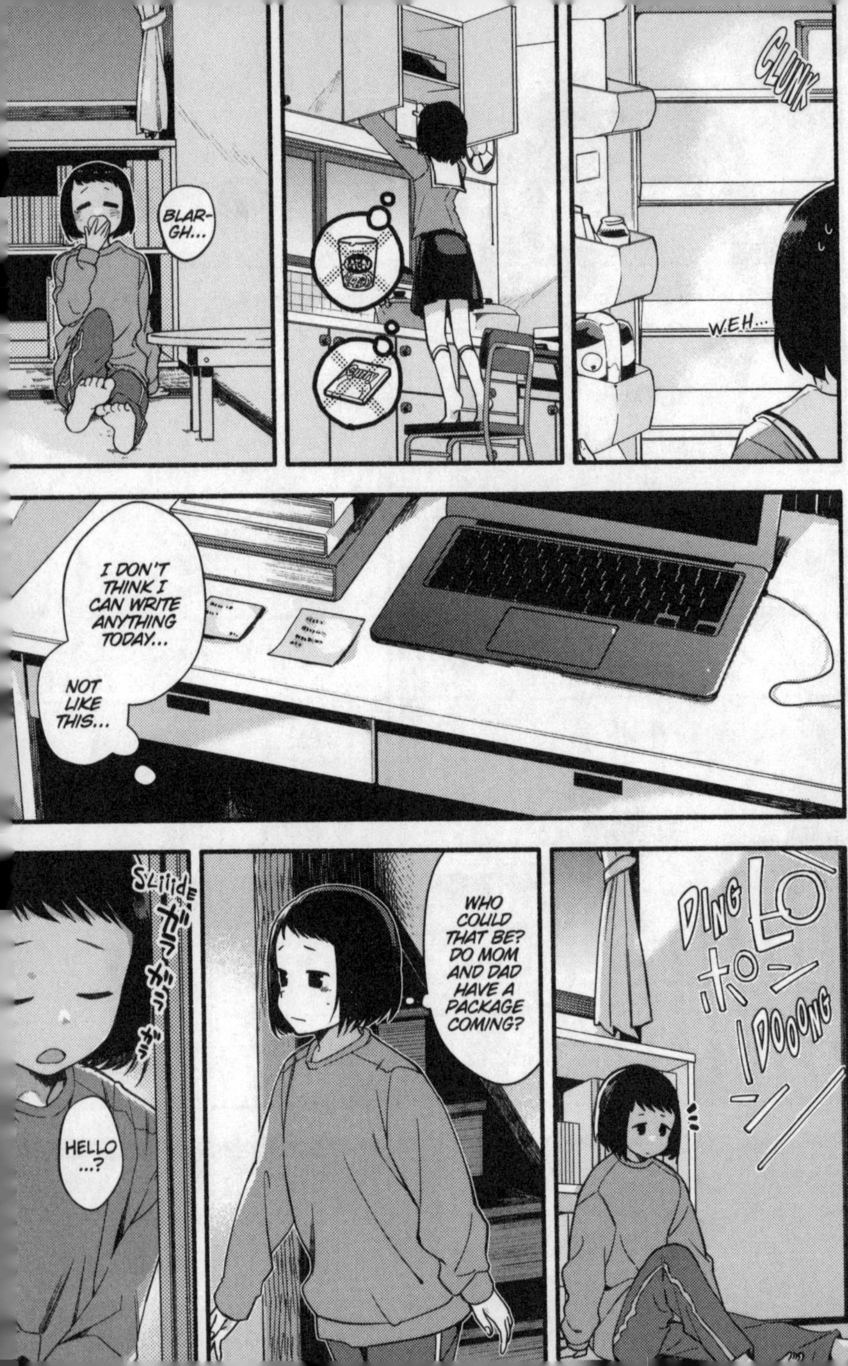
CLUNK
W.E.H...
BLARGH...
I DON'T THINK I CAN WRITE ANYTHING TODAY...
NOT LIKE THIS...
DING
DOOONG
WHO COULD THAT BE? DO MOM AND DAD HAVE A PACKAGE COMING?
SLiiide
HELLO ...?

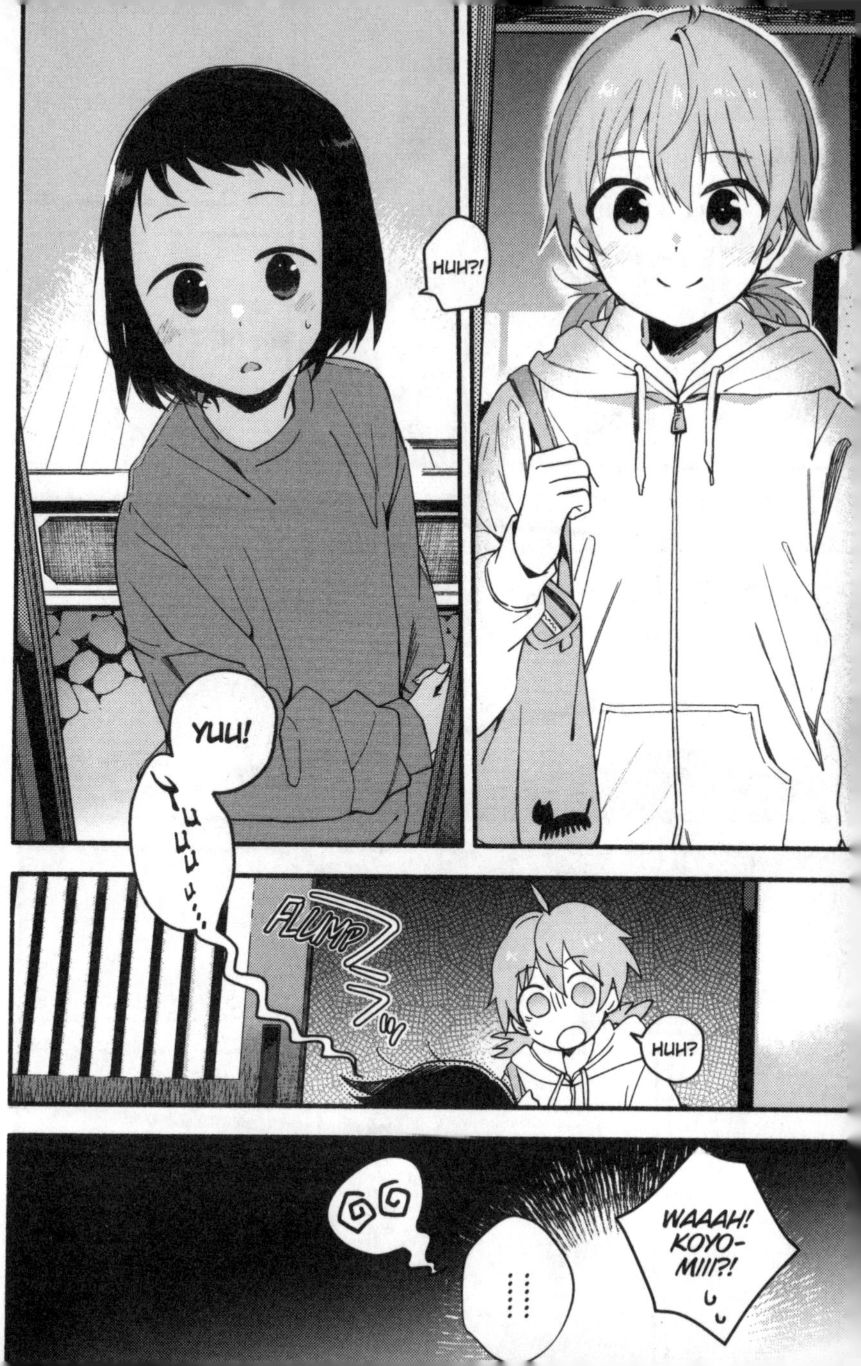
HUH?!
YUU!
FLUMP
HUH?
WAAAH! KOYO-MIII?!
......

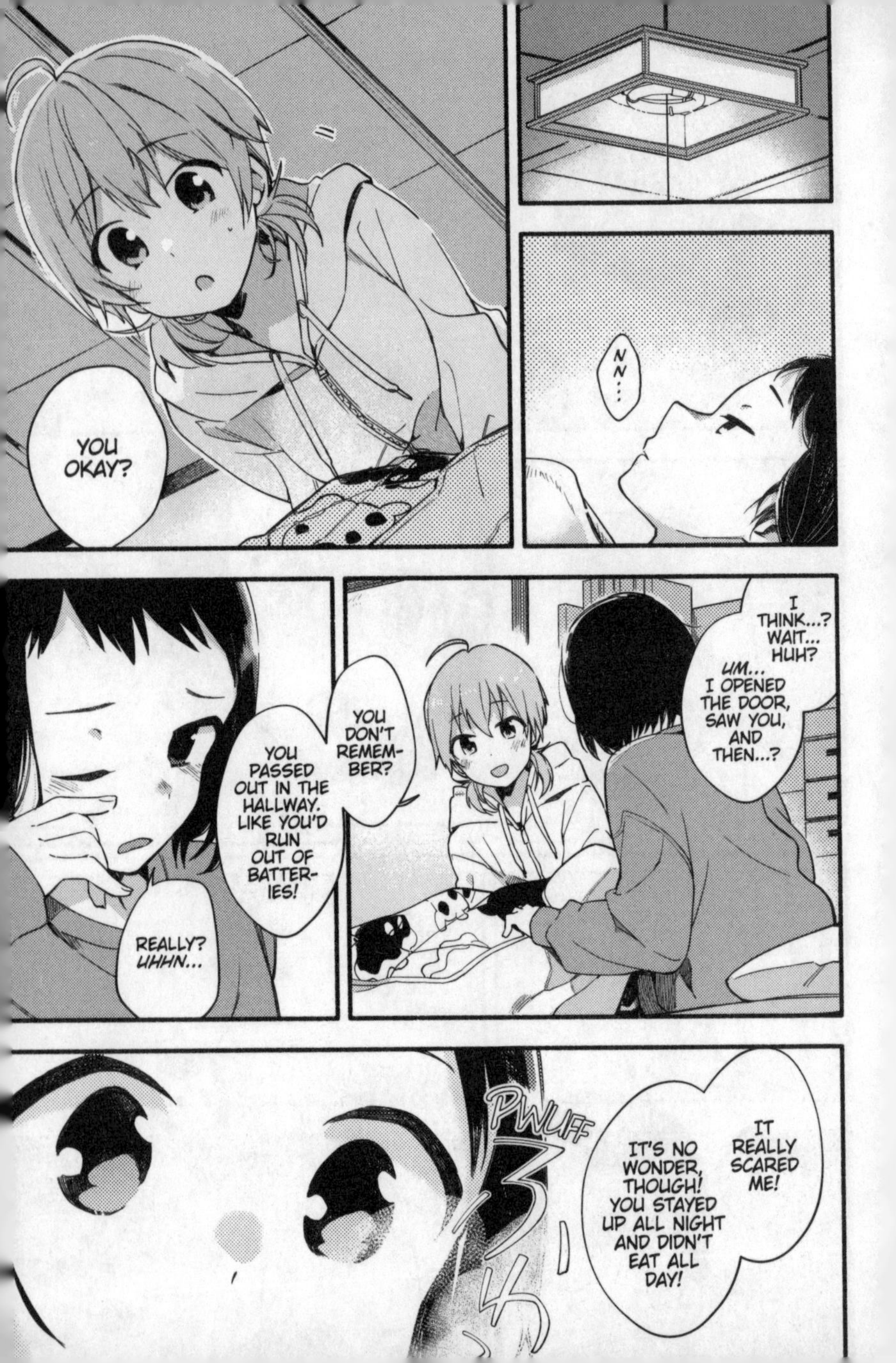
NN...
YOU OKAY?
I THINK...? WAIT... HUH?
UM... I OPENED THE DOOR, SAW YOU, AND THEN...?
YOU DON'T REMEMBER?
YOU PASSED OUT IN THE HALLWAY. LIKE YOU'D RUN OUT OF BATTERIES!
REALLY? UHHN...
IT REALLY SCARED ME!
IT'S NO WONDER, THOUGH! YOU STAYED UP ALL NIGHT AND DIDN'T EAT ALL DAY!
PWUFF

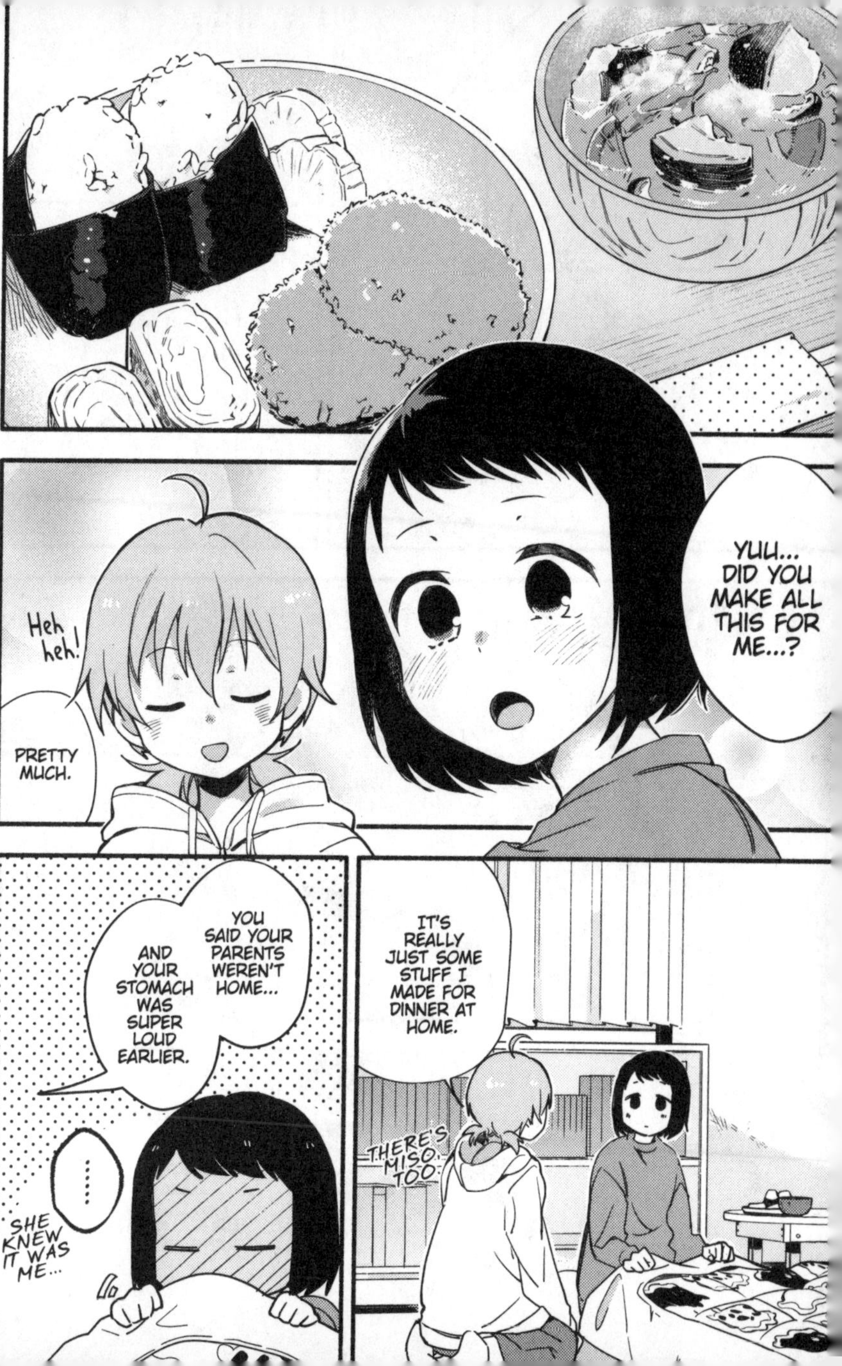
YUU... DID YOU MAKE ALL THIS FOR ME...?
Heh heh!
PRETTY MUCH.
IT'S REALLY JUST SOME STUFF I MADE FOR DINNER AT HOME.
THERE'S MISO TOO
YOU SAID YOUR PARENTS WEREN'T HOME...
AND YOUR STOMACH WAS SUPER LOUD EARLIER.
......
SHE KNEW IT WAS ME...

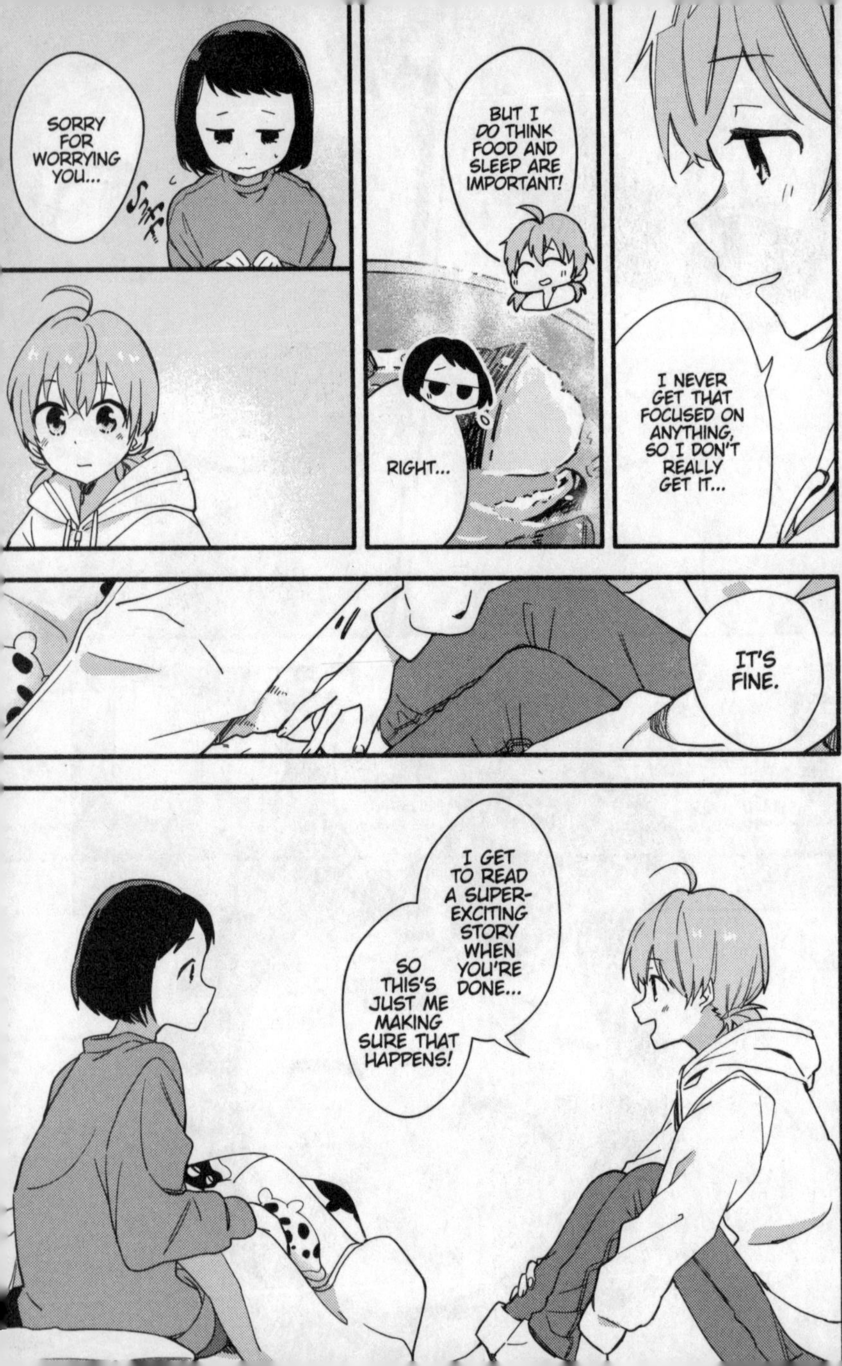
I NEVER GET THAT FOCUSED ON ANYTHING, SO I DON'T REALLY GET IT...
BUT I *DO* THINK FOOD AND SLEEP ARE IMPORTANT!
RIGHT...
SORRY FOR WORRYING YOU...
Sniff
IT'S FINE.
I GET TO READ A SUPER-EXCITING STORY WHEN YOU'RE DONE...
SO THIS'S JUST ME MAKING SURE THAT HAPPENS!

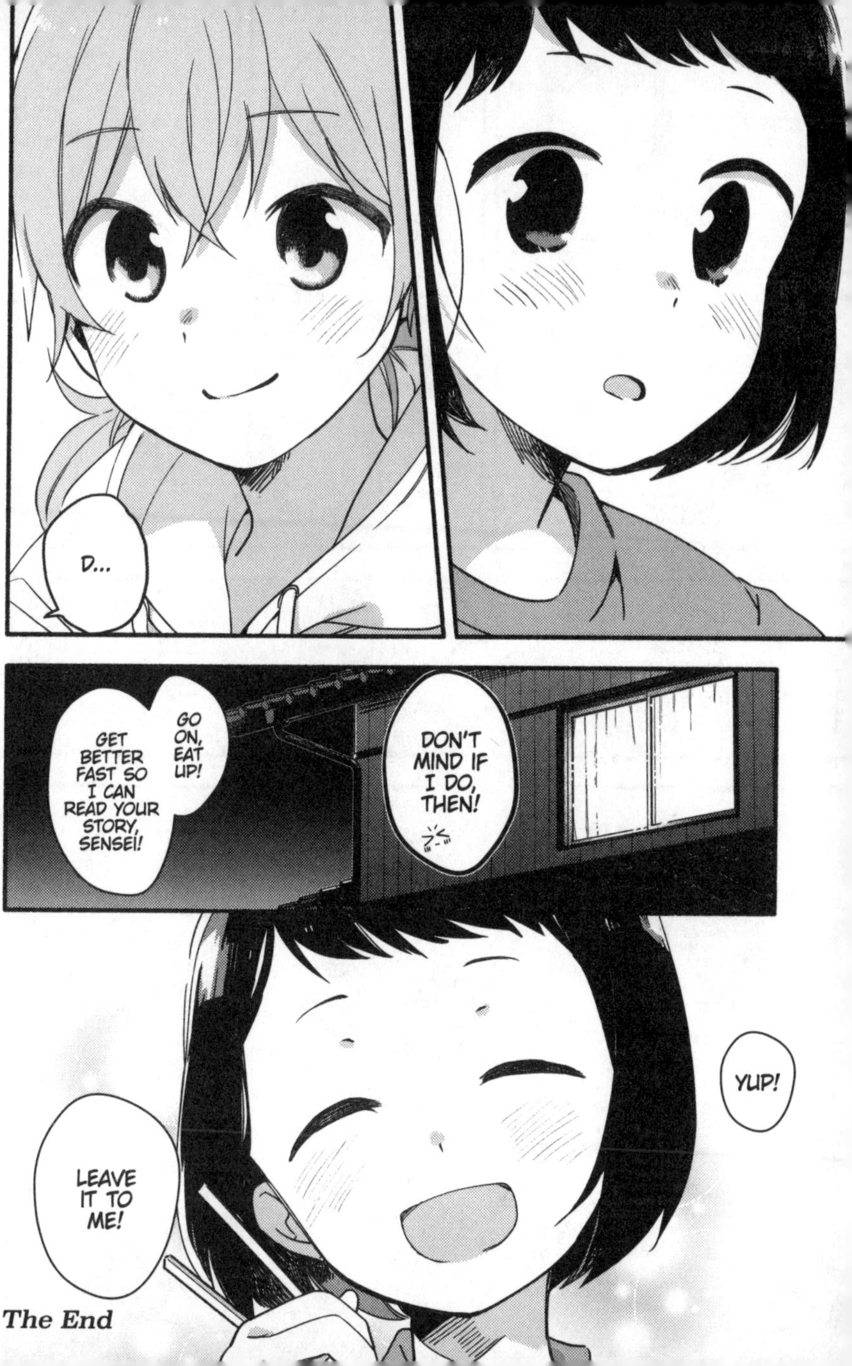
D...
DON'T MIND IF I DO, THEN!
GO ON, EAT UP!
GET BETTER FAST SO I CAN READ YOUR STORY, SENSEI!
YUP!
LEAVE IT TO ME!
The End

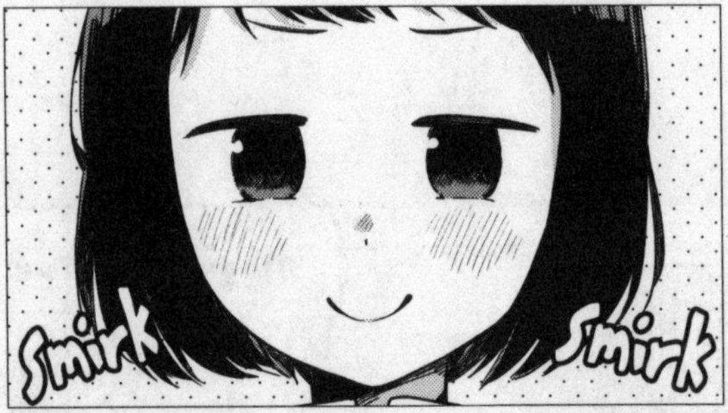
Smirk
Smirk

Okara Miyama

Best known for *Ore no Pantsu ga Nerawareteita (She's Only After My Undies)* (KADOKAWA).

(**Bloom Into You**)

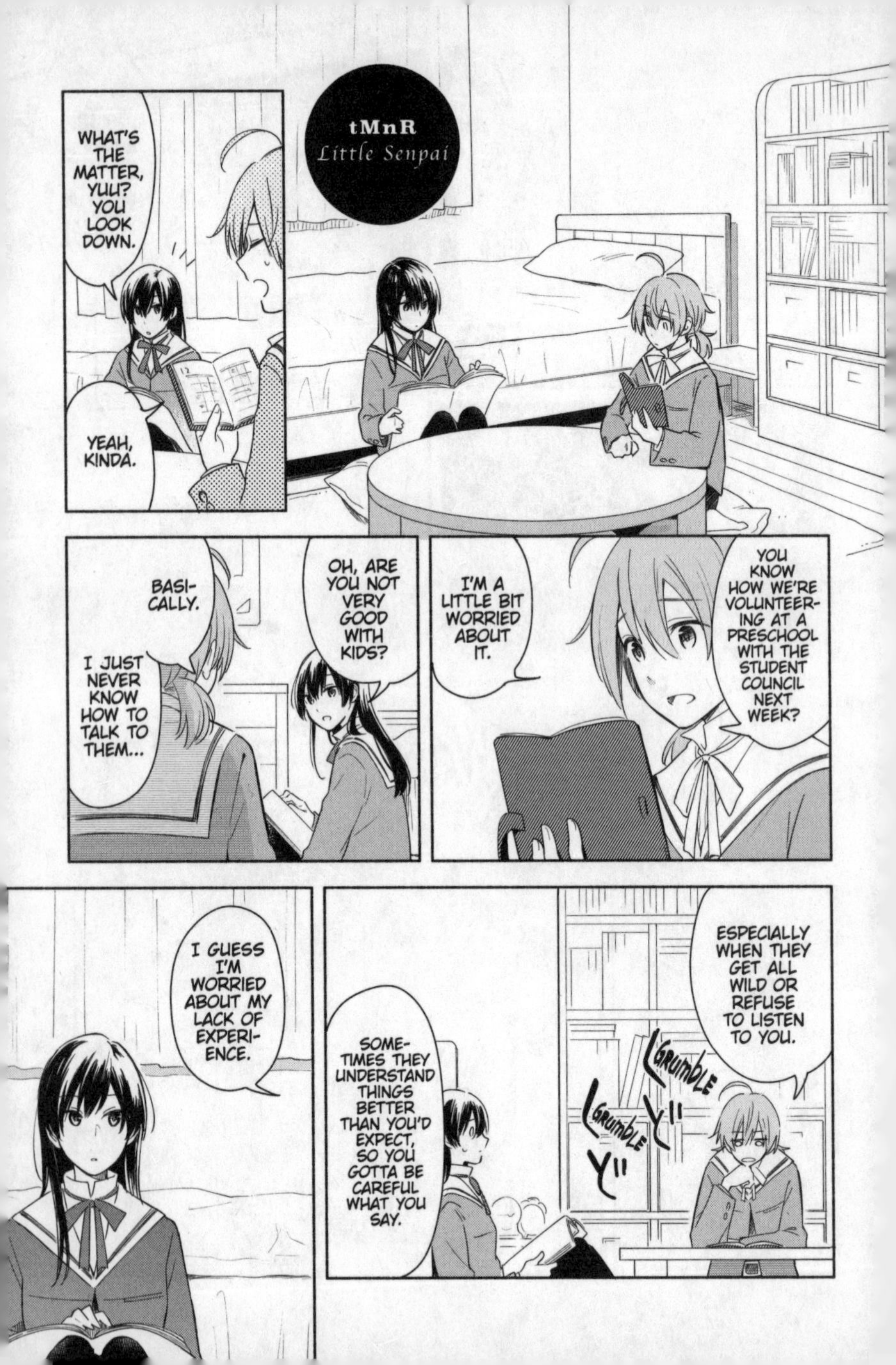
tMnR
Little Senpai
WHAT'S THE MATTER, YUU? YOU LOOK DOWN.
YEAH, KINDA.
YOU KNOW HOW WE'RE VOLUNTEERING AT A PRESCHOOL WITH THE STUDENT COUNCIL NEXT WEEK?
I'M A LITTLE BIT WORRIED ABOUT IT.
OH, ARE YOU NOT VERY GOOD WITH KIDS?
BASICALLY.
I JUST NEVER KNOW HOW TO TALK TO THEM...
ESPECIALLY WHEN THEY GET ALL WILD OR REFUSE TO LISTEN TO YOU.
GRUMBLE
GRUMBLE
SOMETIMES THEY UNDERSTAND THINGS BETTER THAN YOU'D EXPECT, SO YOU GOTTA BE CAREFUL WHAT YOU SAY.
I GUESS I'M WORRIED ABOUT MY LACK OF EXPERIENCE.

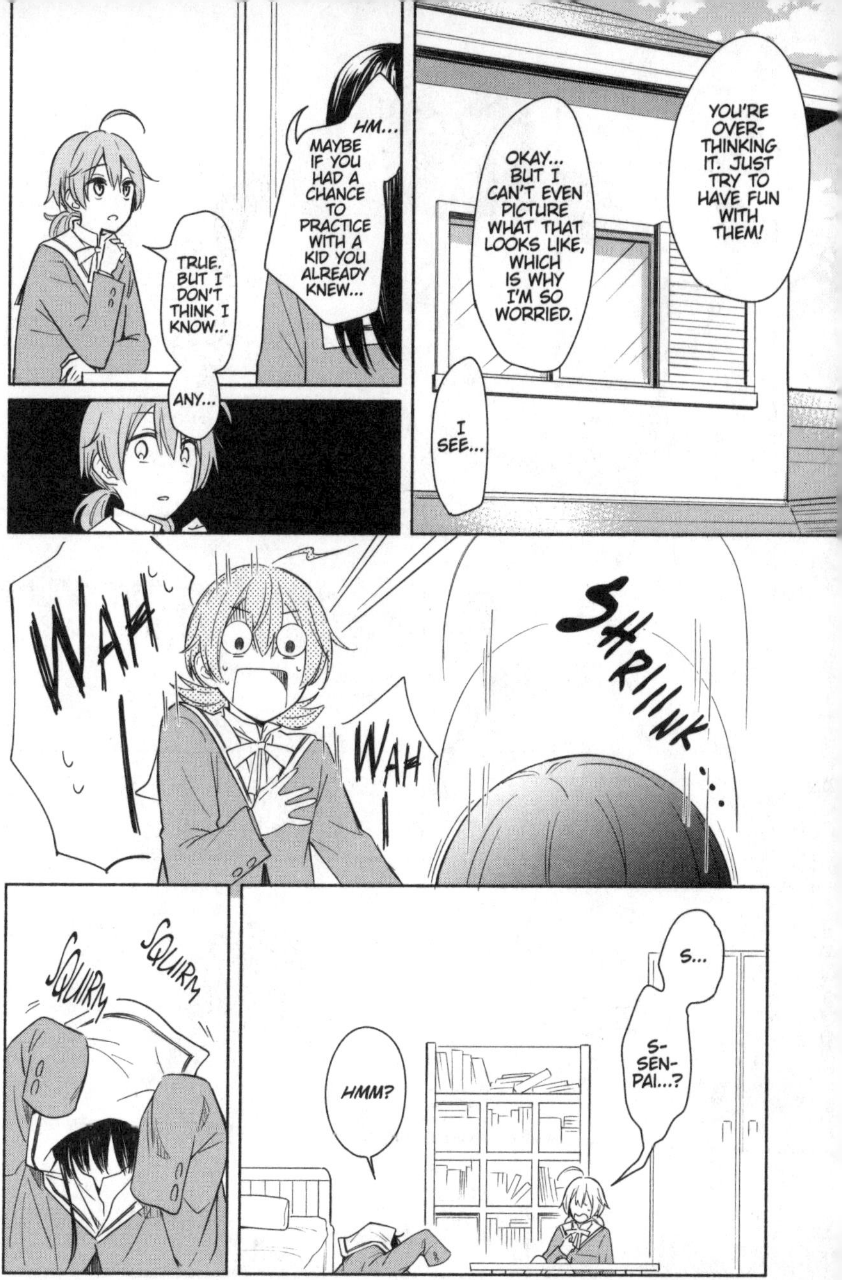
YOU'RE OVER-THINKING IT. JUST TRY TO HAVE FUN WITH THEM!
OKAY... BUT I CAN'T EVEN PICTURE WHAT THAT LOOKS LIKE, WHICH IS WHY I'M SO WORRIED.
I SEE...
HM... MAYBE IF YOU HAD A CHANCE TO PRACTICE WITH A KID YOU ALREADY KNEW...
TRUE. BUT I DON'T THINK I KNOW...
ANY...
SHRIIIINK...
WAH
WAH
S...
S-SEN-PAI...?
HMM?
SQUIRM
SQUIRM

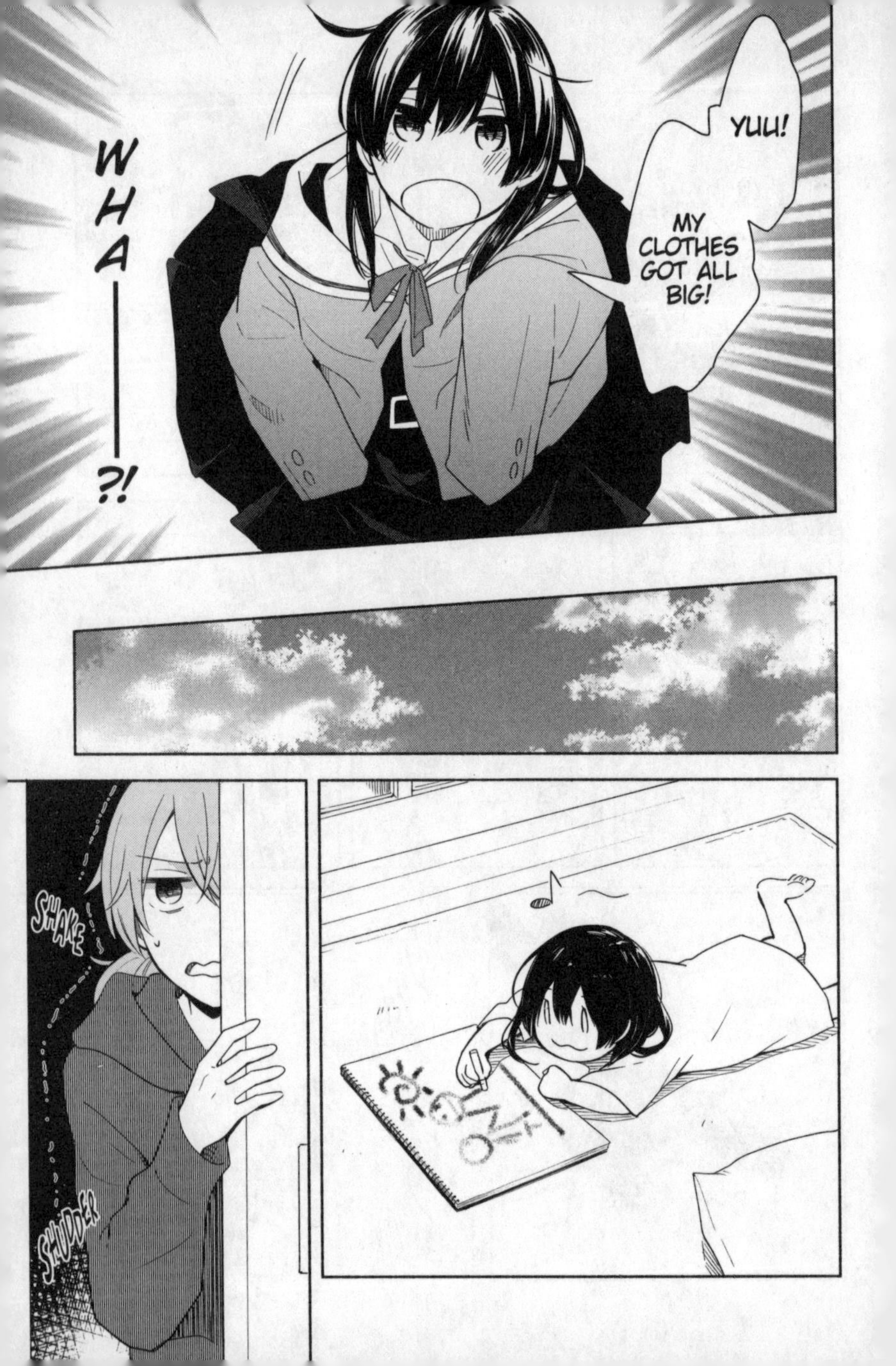
YUU!
MY CLOTHES GOT ALL BIG!
WHA——?!
SHAKE
SHUDDER

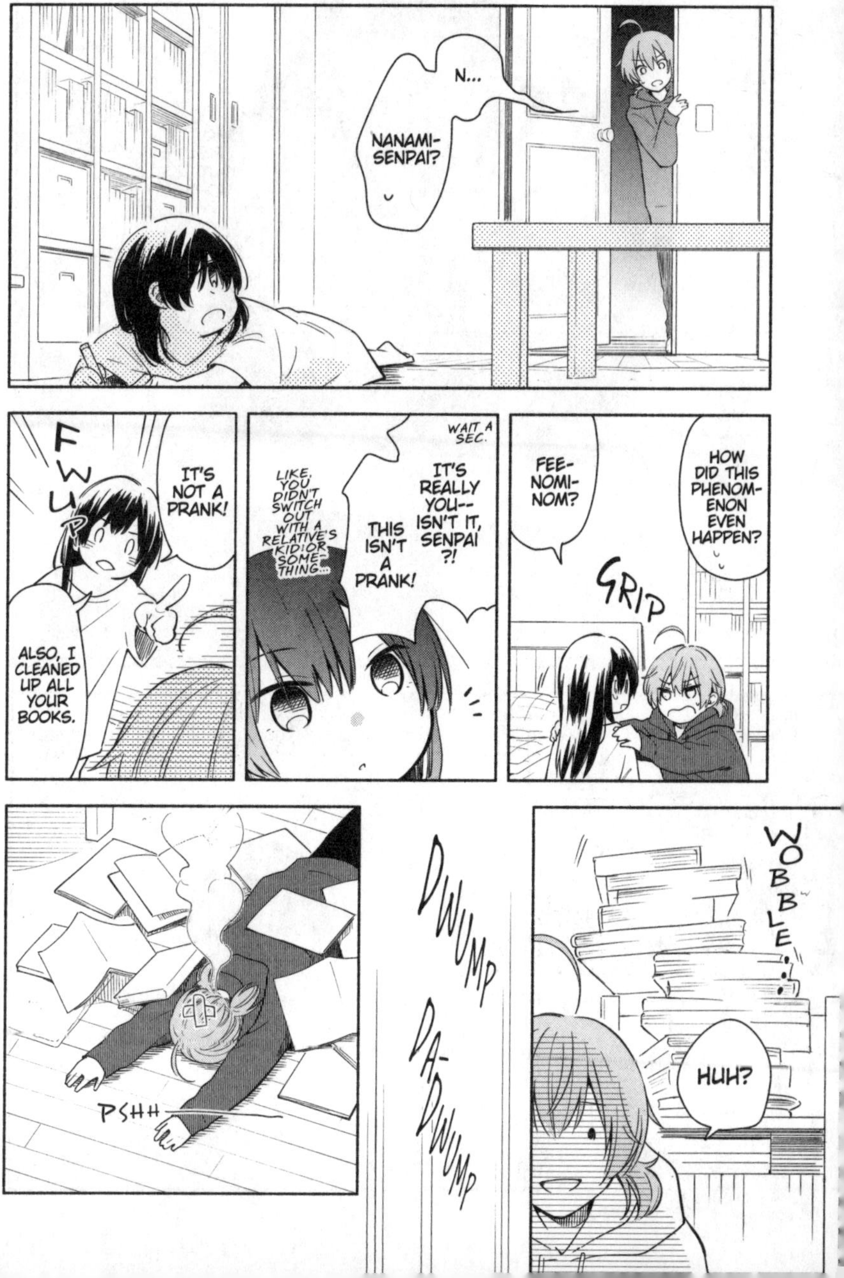
N...
NANAMI-SENPAI?
HOW DID THIS PHENOMENON EVEN HAPPEN?
FEE-NOMI-NOM?
GRIP
WAIT A SEC.
IT'S REALLY YOU-- ISN'T IT, SENPAI?!
THIS ISN'T A PRANK!
LIKE, YOU DIDN'T SWITCH OUT WITH A RELATIVE'S KID OR SOMETHING...
FWUP
IT'S NOT A PRANK!
ALSO, I CLEANED UP ALL YOUR BOOKS.
WOBBLE
HUH?
DWUMP
DA-DWUMP
PSHH

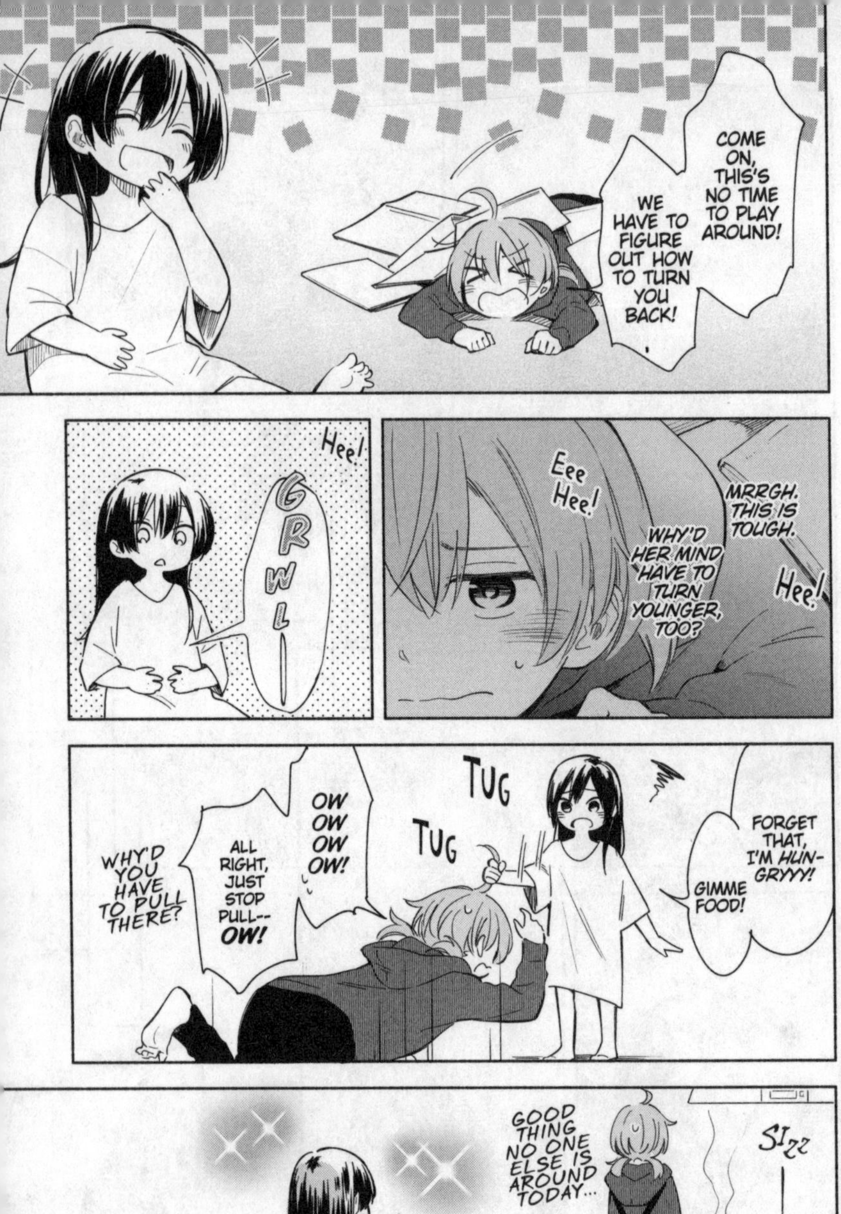
COME ON, THIS'S NO TIME TO PLAY AROUND!
WE HAVE TO FIGURE OUT HOW TO TURN YOU BACK!
MRRGH. THIS IS TOUGH.
WHY'D HER MIND HAVE TO TURN YOUNGER, TOO?
Hee!
Eee Hee!
Hee!
GRWL
FORGET THAT, I'M HUN-GRYYY!
GIMME FOOD!
TUG
TUG
OW OW OW OW!
ALL RIGHT, JUST STOP PULL--OW!
WHY'D YOU HAVE TO PULL THERE?
SIZZ
GOOD THING NO ONE ELSE IS AROUND TODAY...

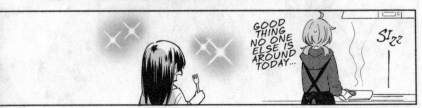

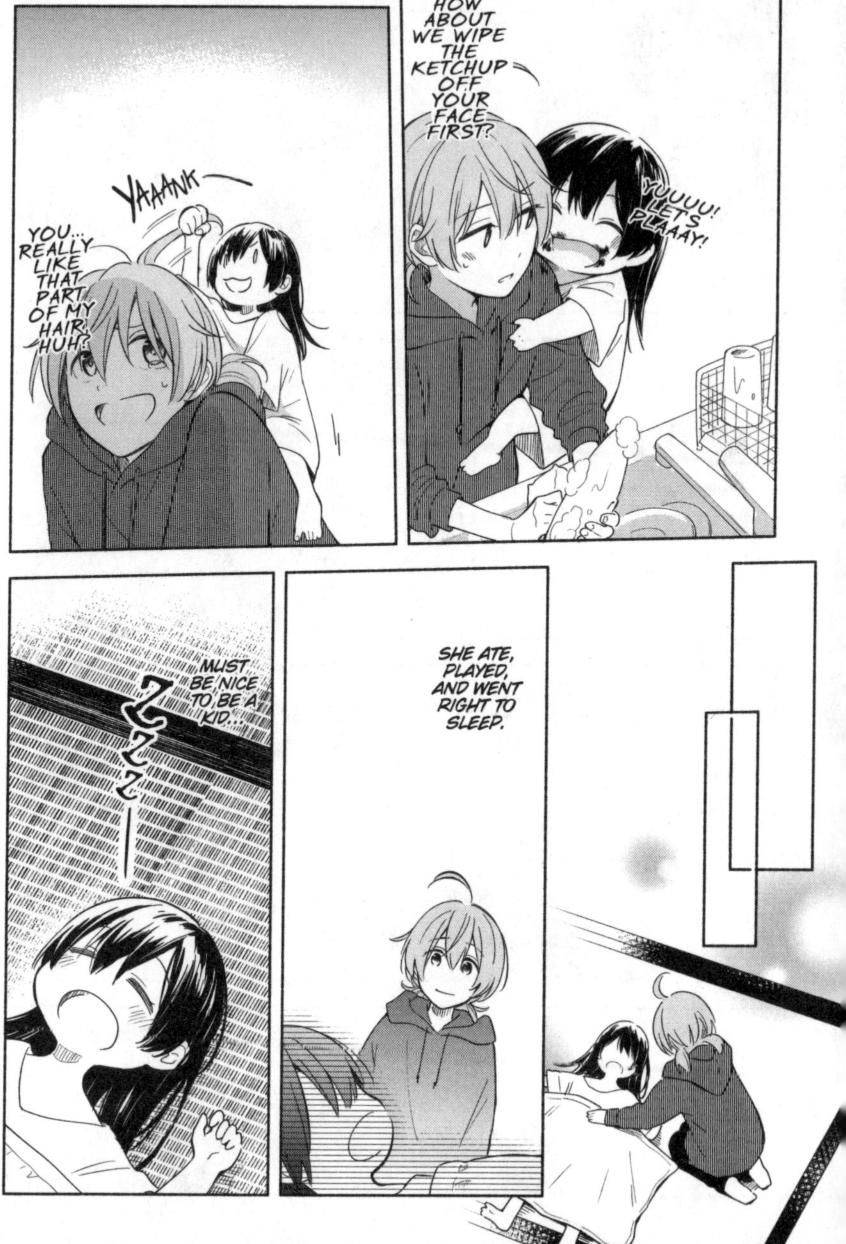
HOW ABOUT WE WIPE THE KETCHUP OFF YOUR FACE FIRST?
YUUUU! LET'S PLAAAY!
YAAANK
YOU... REALLY LIKE THAT PART OF MY HAIR, HUH?
SHE ATE, PLAYED, AND WENT RIGHT TO SLEEP.
MUST BE NICE TO BE A KID...
ZZZZ

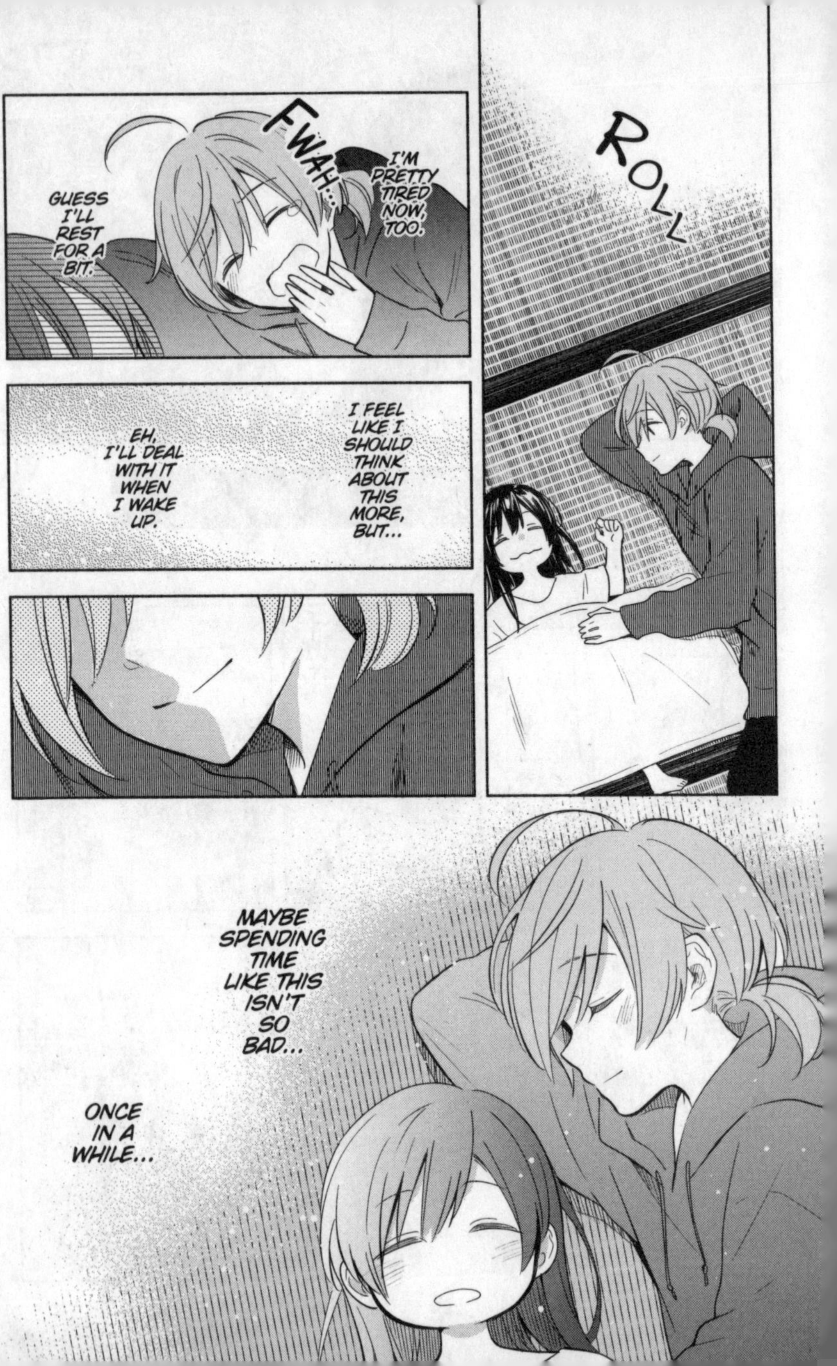
ROLL
FWAH...
I'M PRETTY TIRED NOW, TOO.
GUESS I'LL REST FOR A BIT.
I FEEL LIKE I SHOULD THINK ABOUT THIS MORE, BUT...
EH, I'LL DEAL WITH IT WHEN I WAKE UP.
MAYBE SPENDING TIME LIKE THIS ISN'T SO BAD...
ONCE IN A WHILE...

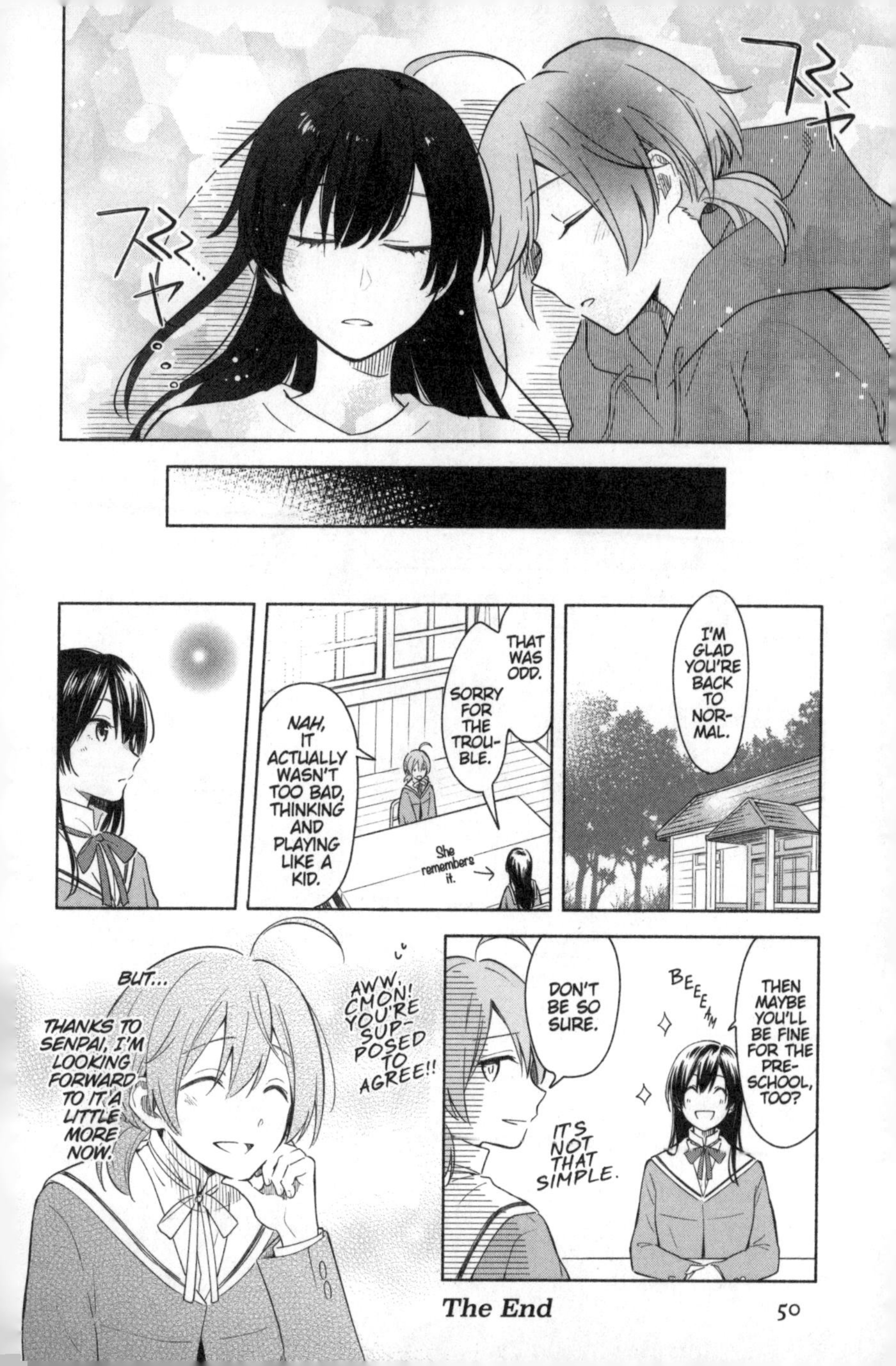
I'M GLAD YOU'RE BACK TO NOR-MAL.
THAT WAS ODD.
SORRY FOR THE TROU-BLE.
NAH, IT ACTUALLY WASN'T TOO BAD, THINKING AND PLAYING LIKE A KID.
She remembers it.
THEN MAYBE YOU'LL BE FINE FOR THE PRE-SCHOOL, TOO?
BEEEAM
DON'T BE SO SURE.
IT'S NOT THAT SIMPLE.
AWW, CMON! YOU'RE SUP-POSED TO AGREE!!
BUT...
THANKS TO SENPAI, I'M LOOKING FORWARD TO IT A LITTLE MORE NOW.

The End

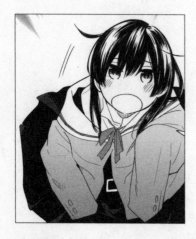

tMnR

Best known for *If I Could Reach You* (Ichijinsha).

(Bloom Into You)

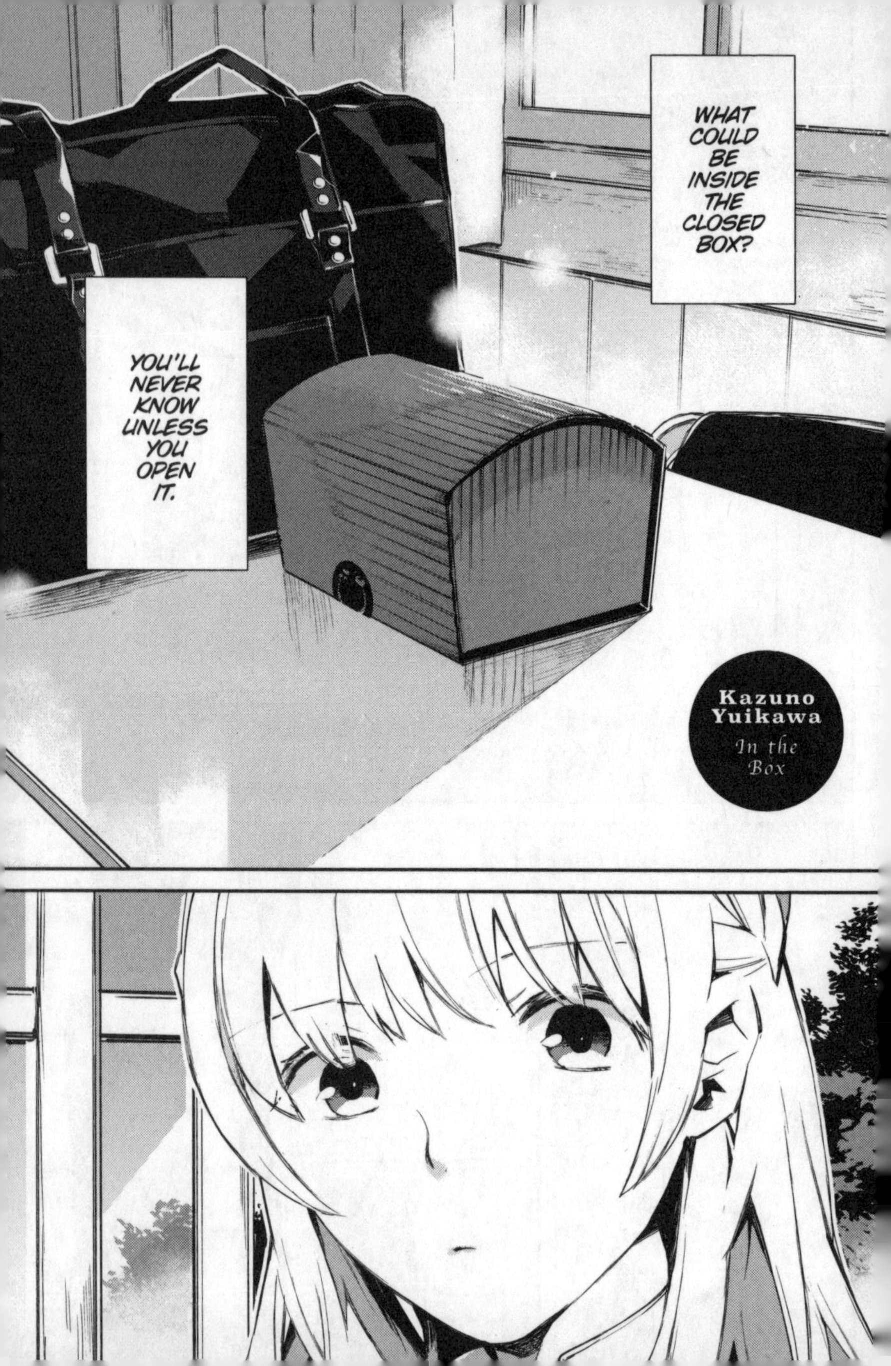
WHAT COULD BE INSIDE THE CLOSED BOX?
YOU'LL NEVER KNOW UNLESS YOU OPEN IT.
Kazuno Yuikawa
In the Box

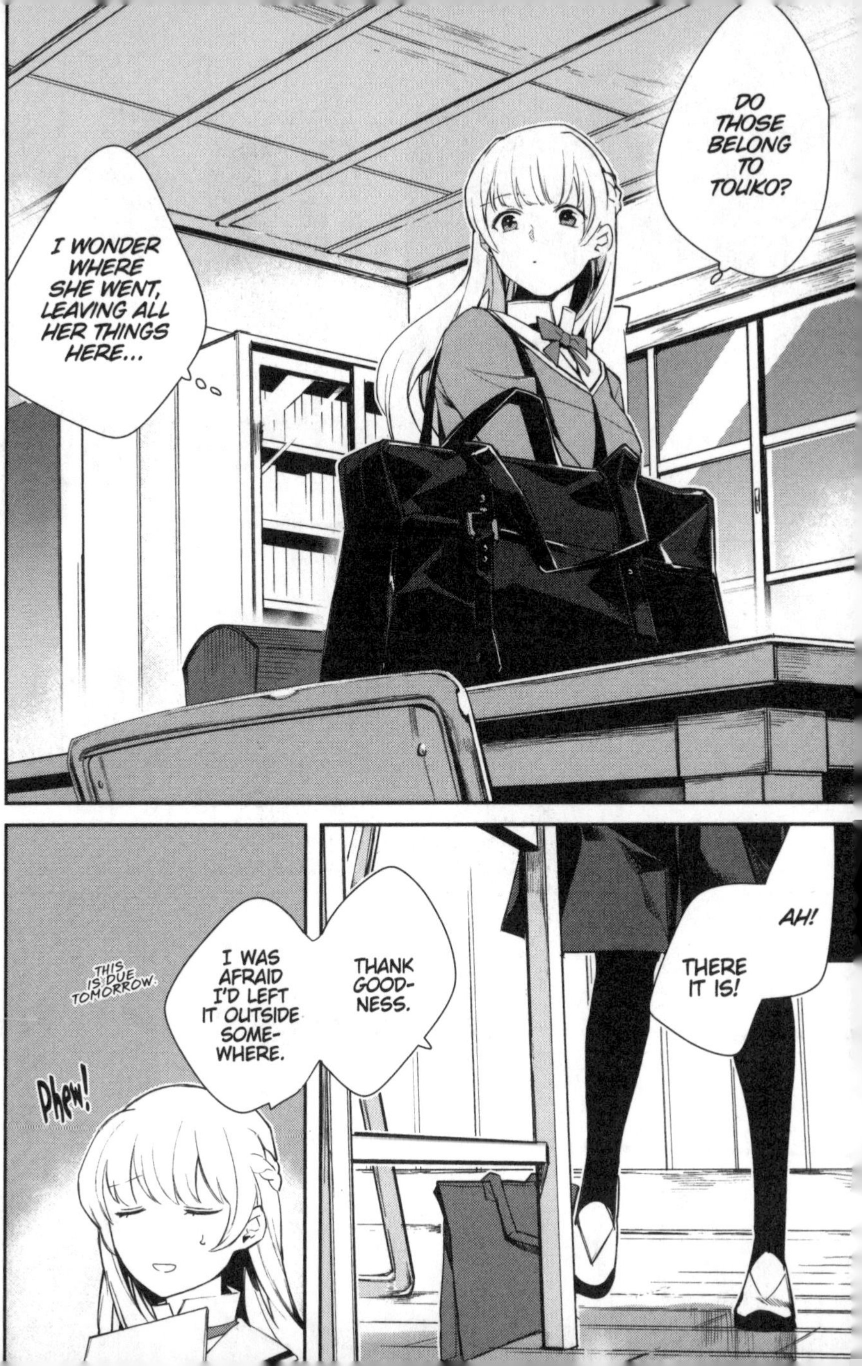
DO THOSE BELONG TO TOUKO?
I WONDER WHERE SHE WENT, LEAVING ALL HER THINGS HERE...
AH!
THERE IT IS!
THANK GOOD-NESS.
I WAS AFRAID I'D LEFT IT OUTSIDE SOME-WHERE.
THIS IS DUE TOMORROW.
Phew!

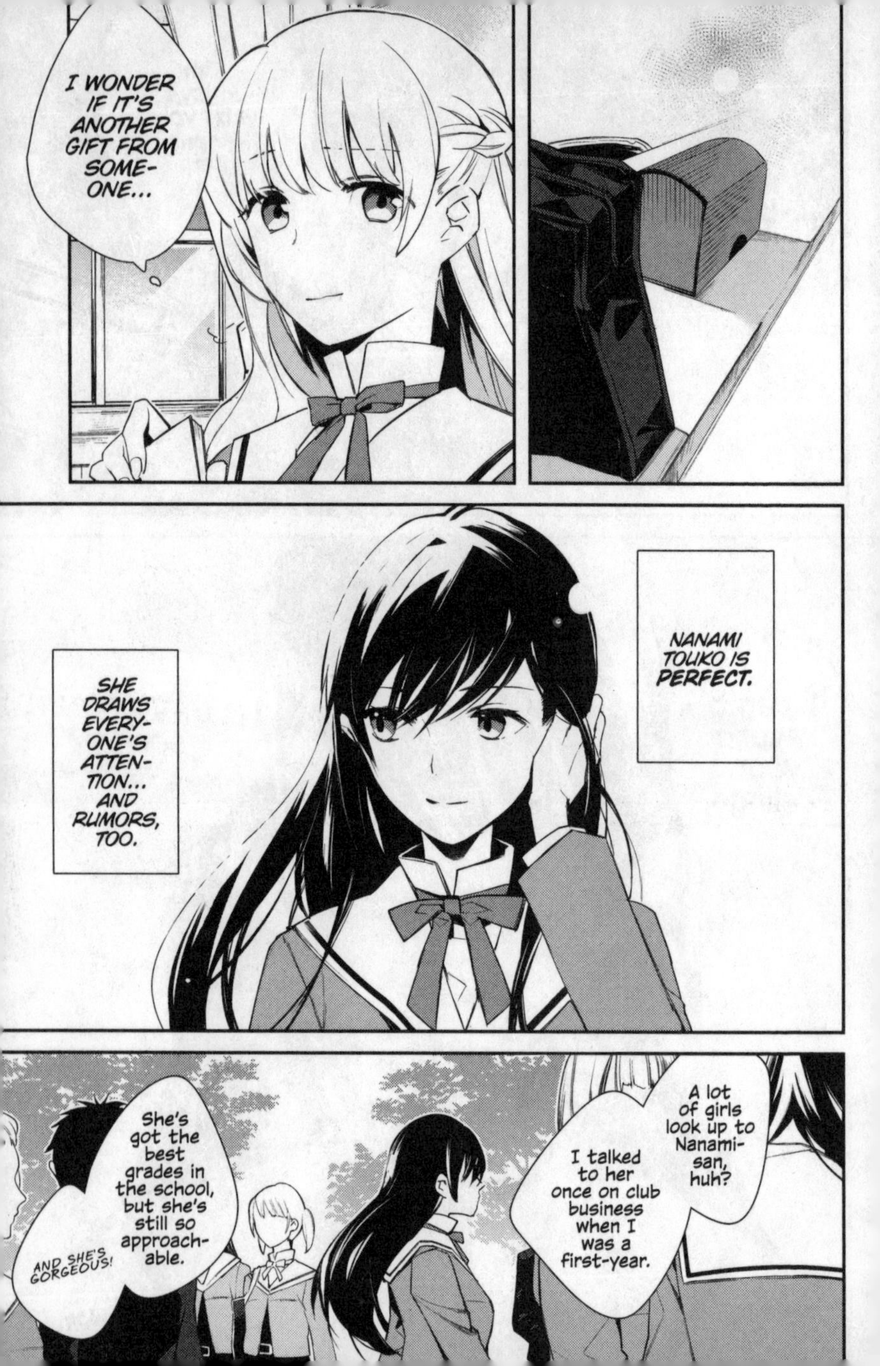

I WONDER IF IT'S ANOTHER GIFT FROM SOME-ONE...
NANAMI TOUKO IS PERFECT.
SHE DRAWS EVERY-ONE'S ATTEN-TION... AND RUMORS, TOO.
A lot of girls look up to Nanami-san, huh?
I talked to her once on club business when I was a first-year.
She's got the best grades in the school, but she's still so approach-able.
AND SHE'S GORGEOUS!

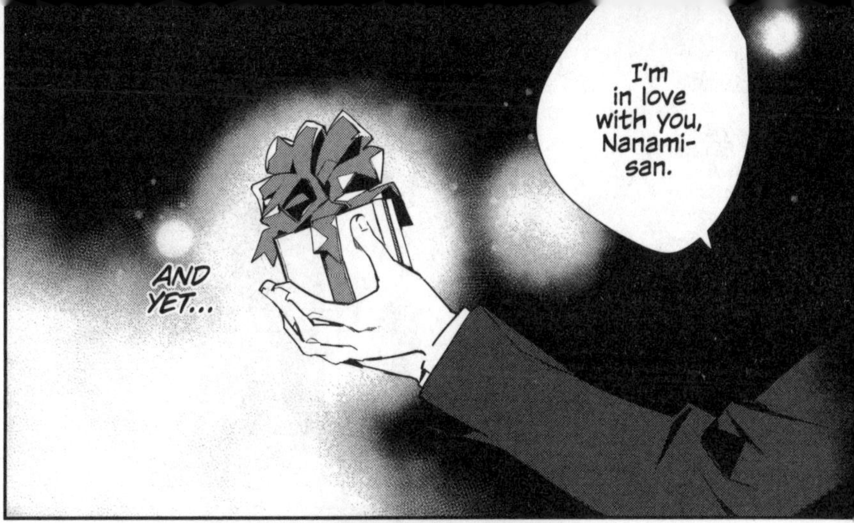
I'm in love with you, Nanami-san.
AND YET...

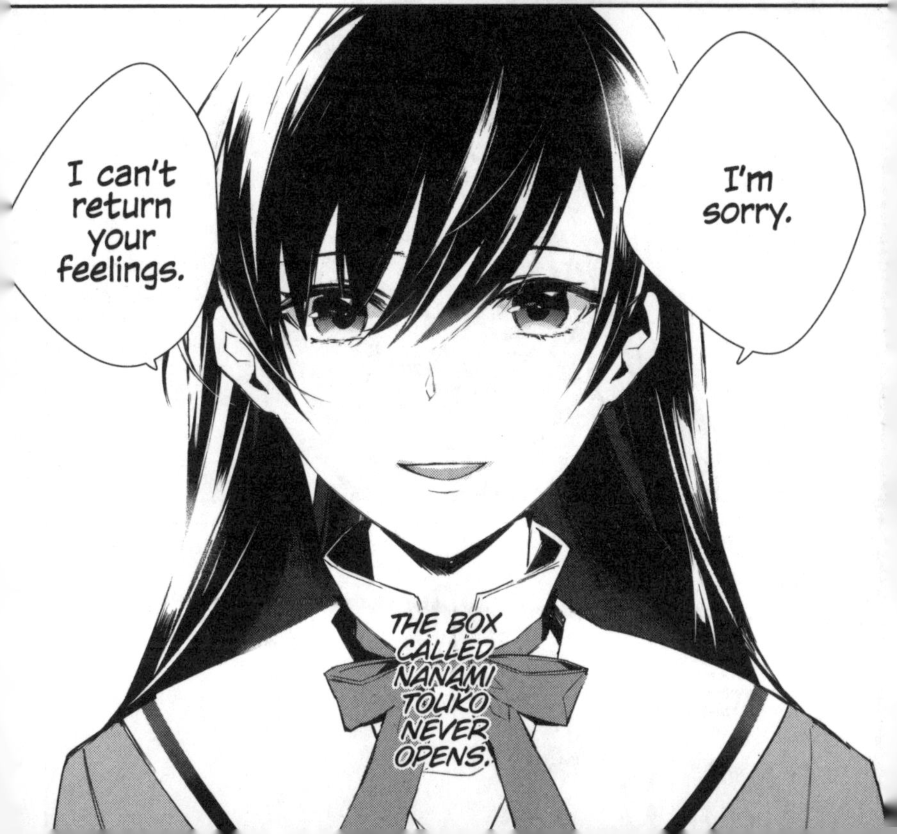
I'm sorry.
I can't return your feelings.
THE BOX CALLED NANAMI TOUKO NEVER OPENS.

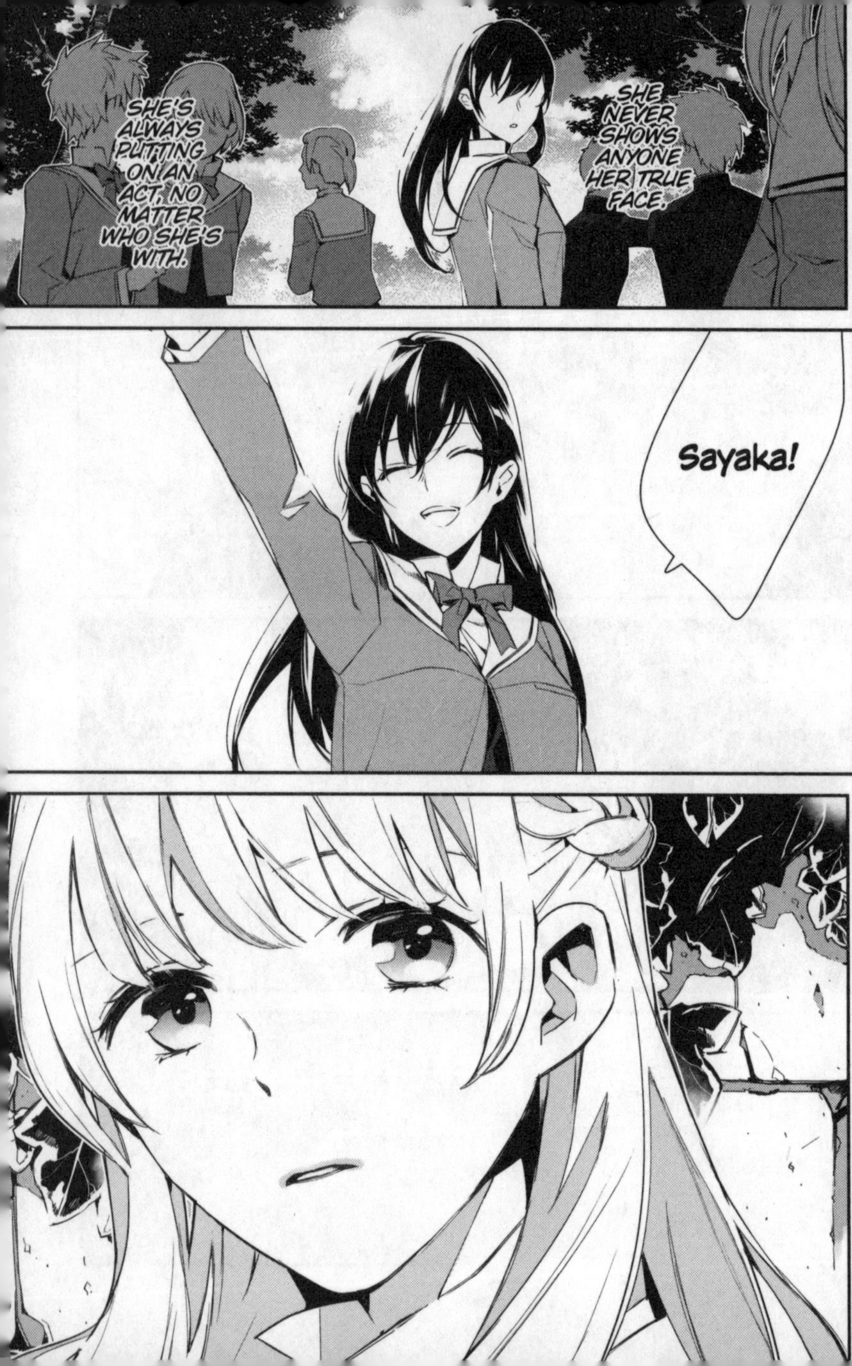
SHE NEVER SHOWS ANYONE HER TRUE FACE.
SHE'S ALWAYS PUTTING ON AN ACT, NO MATTER WHO SHE'S WITH.
Sayaka!

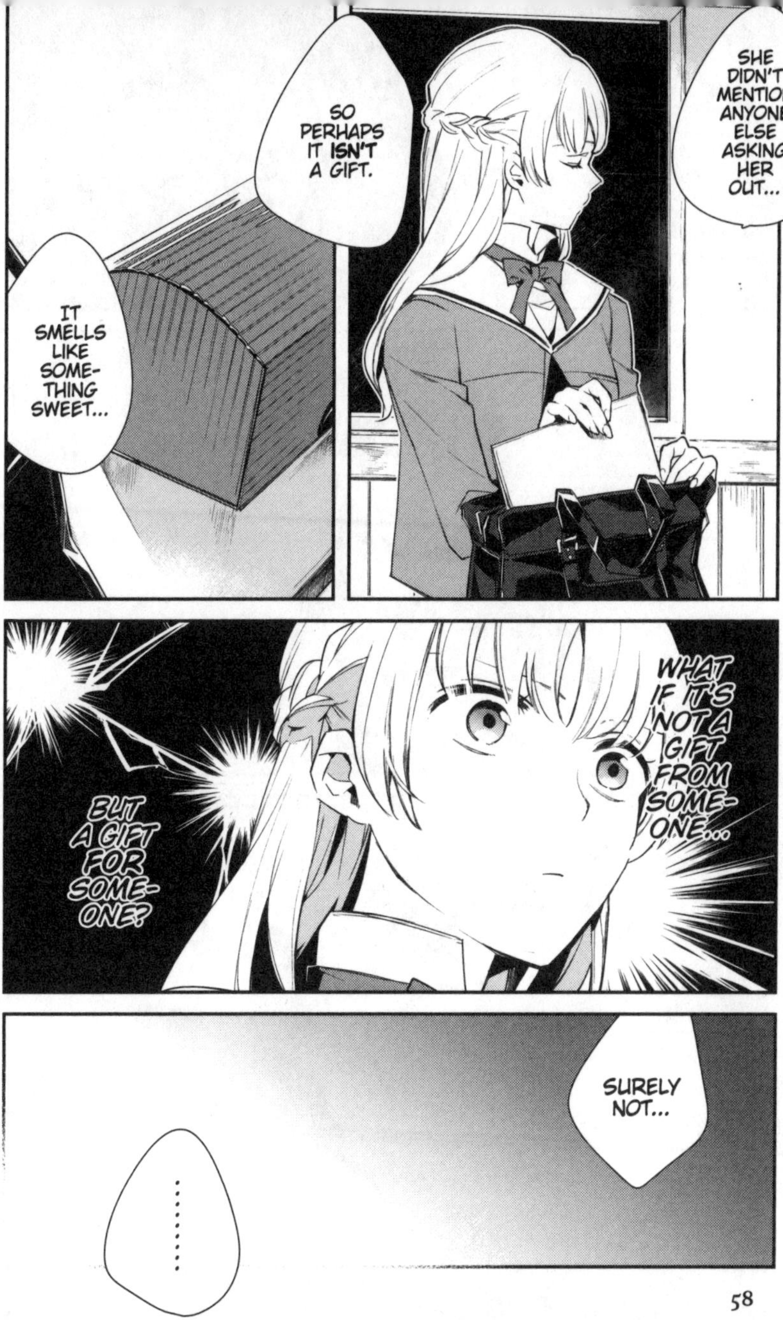
SHE DIDN'T MENTION ANYONE ELSE ASKING HER OUT...
SO PERHAPS IT **ISN'T** A GIFT.
IT SMELLS LIKE SOME-THING SWEET...
WHAT IF IT'S NOT A GIFT FROM SOME-ONE...
BUT A GIFT FOR SOME-ONE?
SURELY NOT...
....

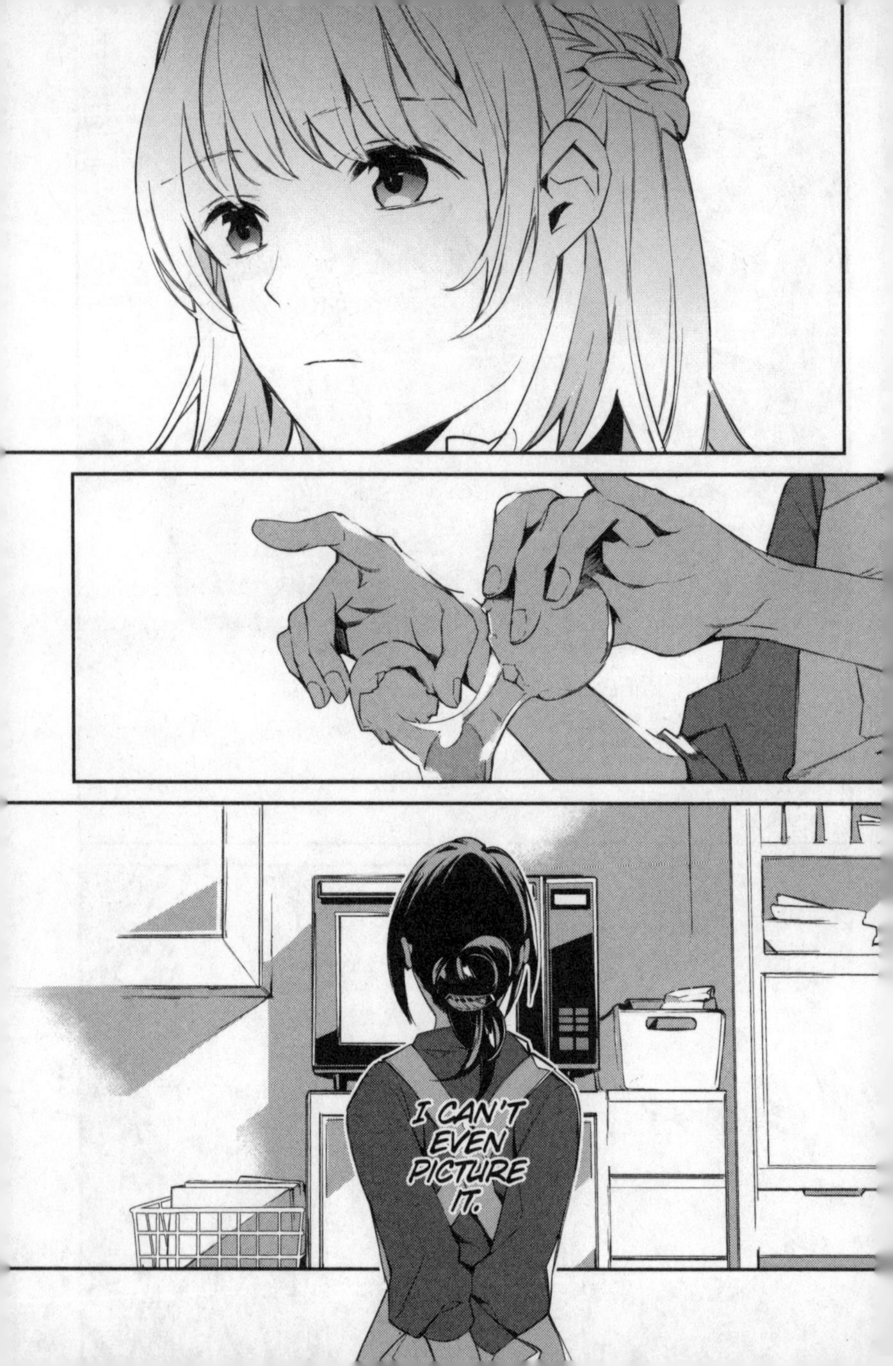
I CAN'T EVEN PICTURE IT.

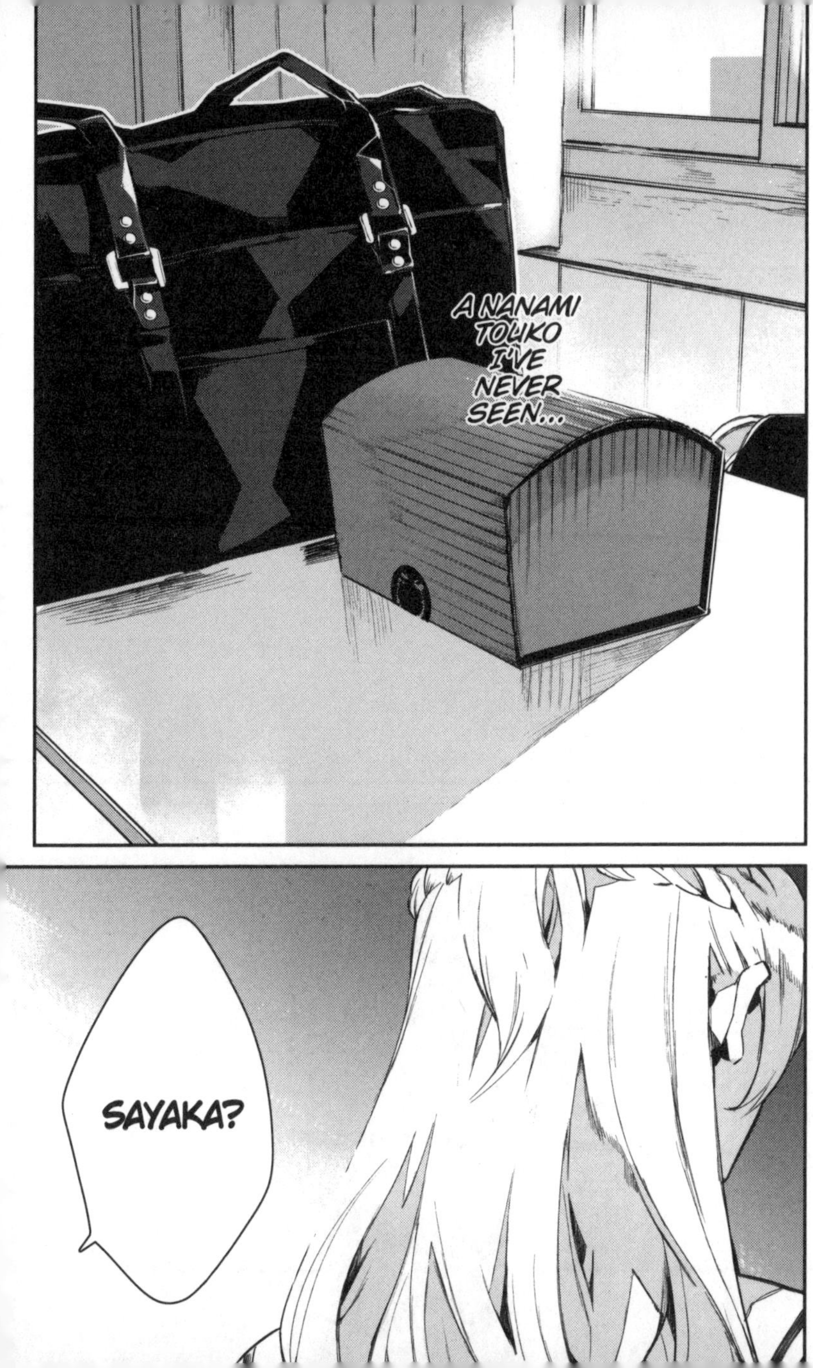
A NANAMI TOUKO I'VE NEVER SEEN...
SAYAKA?

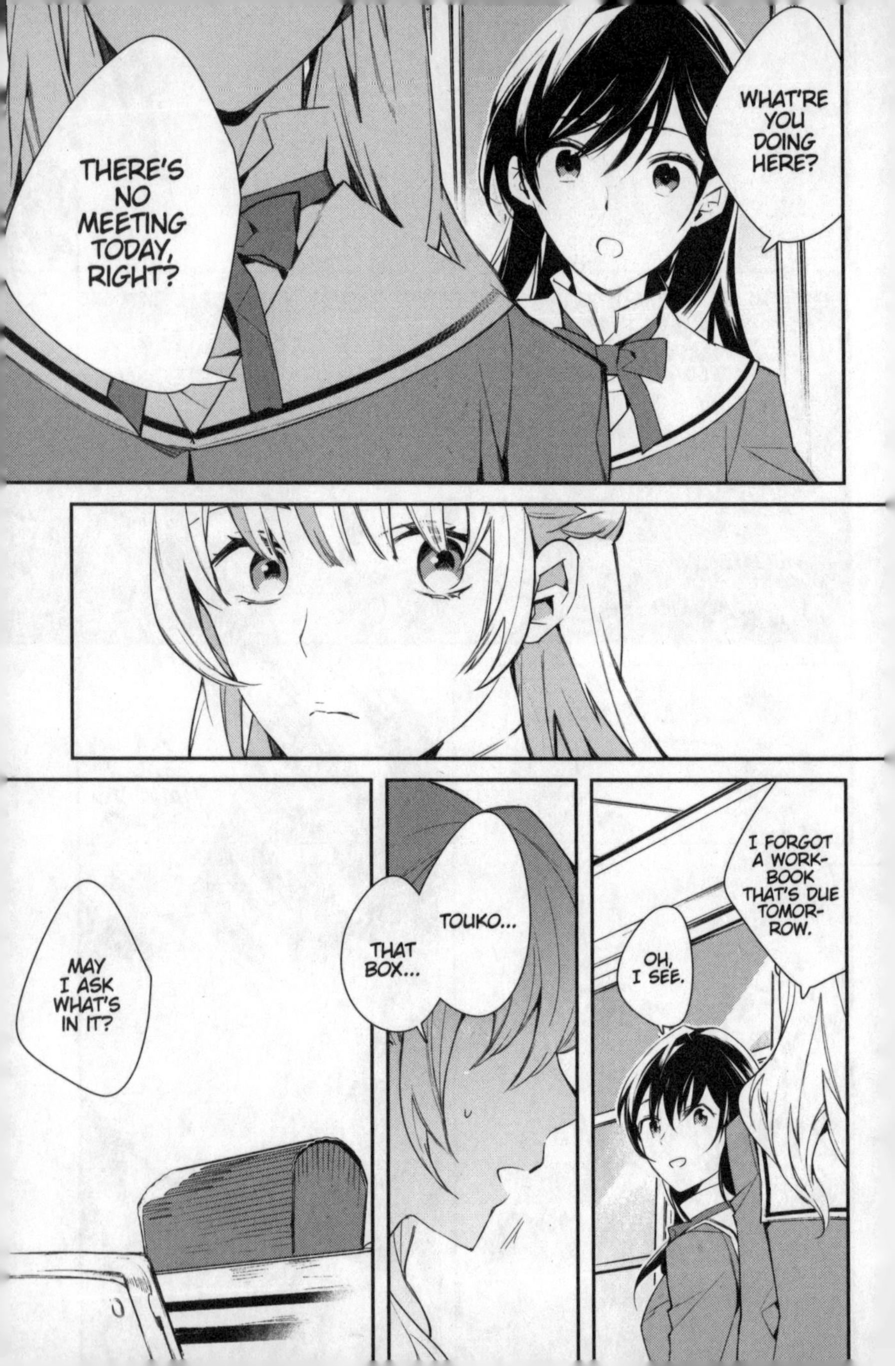
WHAT'RE YOU DOING HERE?
THERE'S NO MEETING TODAY, RIGHT?
I FORGOT A WORK-BOOK THAT'S DUE TOMOR-ROW.
OH, I SEE.
TOUKO...
THAT BOX...
MAY I ASK WHAT'S IN IT?

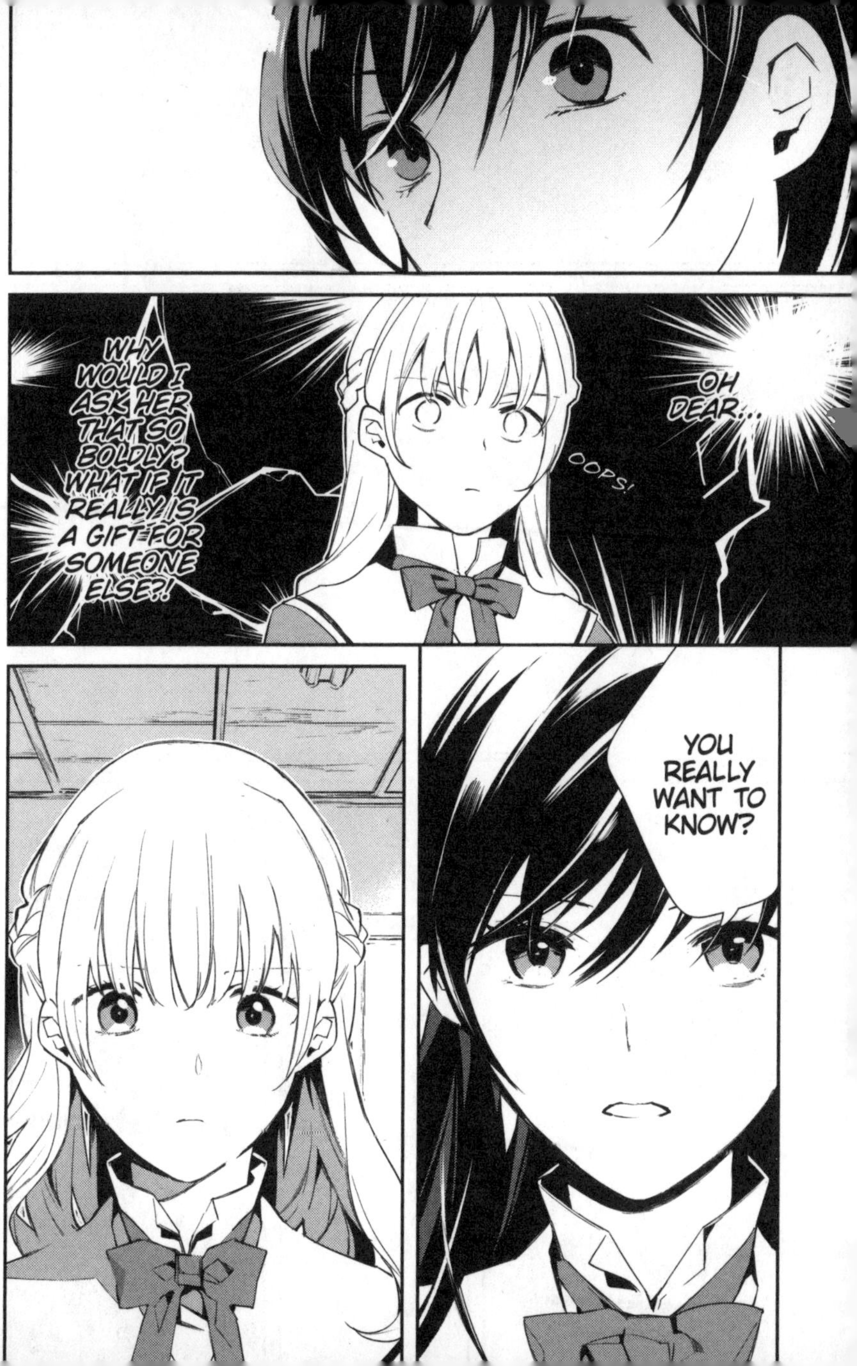
OH DEAR...
OOPS!
WHY WOULD I ASK HER THAT SO BOLDLY? WHAT IF IT REALLY IS A GIFT FOR SOMEONE ELSE?!
YOU REALLY WANT TO KNOW?

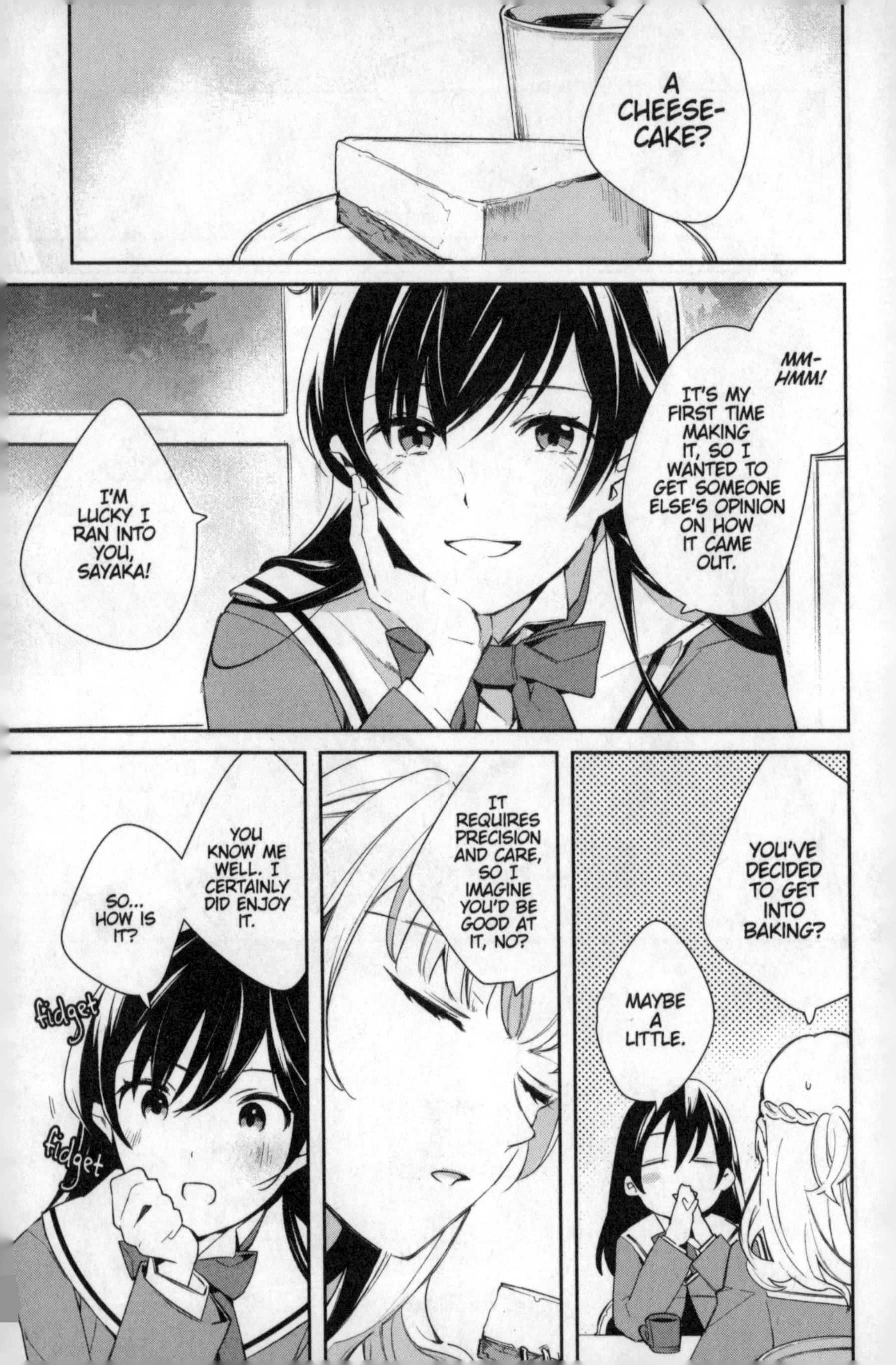
A CHEESE-CAKE?
MM-HMM!
IT'S MY FIRST TIME MAKING IT, SO I WANTED TO GET SOMEONE ELSE'S OPINION ON HOW IT CAME OUT.
I'M LUCKY I RAN INTO YOU, SAYAKA!
YOU'VE DECIDED TO GET INTO BAKING?
MAYBE A LITTLE.
IT REQUIRES PRECISION AND CARE, SO I IMAGINE YOU'D BE GOOD AT IT, NO?
YOU KNOW ME WELL. I CERTAINLY DID ENJOY IT.
SO... HOW IS IT?
fidget
fidget

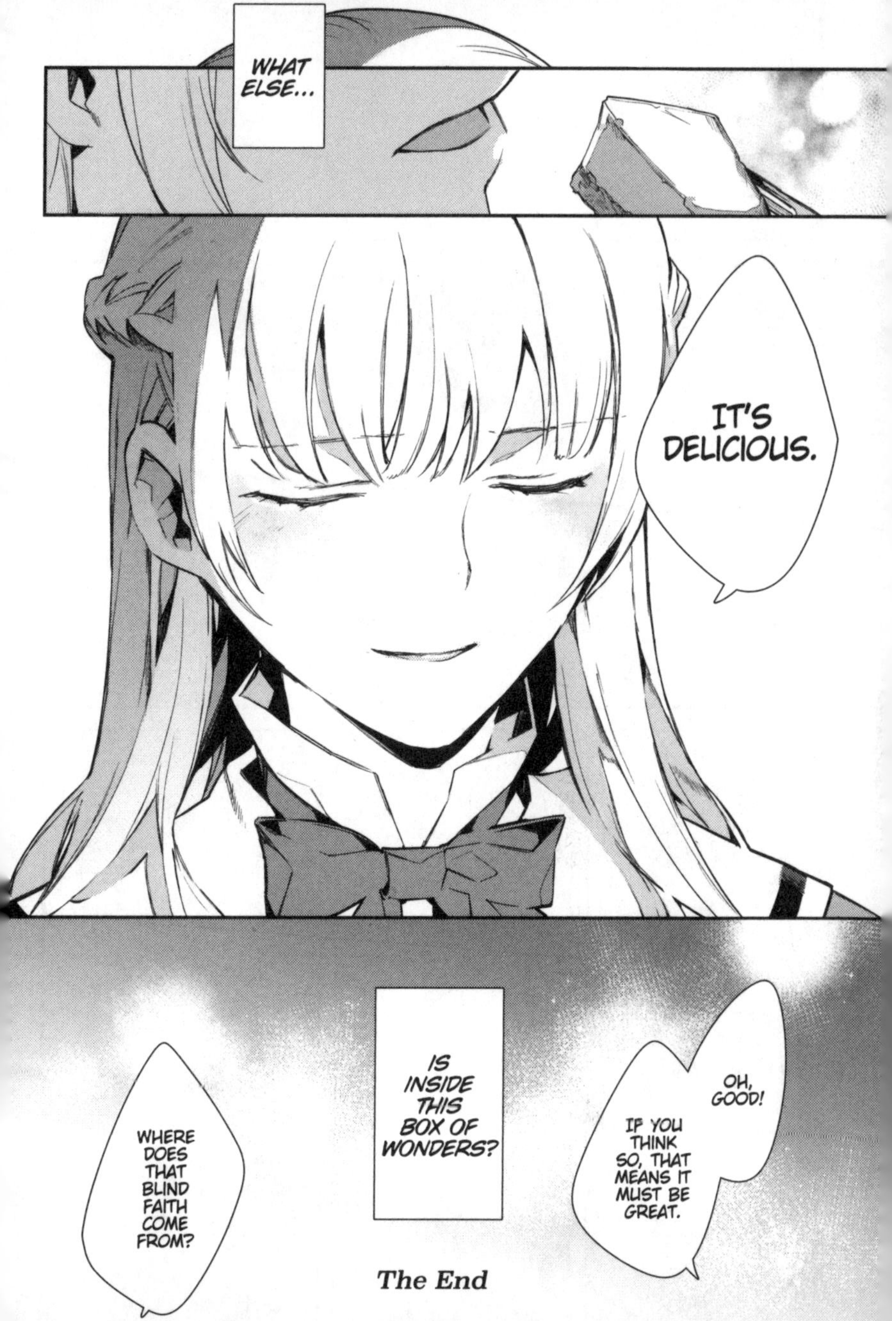
WHAT ELSE...
IT'S DELICIOUS.
OH, GOOD!
IF YOU THINK SO, THAT MEANS IT MUST BE GREAT.
IS INSIDE THIS BOX OF WONDERS?
WHERE DOES THAT BLIND FAITH COME FROM?
The End

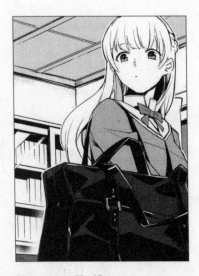

Kazuno Yuikawa

(**Bloom Into You**)

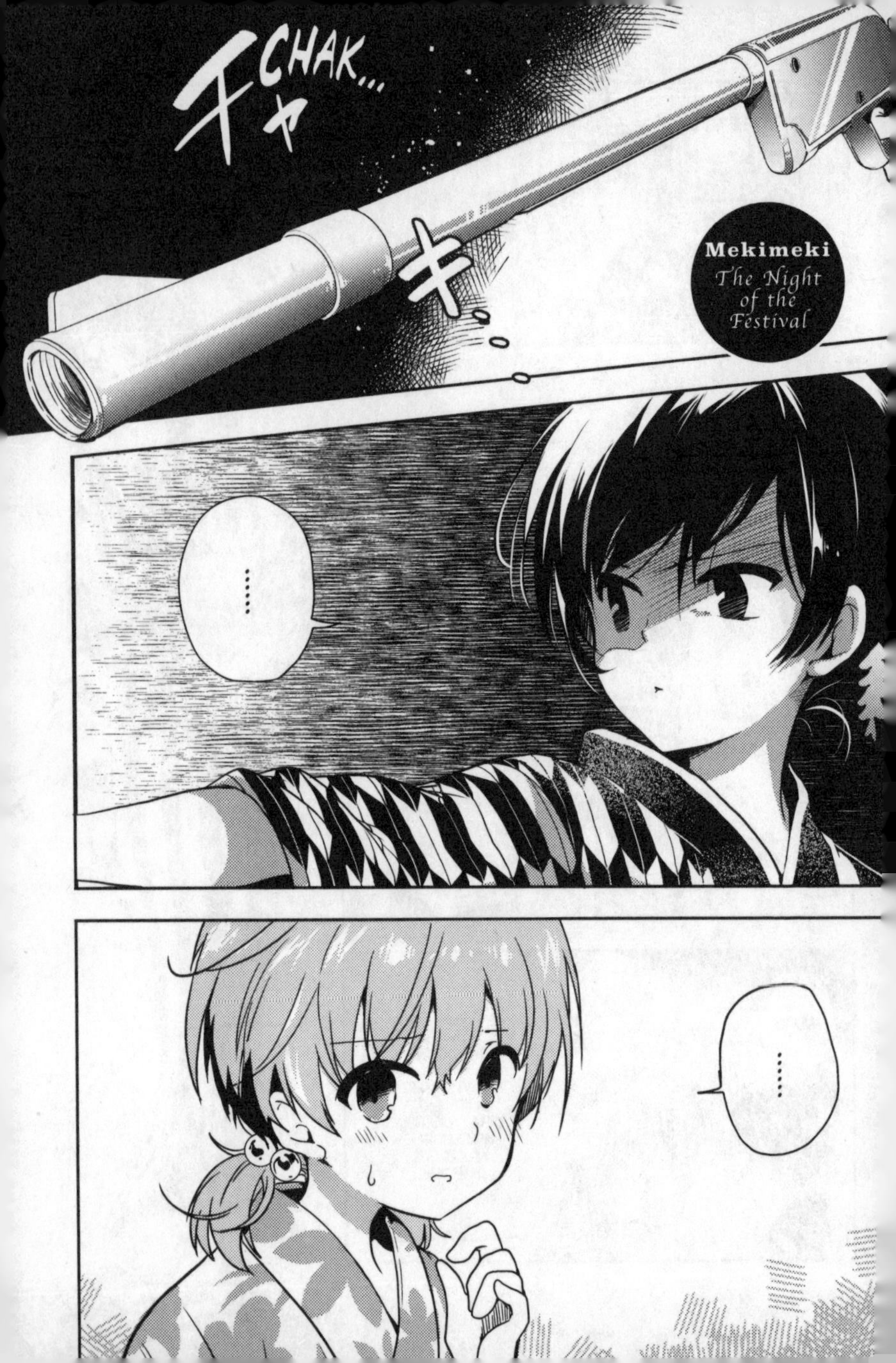
チャ
CHAK...
キ
Mekimeki
The Night of the Festival
......
......

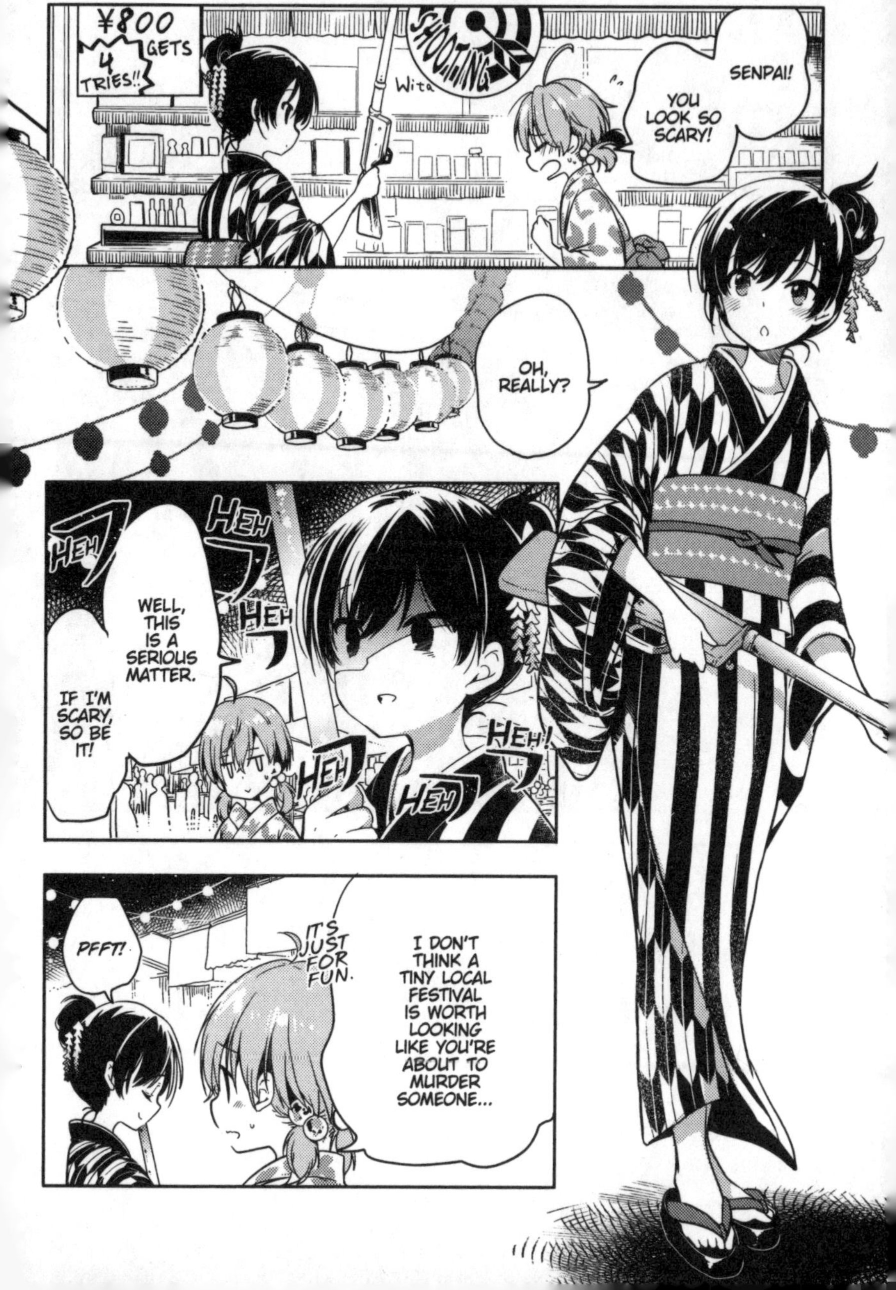
SENPAI! YOU LOOK SO SCARY!
SHOOTING
Wita
¥800 GETS 4 TRIES!!
OH, REALLY?
HEH HEH HEH HEH! HEH HEH
WELL, THIS IS A SERIOUS MATTER.
IF I'M SCARY, SO BE IT!
I DON'T THINK A TINY LOCAL FESTIVAL IS WORTH LOOKING LIKE YOU'RE ABOUT TO MURDER SOMEONE...
IT'S JUST FOR FUN.
PFFT!

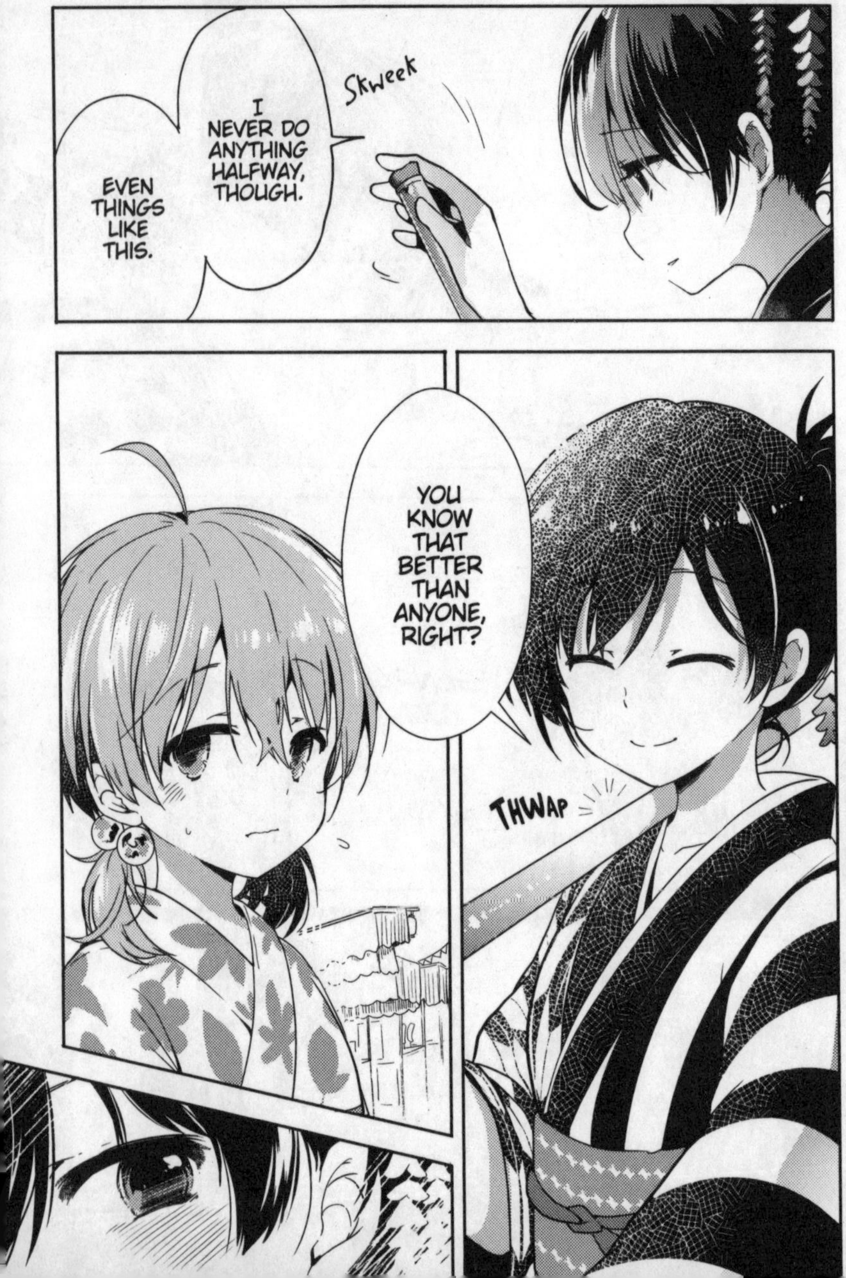
Skweek
I NEVER DO ANYTHING HALFWAY, THOUGH.
EVEN THINGS LIKE THIS.
YOU KNOW THAT BETTER THAN ANYONE, RIGHT?
THWAP

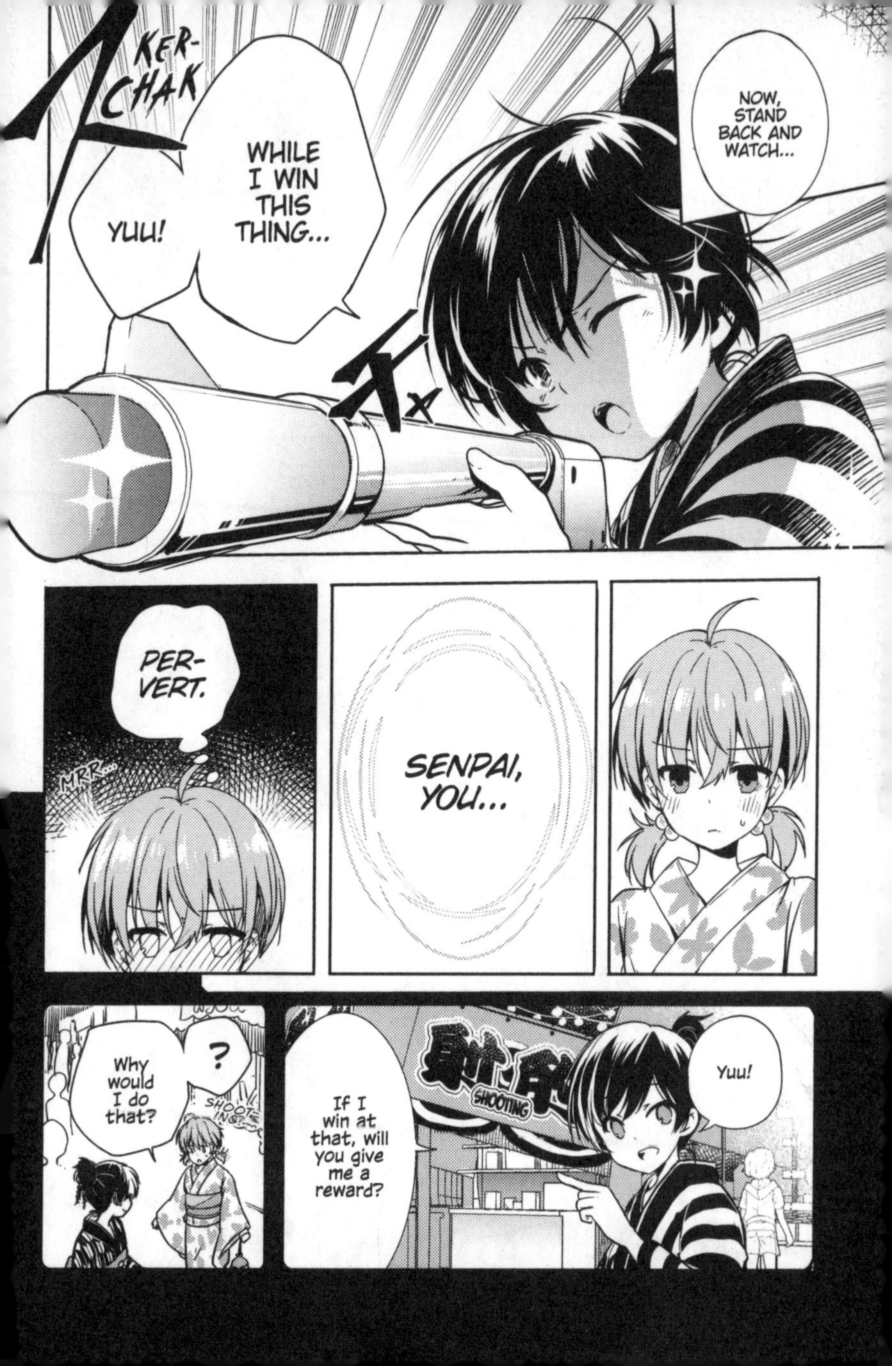
NOW, STAND BACK AND WATCH...
WHILE I WIN THIS THING...
YUU!
KER-CHAK
SENPAI, YOU...
PER-VERT.
MRR...
Yuu!
SHOOTING
If I win at that, will you give me a reward?
?
Why would I do that?
SHOOT-ING!?

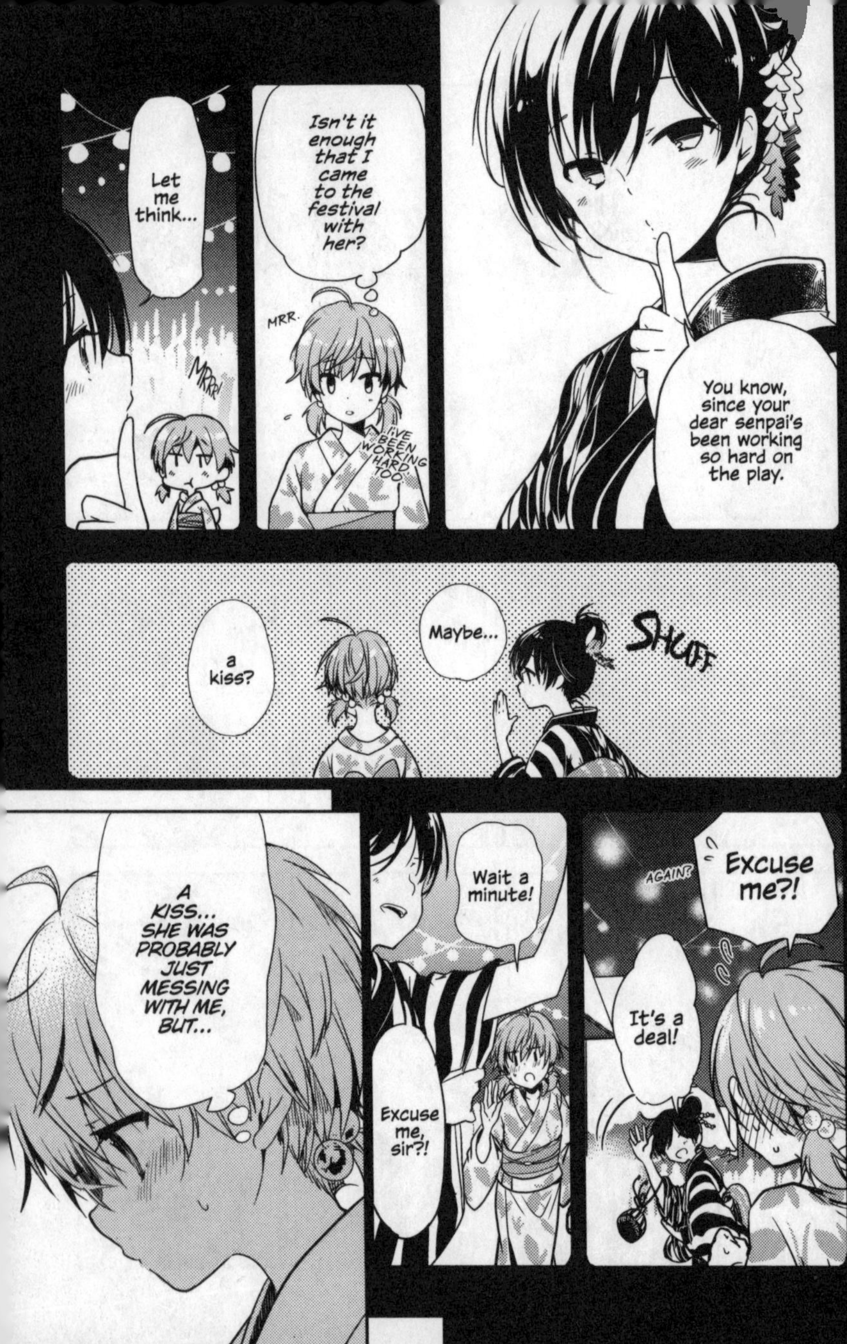

You know, since your dear senpai's been working so hard on the play.
Isn't it enough that I came to the festival with her?
MRR.
I'VE BEEN WORKING HARD TOO
Let me think...
MRRR!
SHUFF
Maybe...
a kiss?
Excuse me?!
AGAIN?
It's a deal!
Wait a minute!
Excuse me, sir?!
A KISS... SHE WAS PROBABLY JUST MESSING WITH ME, BUT...

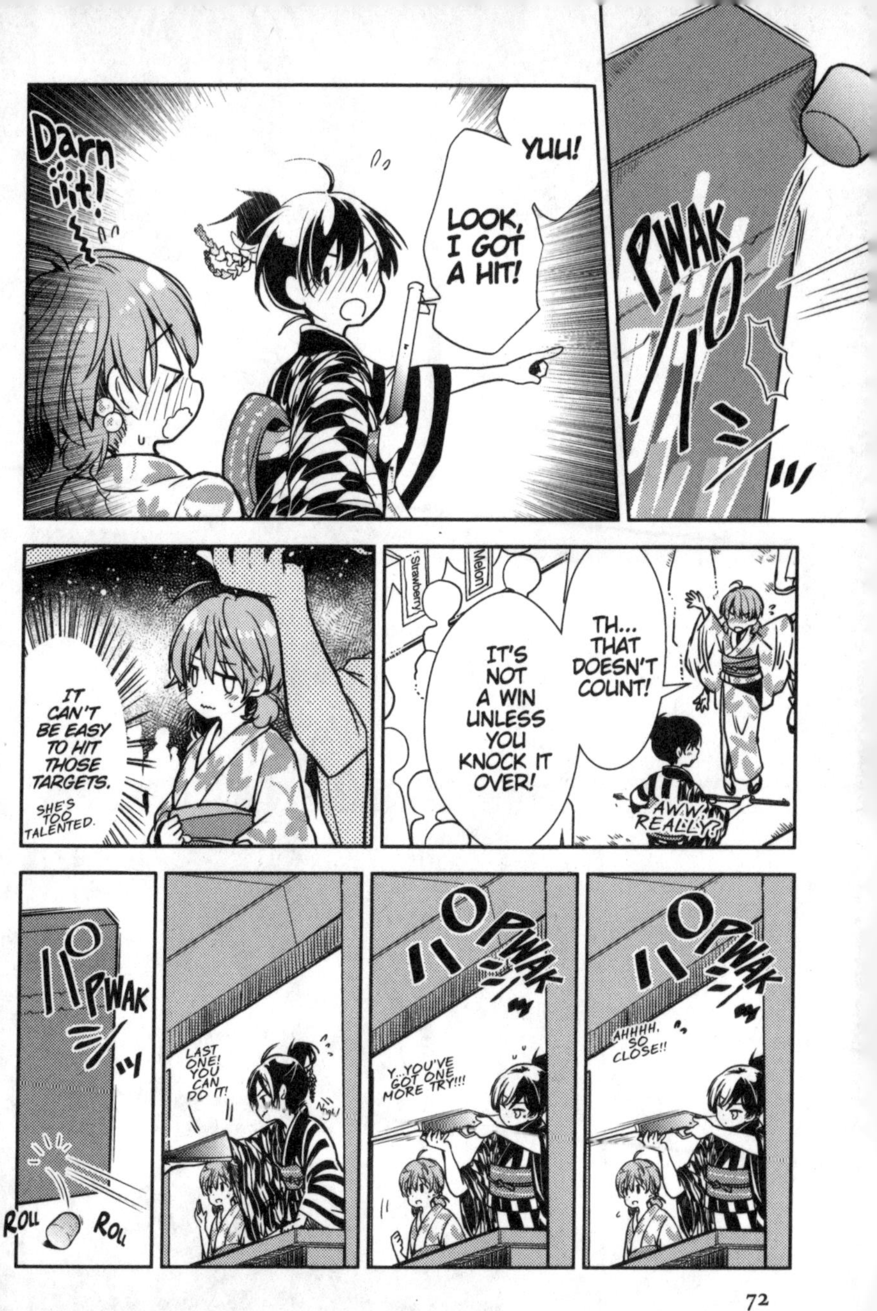
PWAK
YUU!
LOOK, I GOT A HIT!
Darn it!
Strawberry
Melon
TH... THAT DOESN'T COUNT!
IT'S NOT A WIN UNLESS YOU KNOCK IT OVER!
AWW REALLY?
IT CAN'T BE EASY TO HIT THOSE TARGETS.
SHE'S TOO TALENTED.
PWAK
AHHHH. SO CLOSE!!
PWAK
Y..YOU'VE GOT ONE MORE TRY!!!
LAST ONE! YOU CAN DO IT!
Nngh!
PWAK
ROLL
ROLL

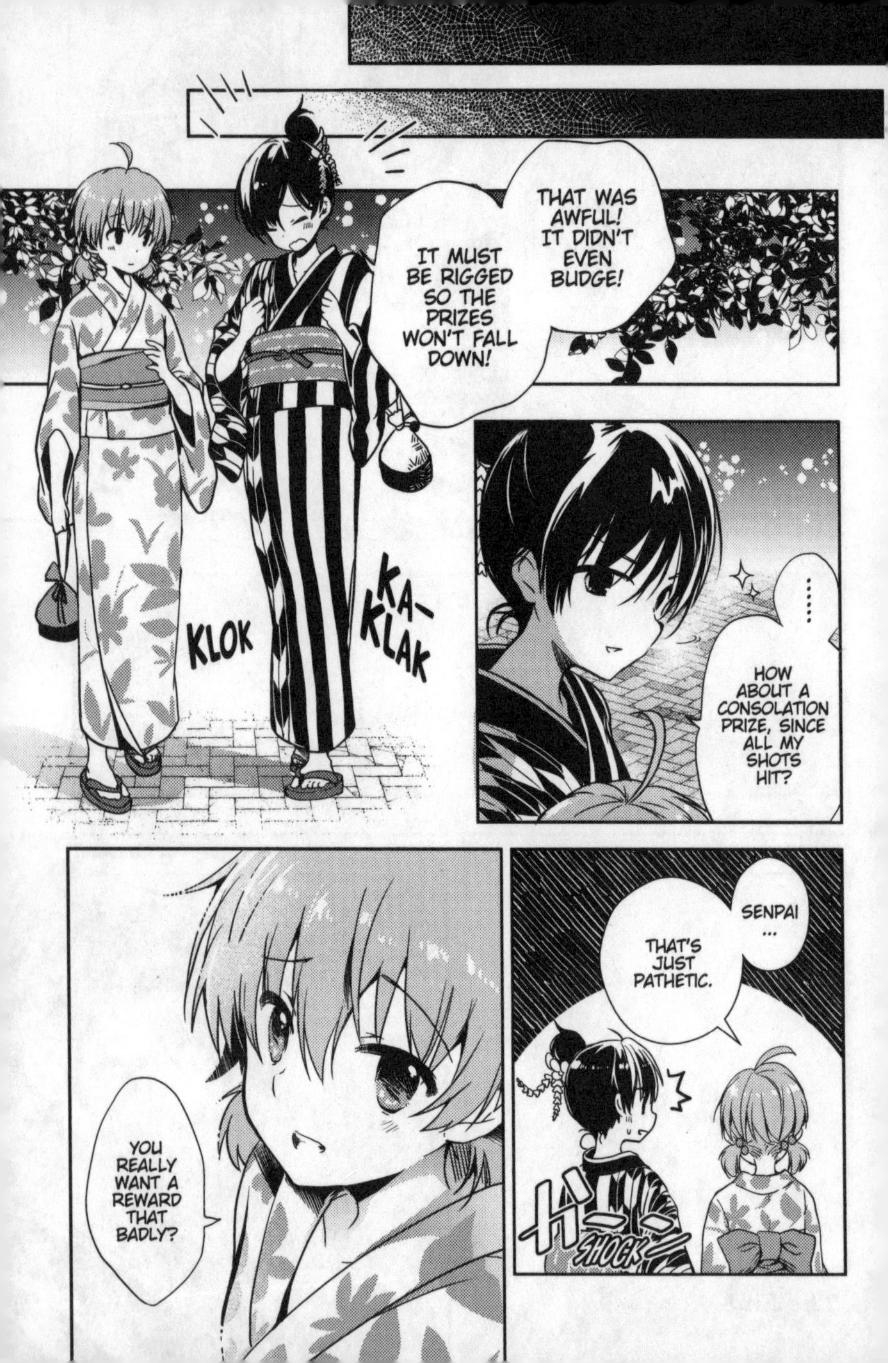
THAT WAS AWFUL! IT DIDN'T EVEN BUDGE!
IT MUST BE RIGGED SO THE PRIZES WON'T FALL DOWN!
KA-KLAK
KLOK
......
HOW ABOUT A CONSOLATION PRIZE, SINCE ALL MY SHOTS HIT?
SENPAI ...
THAT'S JUST PATHETIC.
SHOCK
YOU REALLY WANT A REWARD THAT BADLY?

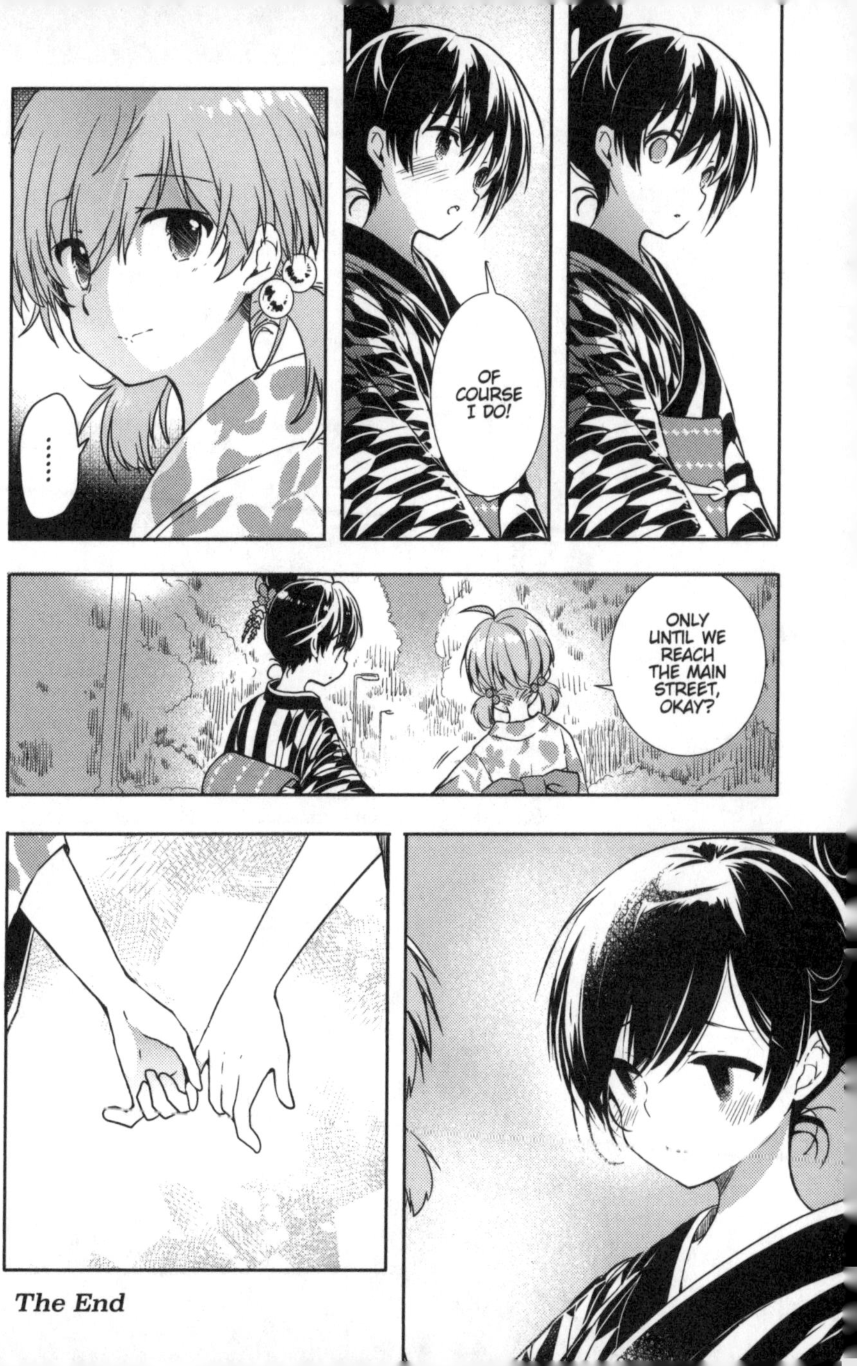
OF COURSE I DO!
......
ONLY UNTIL WE REACH THE MAIN STREET, OKAY?

The End

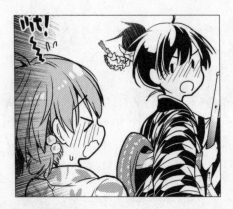

Mekimeki

Best known for *Only You ~Anata to Watashi no Futari Bocchi Keikaku~* (KADOKAWA).

(**Bloom Into You**)

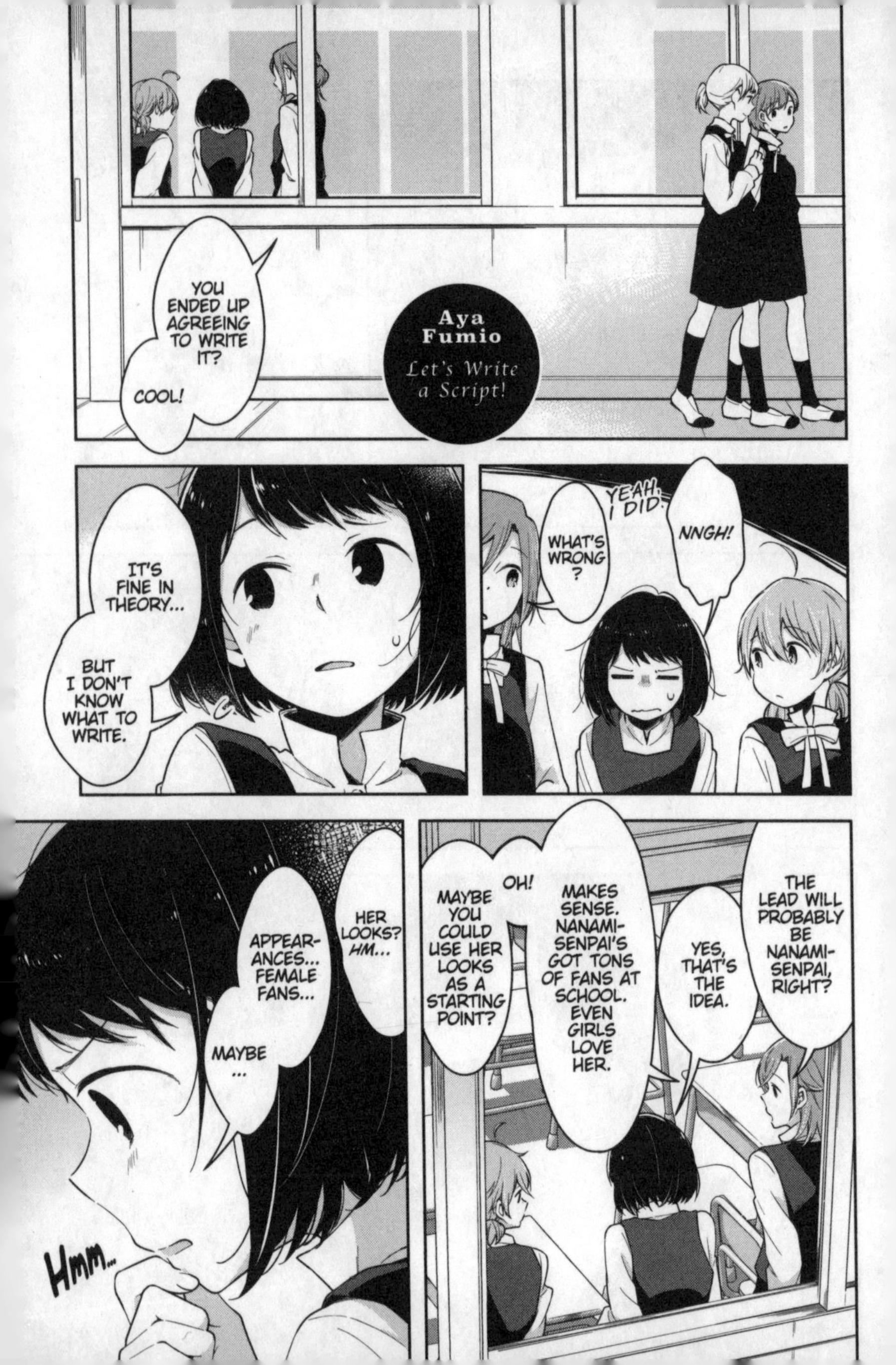

YOU ENDED UP AGREEING TO WRITE IT?
COOL!
Aya Fumio
Let's Write a Script!
NNGH!
YEAH, I DID.
WHAT'S WRONG?
IT'S FINE IN THEORY...
BUT I DON'T KNOW WHAT TO WRITE.
THE LEAD WILL PROBABLY BE NANAMI-SENPAI, RIGHT?
YES, THAT'S THE IDEA.
MAKES SENSE. NANAMI-SENPAI'S GOT TONS OF FANS AT SCHOOL. EVEN GIRLS LOVE HER.
OH!
MAYBE YOU COULD USE HER LOOKS AS A STARTING POINT?
HER LOOKS? HM...
APPEARANCES... FEMALE FANS...
MAYBE...
Hmm...

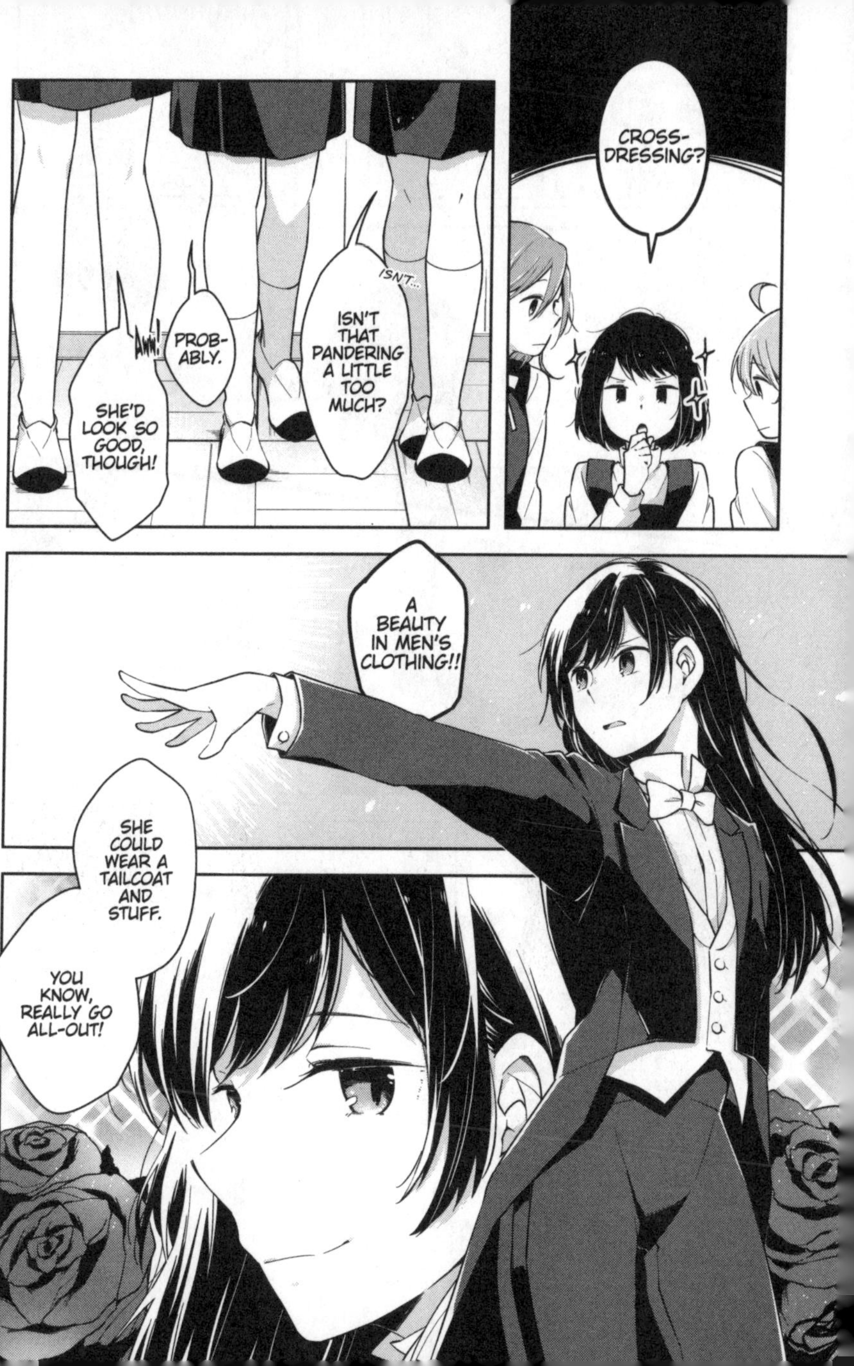
CROSS-DRESSING?
ISN'T...
ISN'T THAT PANDERING A LITTLE TOO MUCH?
PROB-ABLY.
Aww!
SHE'D LOOK SO GOOD, THOUGH!
A BEAUTY IN MEN'S CLOTHING!!
SHE COULD WEAR A TAILCOAT AND STUFF.
YOU KNOW, REALLY GO ALL-OUT!

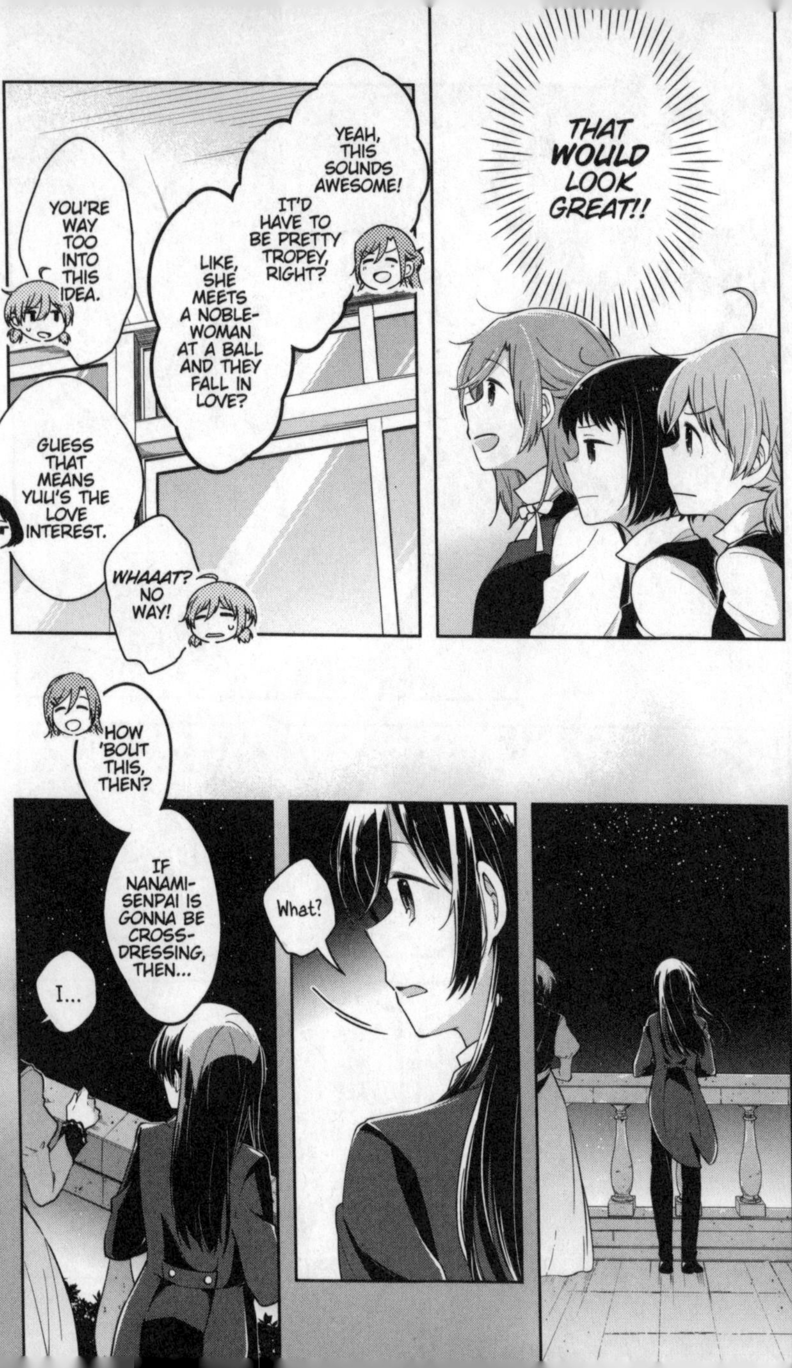
THAT WOULD LOOK GREAT!!
YEAH, THIS SOUNDS AWESOME!
IT'D HAVE TO BE PRETTY TROPEY, RIGHT?
LIKE, SHE MEETS A NOBLE-WOMAN AT A BALL AND THEY FALL IN LOVE?
YOU'RE WAY TOO INTO THIS IDEA.
GUESS THAT MEANS YUU'S THE LOVE INTEREST.
WHAAAT? NO WAY!
HOW 'BOUT THIS, THEN?
IF NANAMI-SENPAI IS GONNA BE CROSS-DRESSING, THEN...
What?
I...

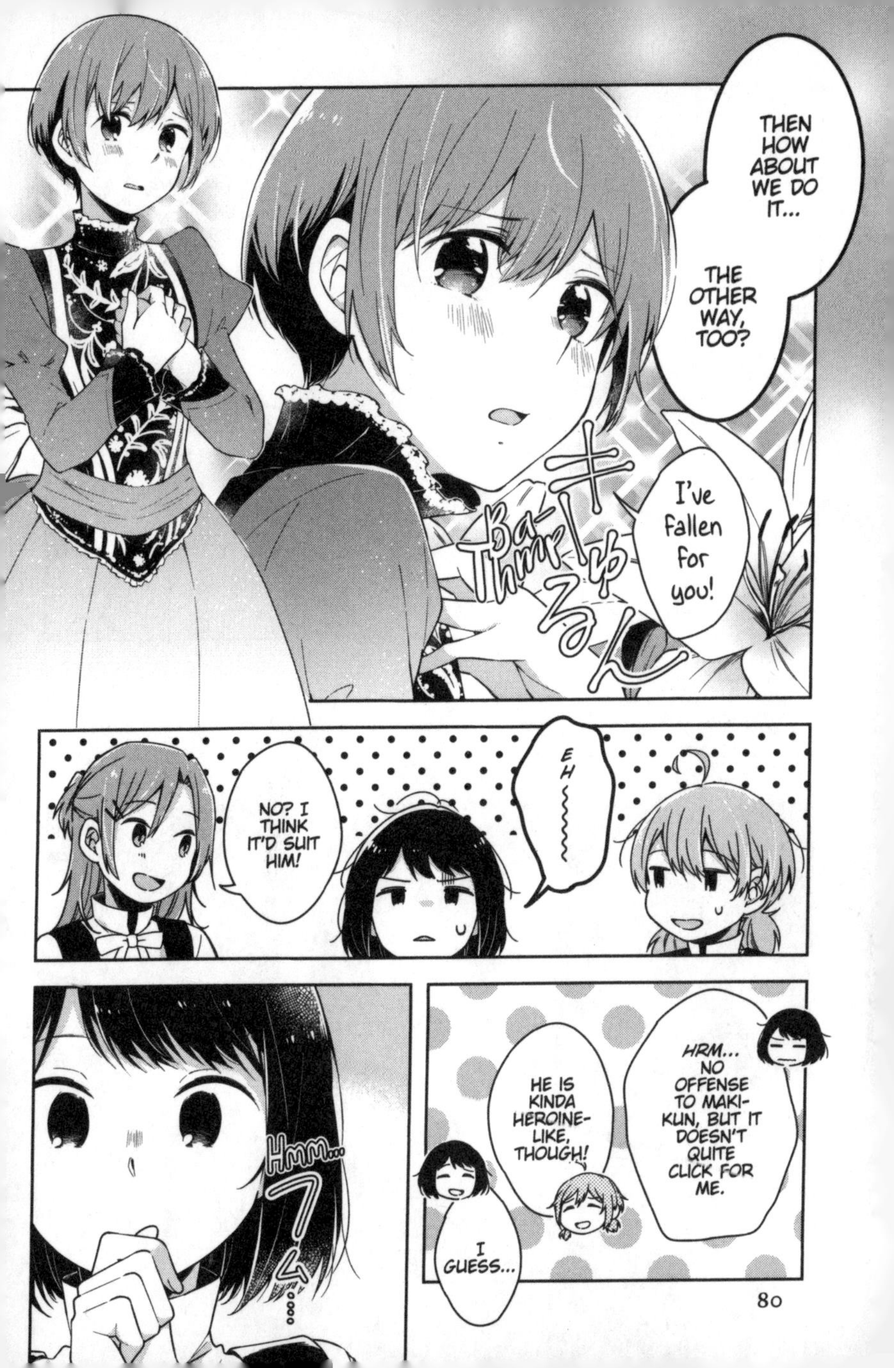
THEN HOW ABOUT WE DO IT...
THE OTHER WAY, TOO?
I've fallen for you!
EH~
NO? I THINK IT'D SUIT HIM!
HRM... NO OFFENSE TO MAKI-KUN, BUT IT DOESN'T QUITE CLICK FOR ME.
HE IS KINDA HEROINE-LIKE, THOUGH!
I GUESS...
Hmm...
フム...

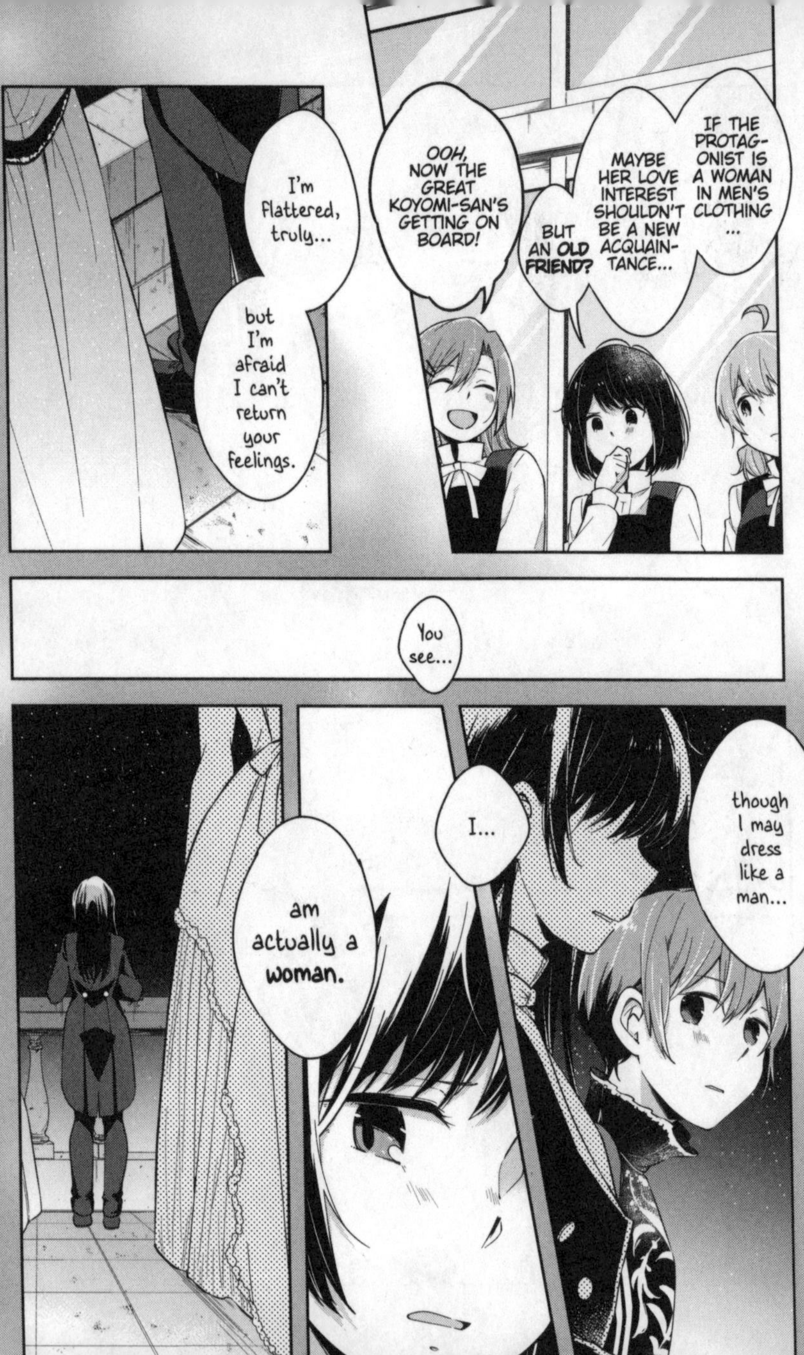
IF THE PROTAGONIST IS A WOMAN IN MEN'S CLOTHING...
MAYBE HER LOVE INTEREST SHOULDN'T BE A NEW ACQUAINTANCE...
BUT AN **OLD FRIEND?**
OOH, NOW THE GREAT KOYOMI-SAN'S GETTING ON BOARD!
I'm flattered, truly...
but I'm afraid I can't return your feelings.
You see...
though I may dress like a man...
I...
am actually a **woman.**

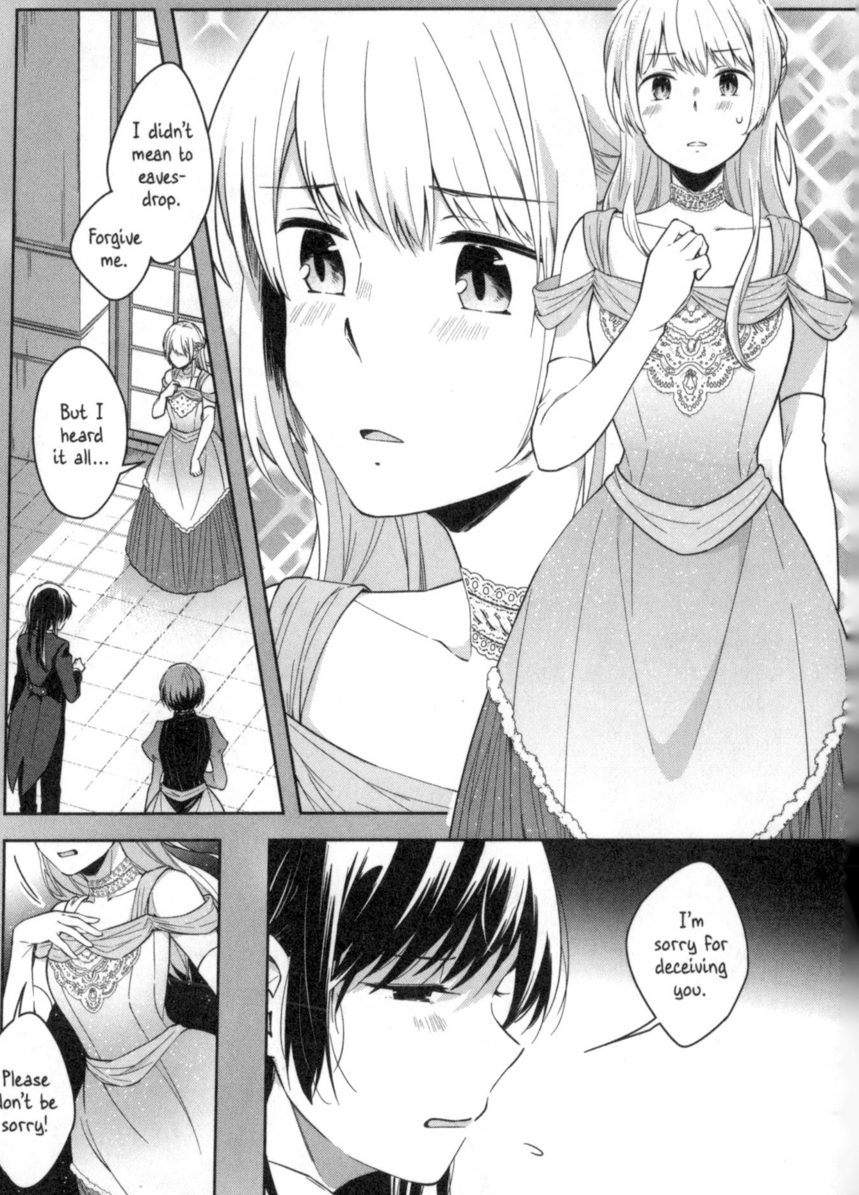
I didn't mean to eaves-drop.
Forgive me.
But I heard it all...
I'm sorry for deceiving you.
Please don't be sorry!

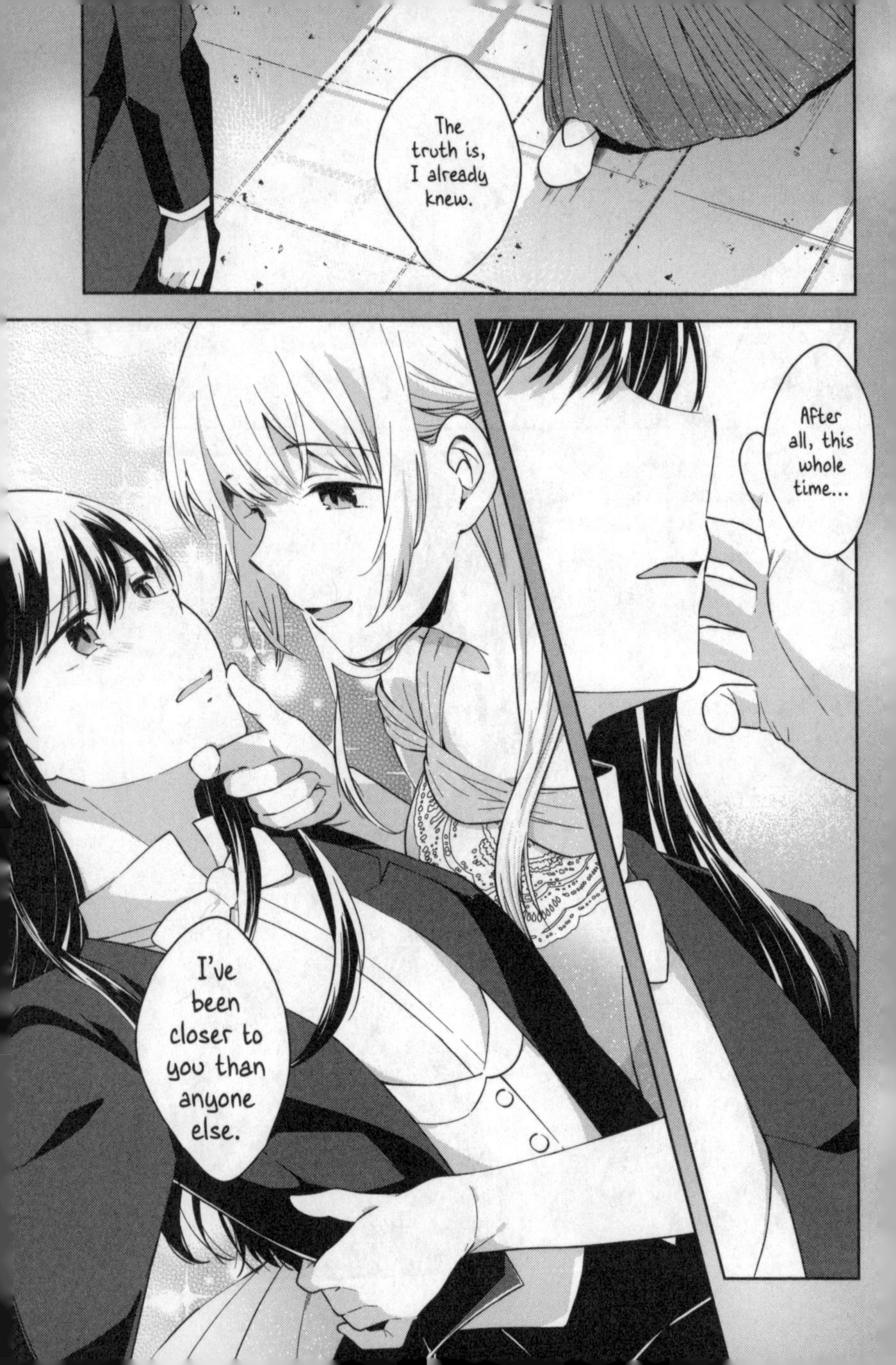
The truth is, I already knew.
After all, this whole time...
I've been closer to you than anyone else.

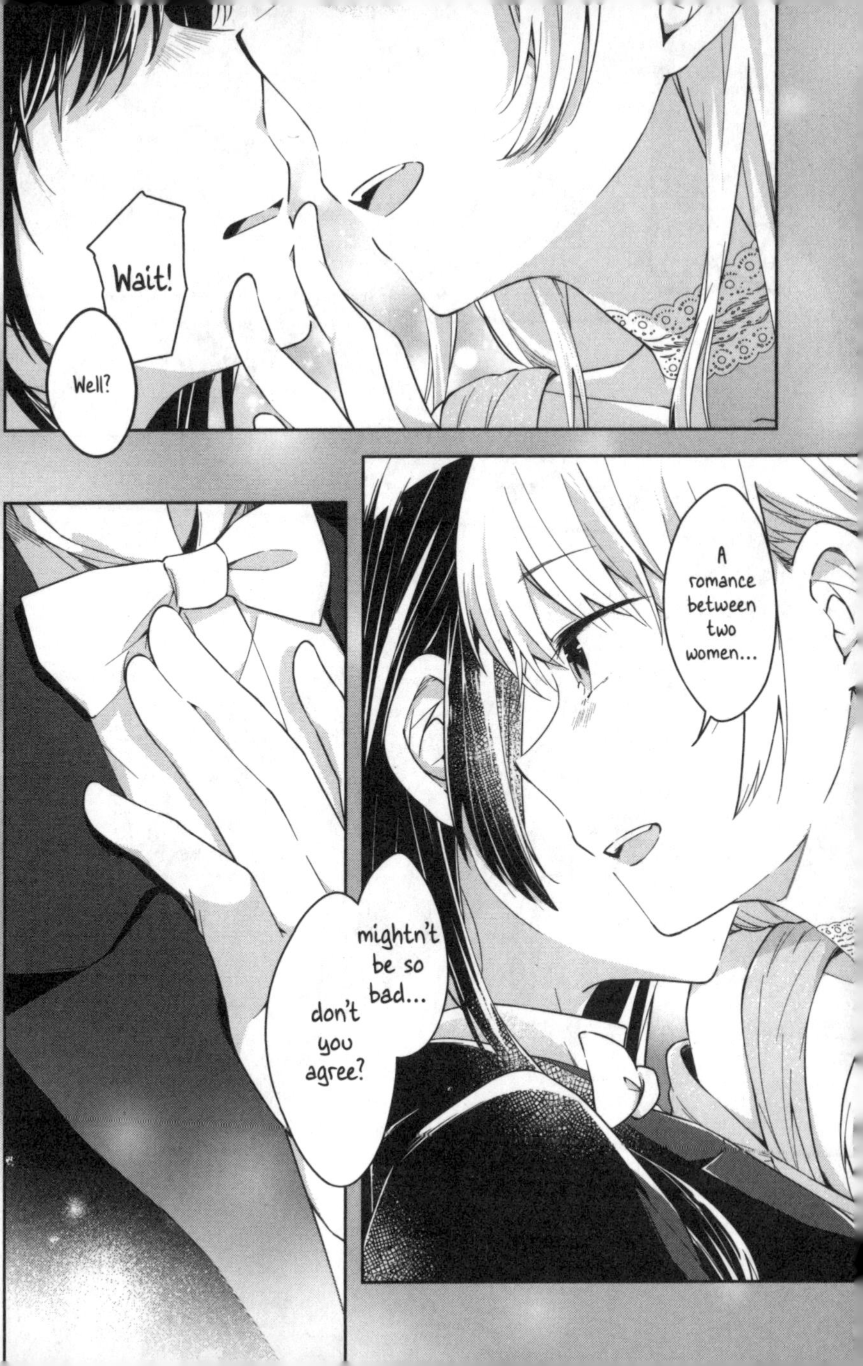
Wait!
Well?
A romance between two women...
mightn't be so bad...
don't you agree?

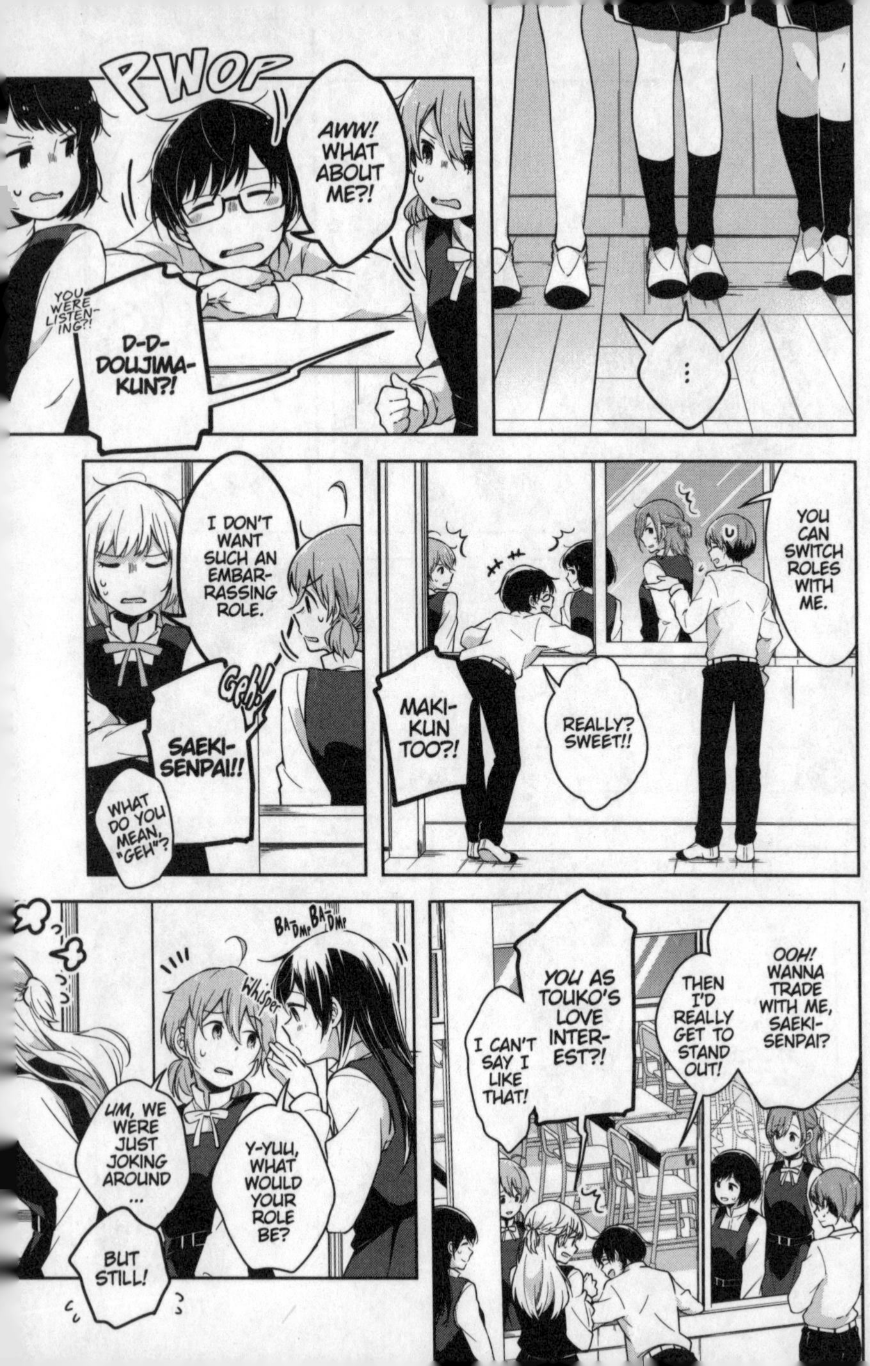
…
PWOP
AWW! WHAT ABOUT ME?!
YOU WERE LISTENING?!
D-D-DOUJIMA-KUN?!
YOU CAN SWITCH ROLES WITH ME.
REALLY? SWEET!!
MAKI-KUN TOO?!
I DON'T WANT SUCH AN EMBARRASSING ROLE.
GEH!
SAEKI-SENPAI!!
WHAT DO YOU MEAN, "GEH"?
OOH! WANNA TRADE WITH ME, SAEKI-SENPAI?
THEN I'D REALLY GET TO STAND OUT!
YOU AS TOUKO'S LOVE INTEREST?!
I CAN'T SAY I LIKE THAT!
BA-DMP BA-DMP
WHISPER
Y-YUU, WHAT WOULD YOUR ROLE BE?
UM, WE WERE JUST JOKING AROUND...
BUT STILL!

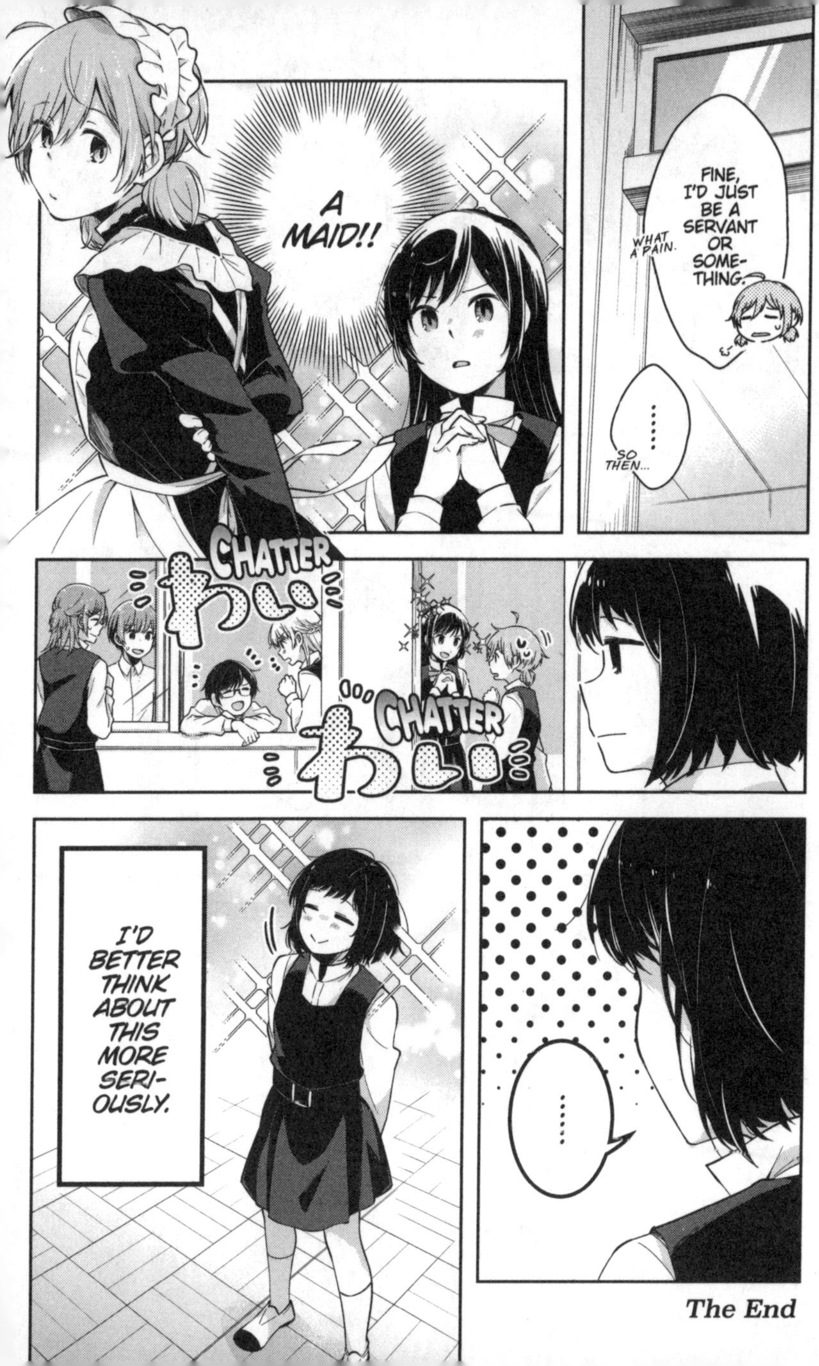
FINE, I'D JUST BE A SERVANT OR SOME-THING.
WHAT A PAIN.
......
SO THEN...
A MAID!!
CHATTER
わいわい
CHATTER
わいわい
......
I'D BETTER THINK ABOUT THIS MORE SERI-OUSLY.
The End

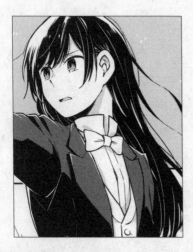

Aya Fumio

Best known for *Watashi wa Kimi wo Nakasetai*
(*I Want to Make You Cry*) (Hakusensha).

(Bloom Into You)

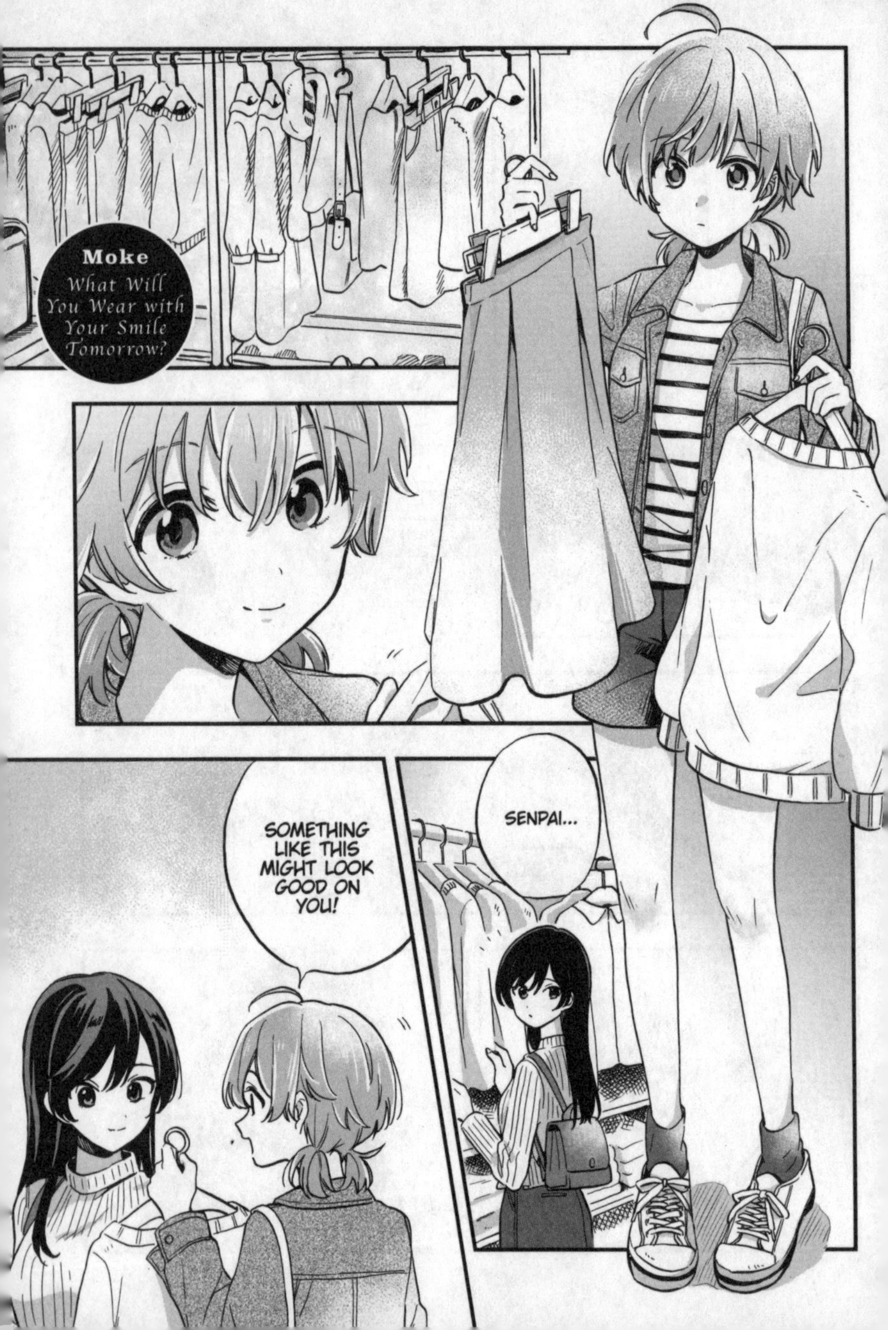
Moke
What Will You Wear with Your Smile Tomorrow?
SENPAI...
SOMETHING LIKE THIS MIGHT LOOK GOOD ON YOU!

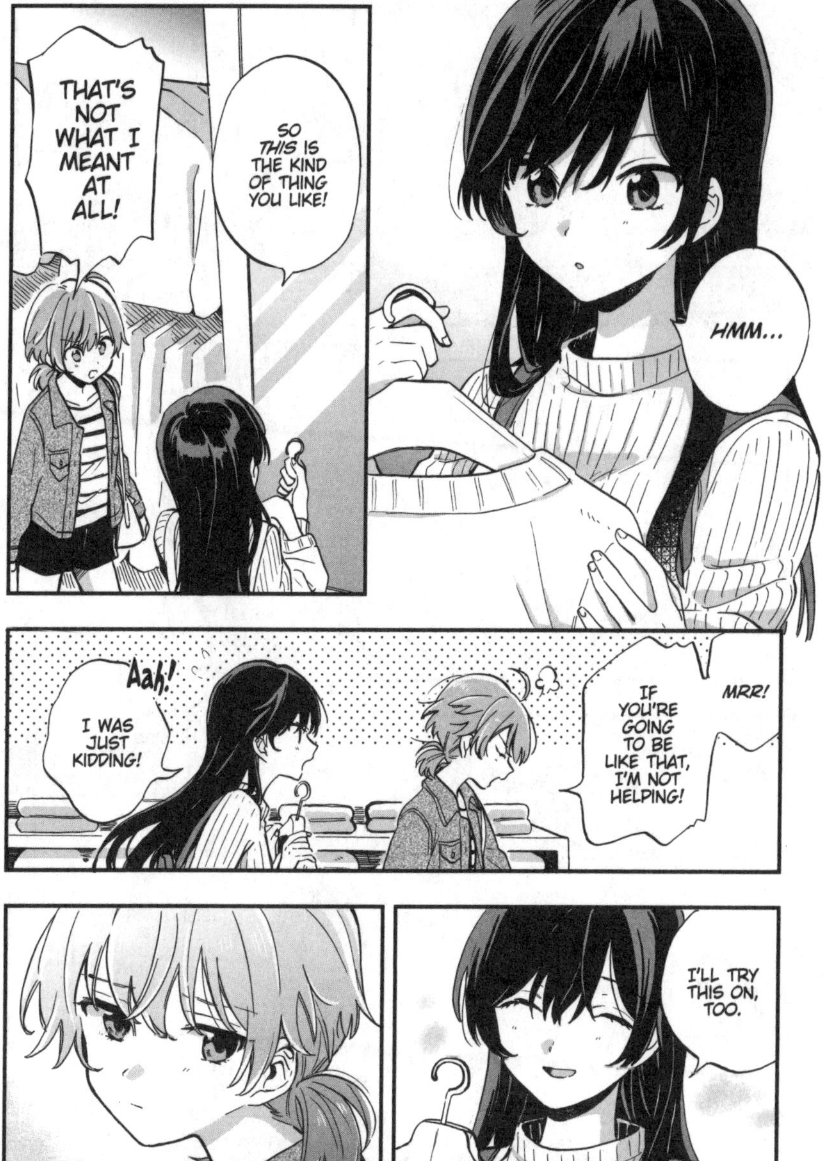
HMM...
SO *THIS* IS THE KIND OF THING YOU LIKE!
THAT'S NOT WHAT I MEANT AT ALL!
MRR!
IF YOU'RE GOING TO BE LIKE THAT, I'M NOT HELPING!
Aah!
I WAS JUST KIDDING!
I'LL TRY THIS ON, TOO.

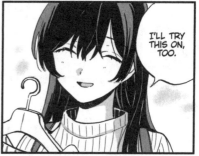

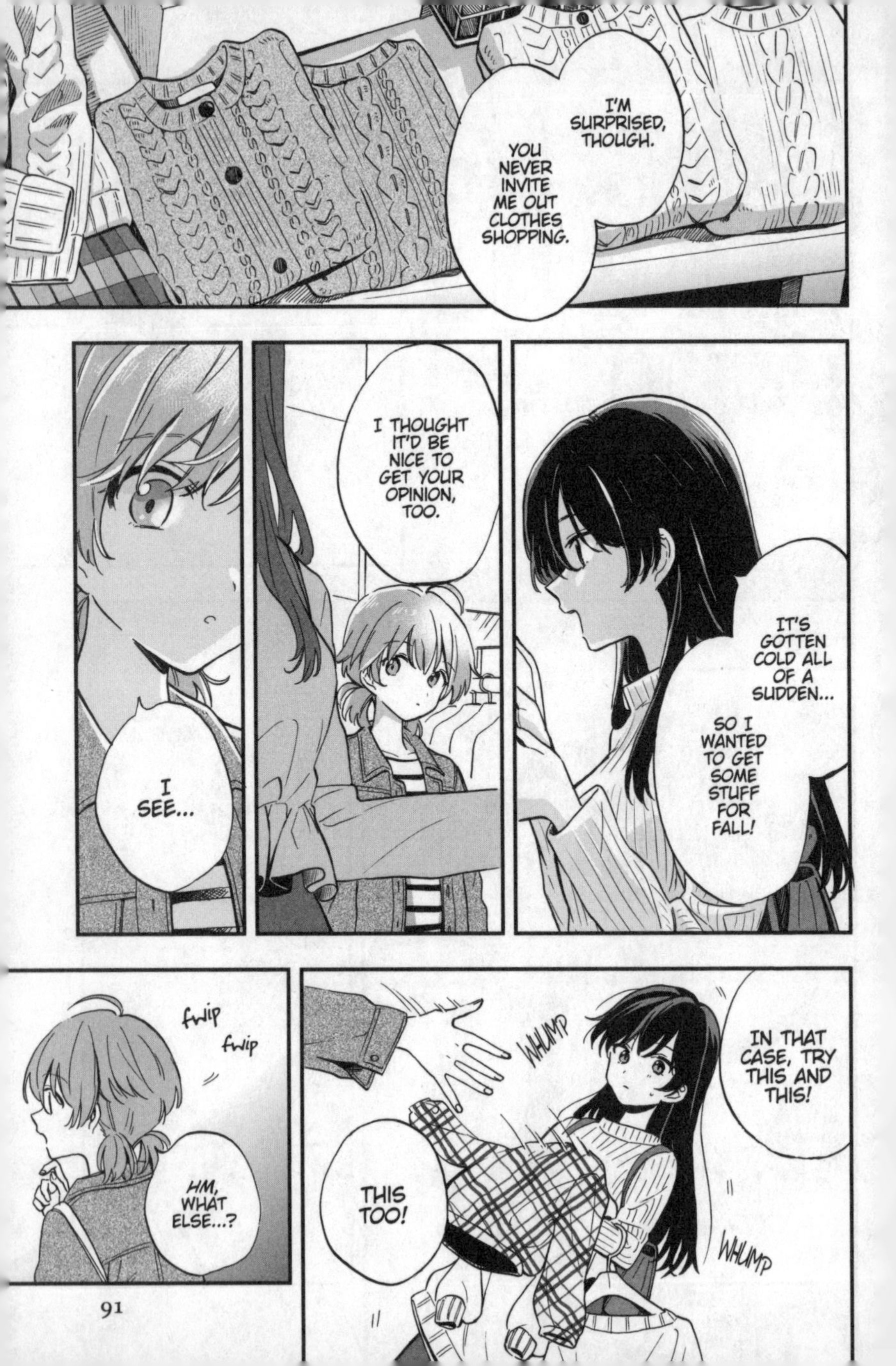
I'M SURPRISED, THOUGH.
YOU NEVER INVITE ME OUT CLOTHES SHOPPING.
IT'S GOTTEN COLD ALL OF A SUDDEN...
SO I WANTED TO GET SOME STUFF FOR FALL!
I THOUGHT IT'D BE NICE TO GET YOUR OPINION, TOO.
I SEE...
IN THAT CASE, TRY THIS AND THIS!
WHUMP
THIS TOO!
WHUMP
fwip
fwip
HM, WHAT ELSE...?

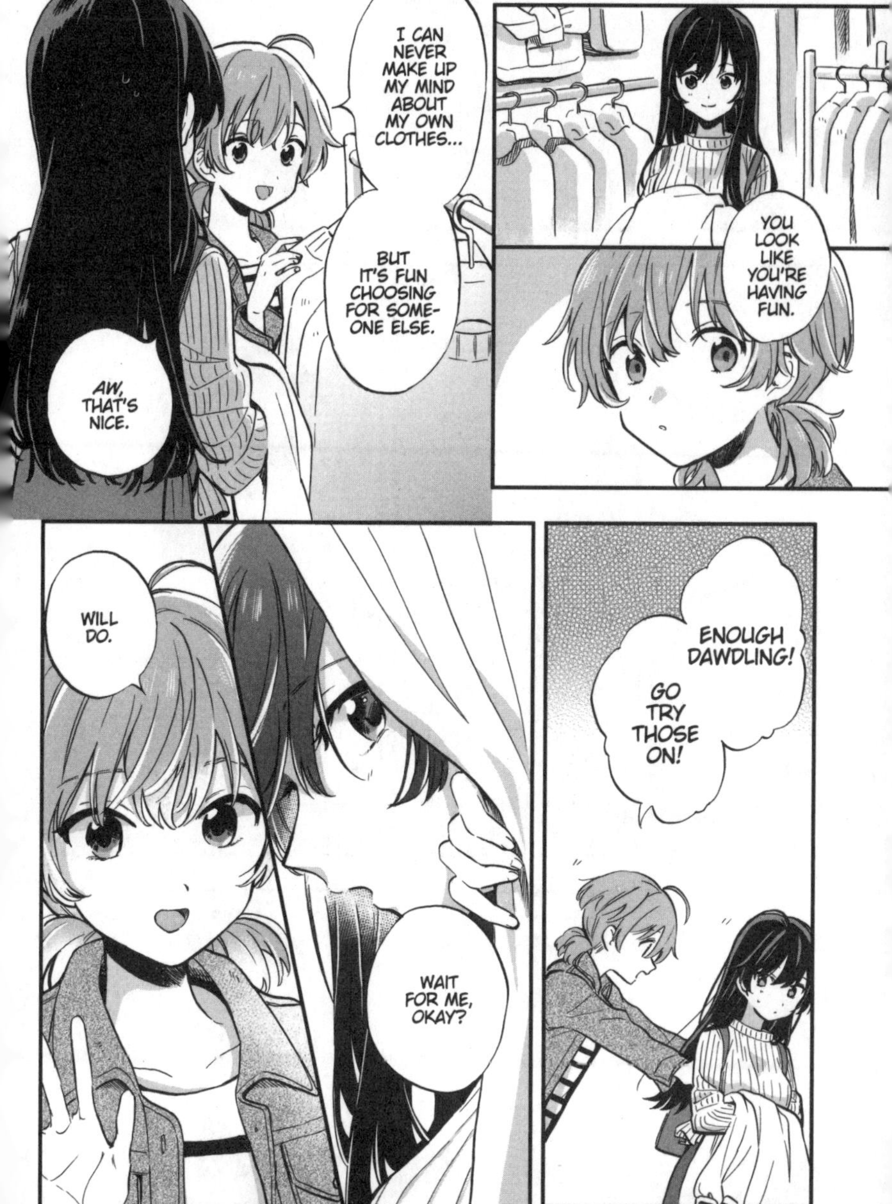
YOU LOOK LIKE YOU'RE HAVING FUN.
I CAN NEVER MAKE UP MY MIND ABOUT MY OWN CLOTHES...
BUT IT'S FUN CHOOSING FOR SOME-ONE ELSE.
AW, THAT'S NICE.
ENOUGH DAWDLING!
GO TRY THOSE ON!
WAIT FOR ME, OKAY?
WILL DO.

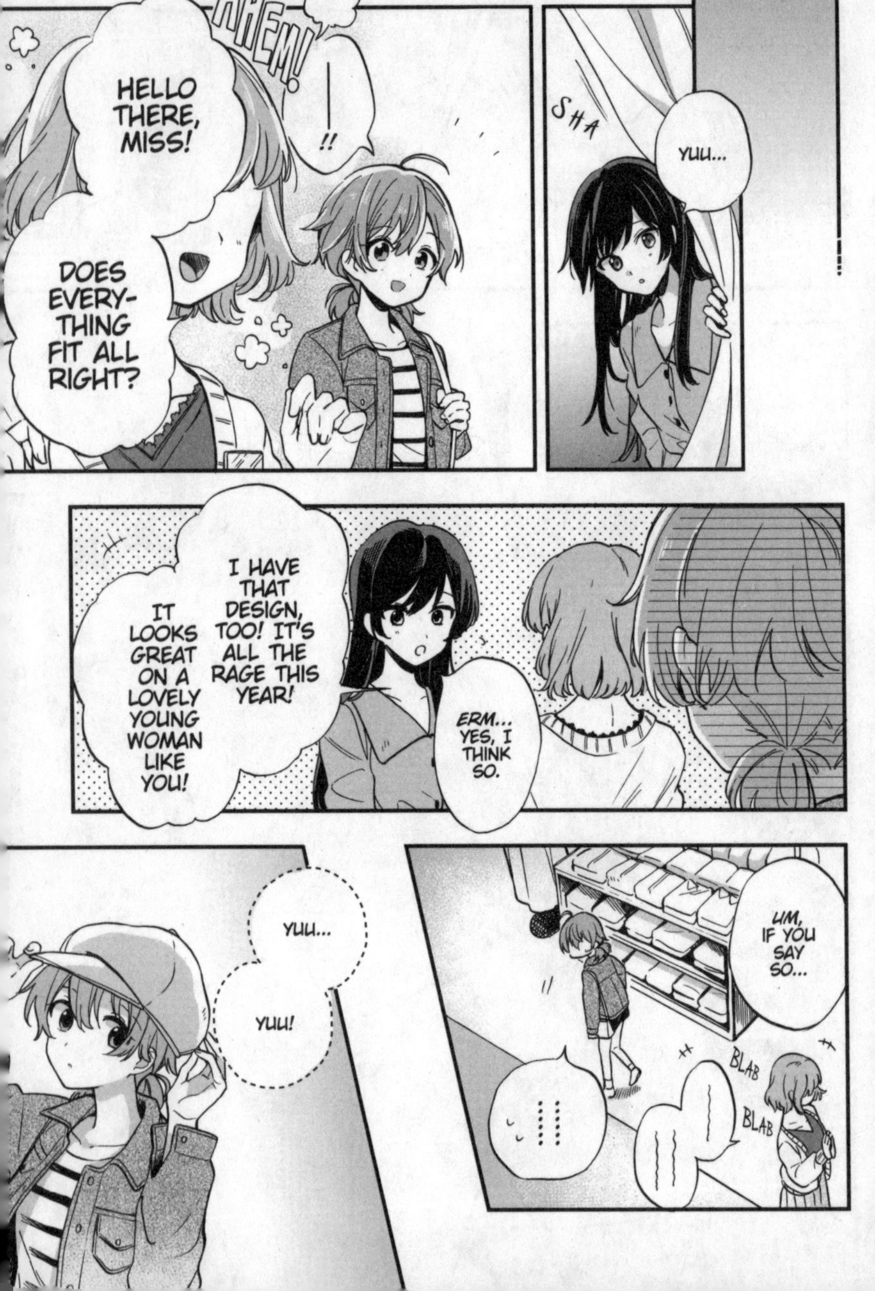
SHA
YUU...
AHEM!
—!!
HELLO THERE, MISS!
DOES EVERY-THING FIT ALL RIGHT?
ERM... YES, I THINK SO.
I HAVE THAT DESIGN, TOO! IT'S ALL THE RAGE THIS YEAR!
IT LOOKS GREAT ON A LOVELY YOUNG WOMAN LIKE YOU!
UM, IF YOU SAY SO...
BLAB
BLAB
YUU...
YUU!

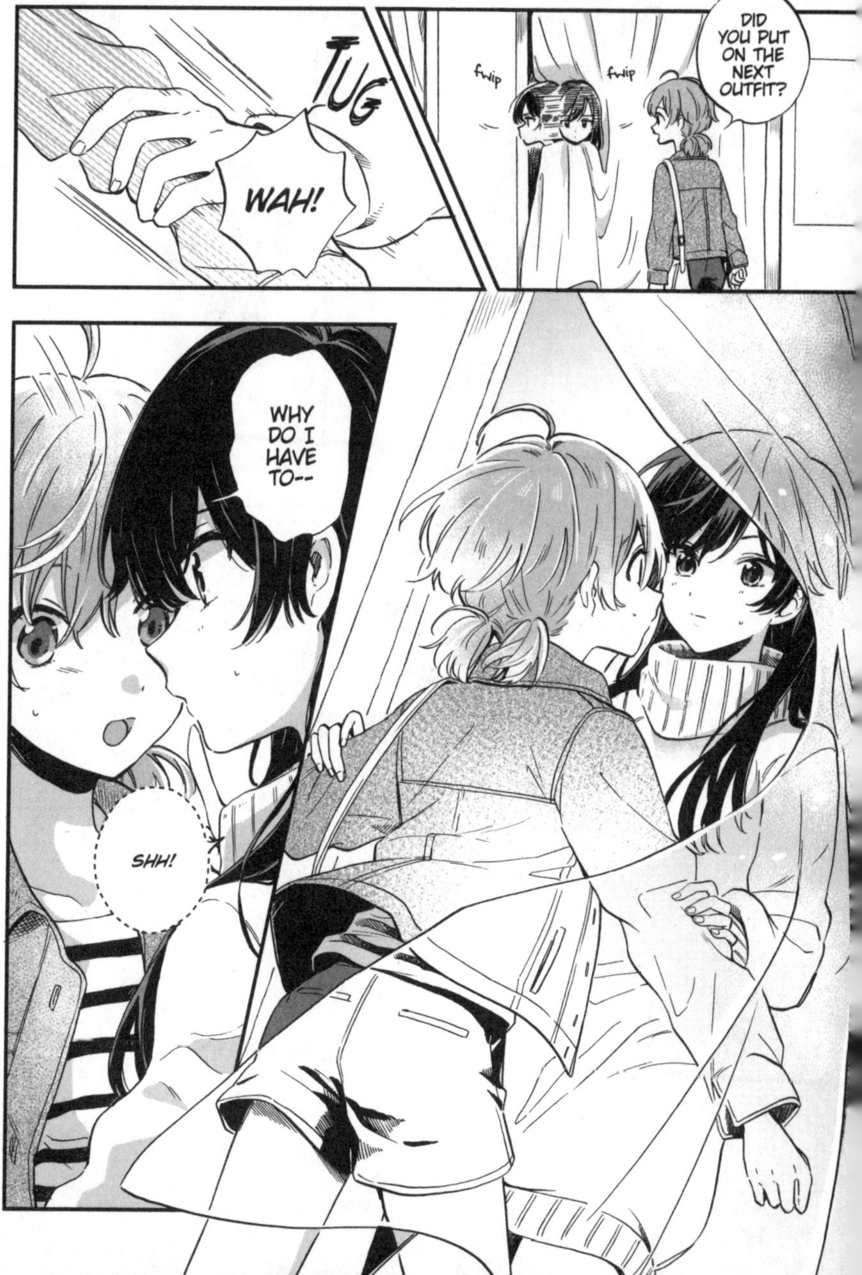
fwip
fwip
DID YOU PUT ON THE NEXT OUTFIT?
TUG
WAH!
WHY DO I HAVE TO--
SHH!

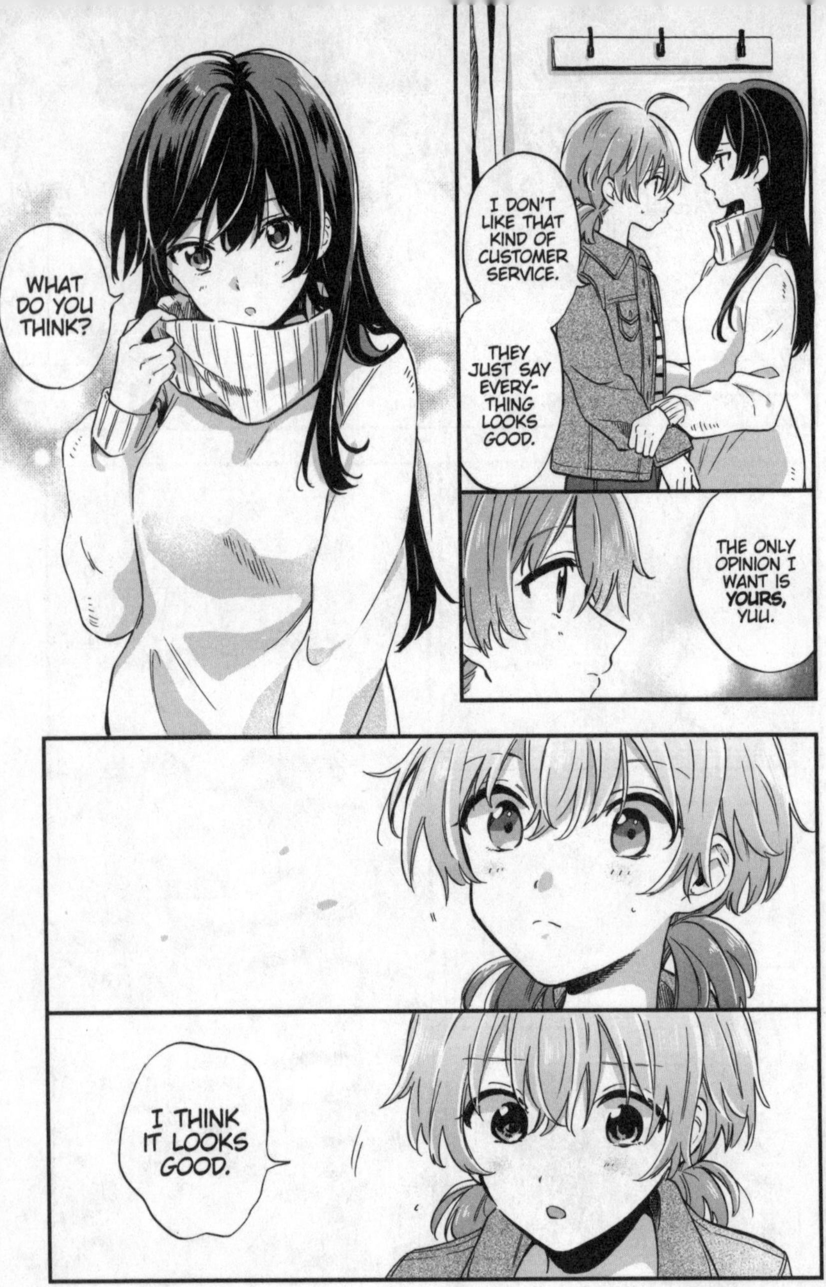
I DON'T LIKE THAT KIND OF CUSTOMER SERVICE.
THEY JUST SAY EVERY-THING LOOKS GOOD.
THE ONLY OPINION I WANT IS **YOURS,** YUU.
WHAT DO YOU THINK?
I THINK IT LOOKS GOOD.

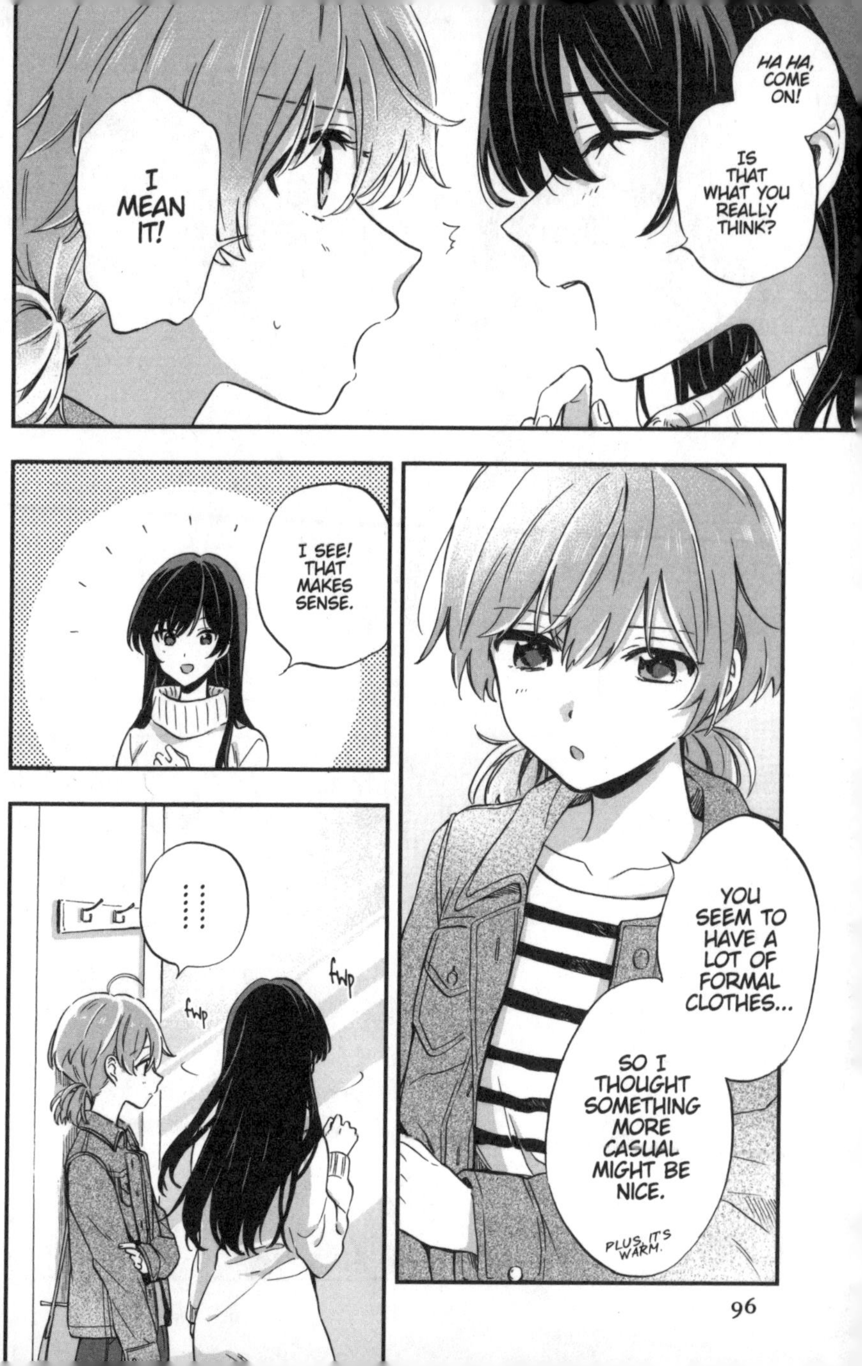
HA HA, COME ON!
IS THAT WHAT YOU REALLY THINK?
I MEAN IT!
YOU SEEM TO HAVE A LOT OF FORMAL CLOTHES...
SO I THOUGHT SOMETHING MORE CASUAL MIGHT BE NICE.
PLUS, IT'S WARM.
I SEE! THAT MAKES SENSE.
......
fwp
fwp

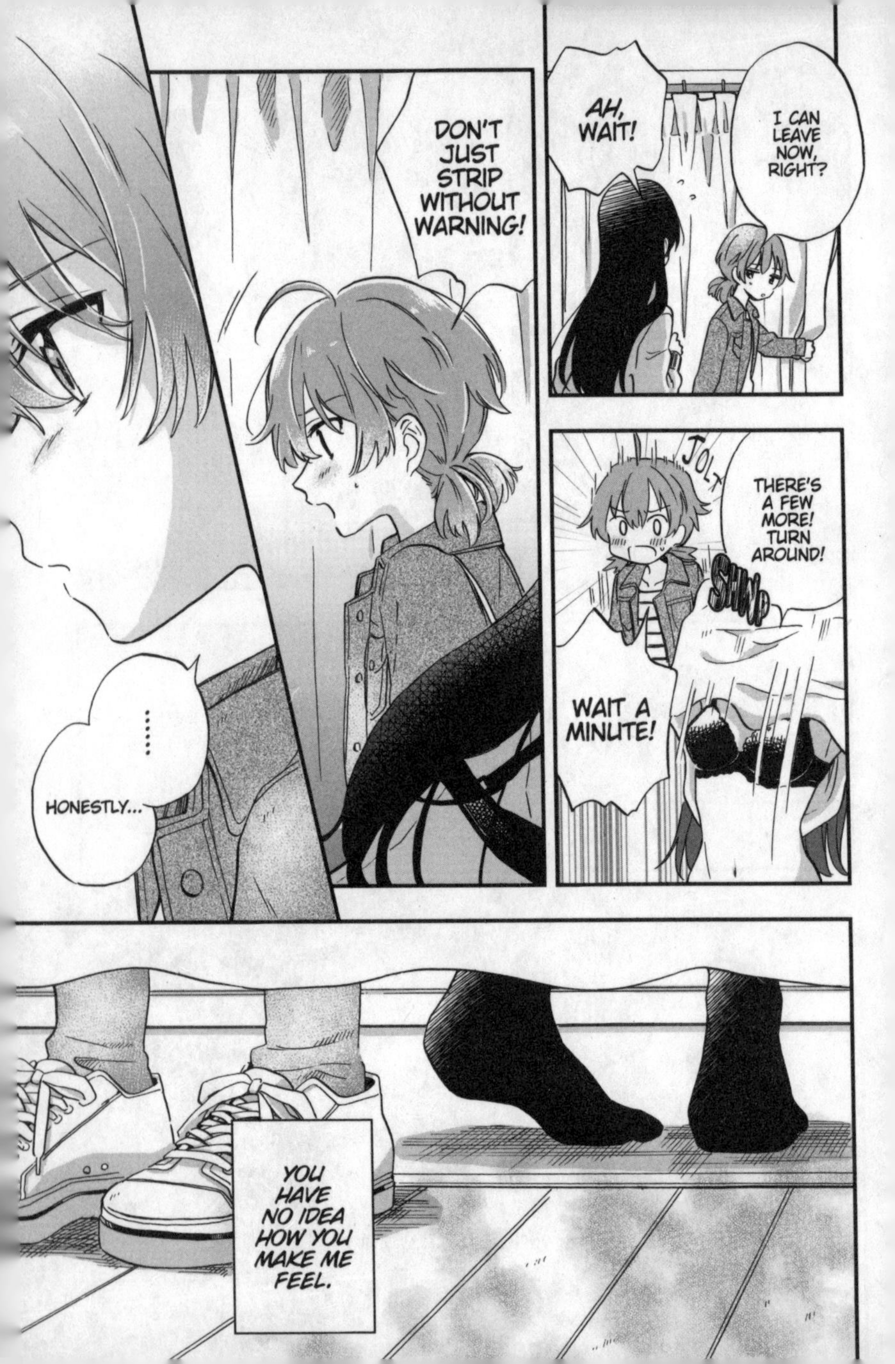
I CAN LEAVE NOW, RIGHT?
AH, WAIT!
THERE'S A FEW MORE! TURN AROUND!
JOLT
SHWP
WAIT A MINUTE!
DON'T JUST STRIP WITHOUT WARNING!
......
HONESTLY...
YOU HAVE NO IDEA HOW YOU MAKE ME FEEL.

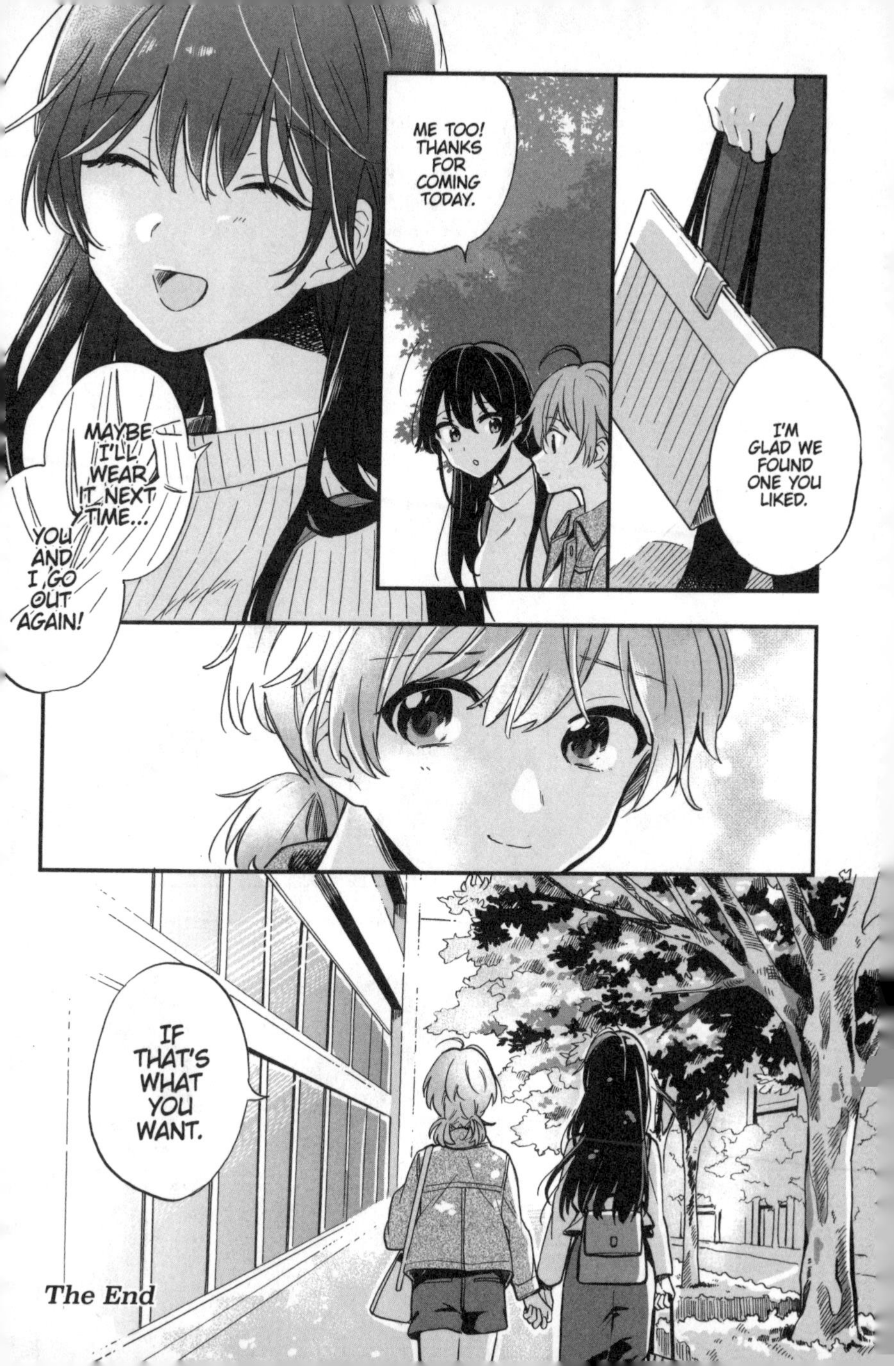
I'M GLAD WE FOUND ONE YOU LIKED.
ME TOO! THANKS FOR COMING TODAY.
MAYBE I'LL WEAR IT NEXT TIME...
YOU AND I GO OUT AGAIN!
IF THAT'S WHAT YOU WANT.
The End

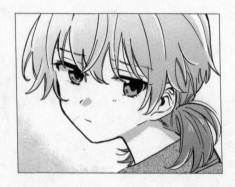

Moke

(Bloom Into You)

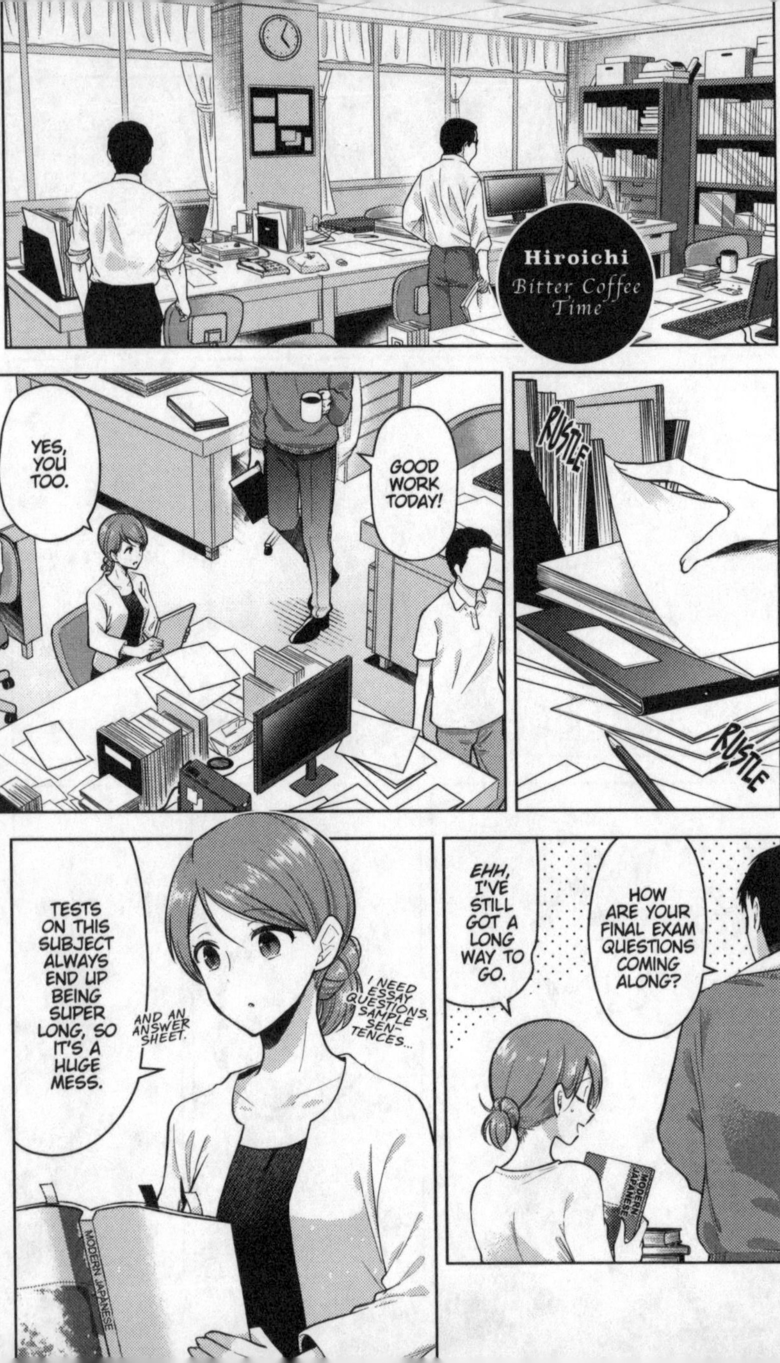
Hiroichi
Bitter Coffee Time
RUSTLE
RUSTLE
GOOD WORK TODAY!
YES, YOU TOO.
HOW ARE YOUR FINAL EXAM QUESTIONS COMING ALONG?
EHH, I'VE STILL GOT A LONG WAY TO GO.
MODERN JAPANESE
I NEED ESSAY QUESTIONS, SAMPLE SEN-TENCES...
AND AN ANSWER SHEET.
TESTS ON THIS SUBJECT ALWAYS END UP BEING SUPER LONG, SO IT'S A HUGE MESS.
MODERN JAPANESE

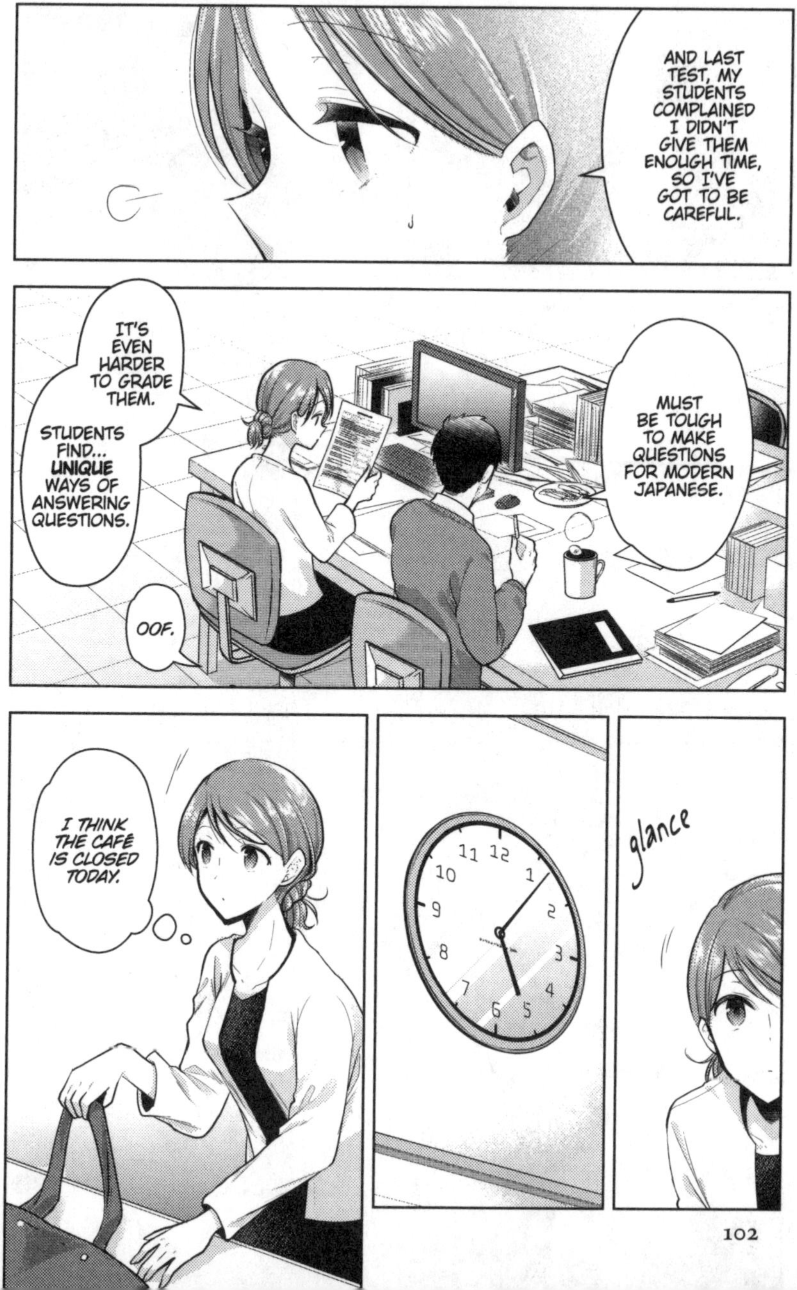
AND LAST TEST, MY STUDENTS COMPLAINED I DIDN'T GIVE THEM ENOUGH TIME, SO I'VE GOT TO BE CAREFUL.
MUST BE TOUGH TO MAKE QUESTIONS FOR MODERN JAPANESE.
IT'S EVEN HARDER TO GRADE THEM.
STUDENTS FIND... **UNIQUE** WAYS OF ANSWERING QUESTIONS.
OOF.
glance
I THINK THE CAFÉ IS CLOSED TODAY.

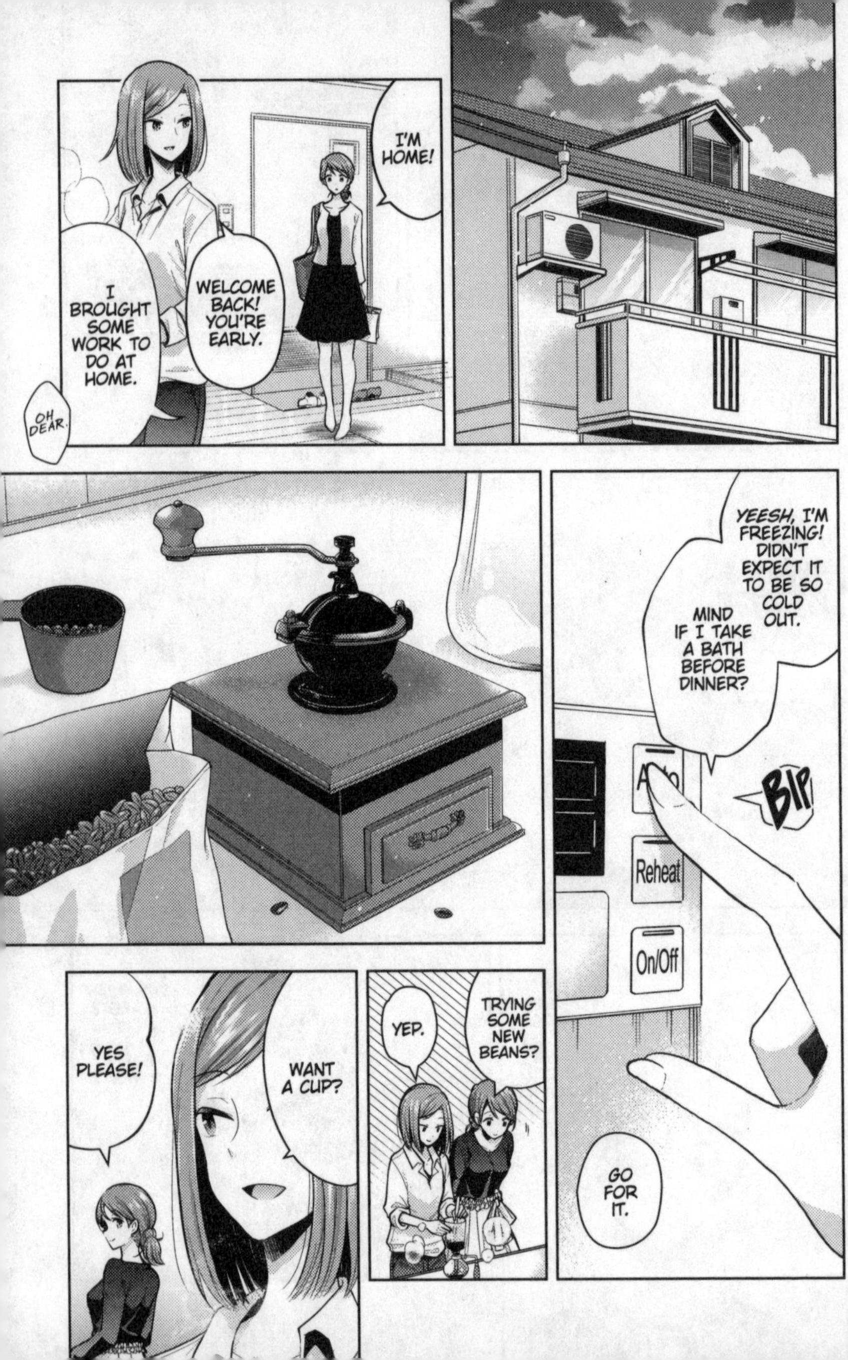
I'M HOME!
WELCOME BACK! YOU'RE EARLY.
I BROUGHT SOME WORK TO DO AT HOME.
OH DEAR.
YEESH, I'M FREEZING! DIDN'T EXPECT IT TO BE SO COLD OUT.
MIND IF I TAKE A BATH BEFORE DINNER?
BIP
Reheat
On/Off
GO FOR IT.
TRYING SOME NEW BEANS?
YEP.
WANT A CUP?
YES PLEASE!

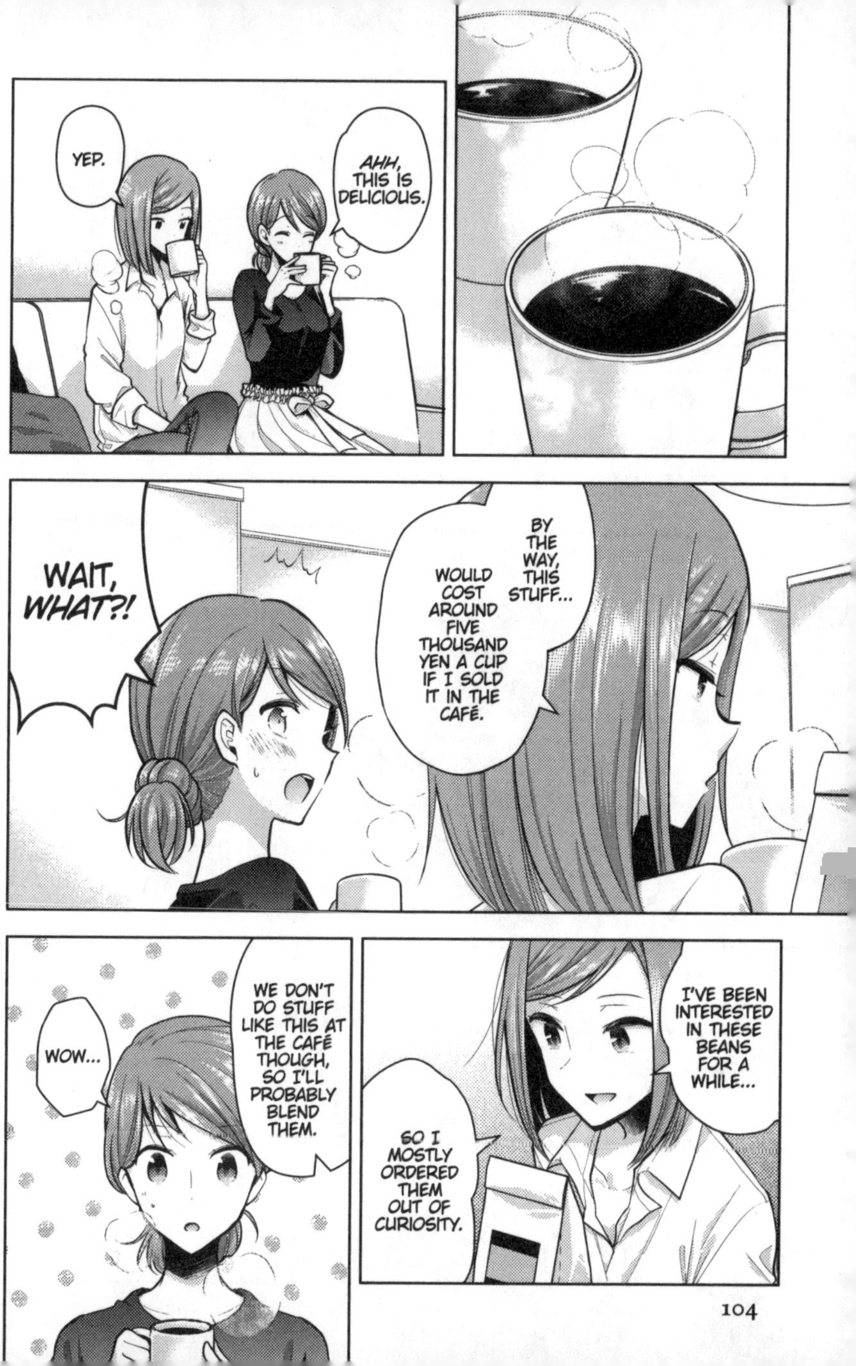
AHH, THIS IS DELICIOUS.
YEP.
BY THE WAY, THIS STUFF...
WOULD COST AROUND FIVE THOUSAND YEN A CUP IF I SOLD IT IN THE CAFÉ.
WAIT, WHAT?!
I'VE BEEN INTERESTED IN THESE BEANS FOR A WHILE...
SO I MOSTLY ORDERED THEM OUT OF CURIOSITY.
WE DON'T DO STUFF LIKE THIS AT THE CAFÉ THOUGH, SO I'LL PROBABLY BLEND THEM.
WOW...

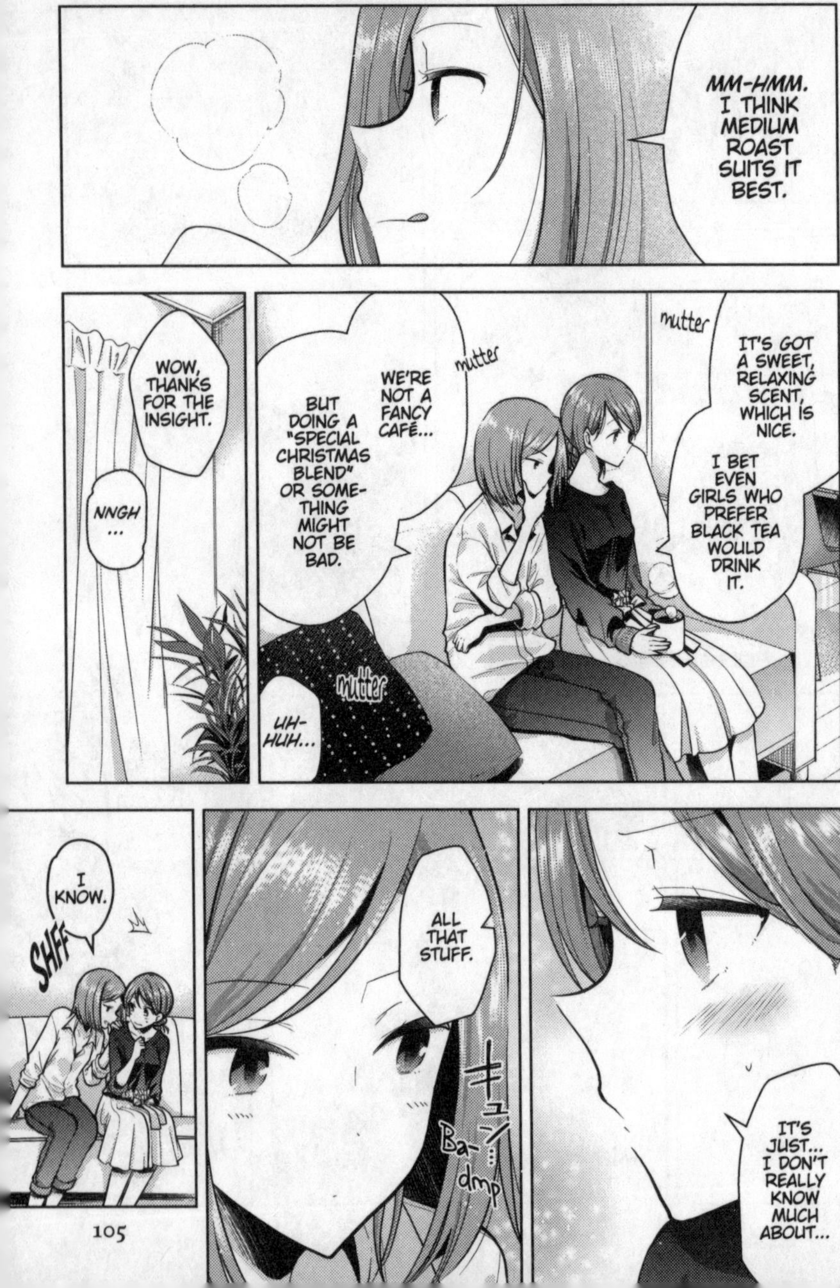
MM-HMM. I THINK MEDIUM ROAST SUITS IT BEST.
mutter
IT'S GOT A SWEET, RELAXING SCENT, WHICH IS NICE.
I BET EVEN GIRLS WHO PREFER BLACK TEA WOULD DRINK IT.
mutter
WE'RE NOT A FANCY CAFÉ...
BUT DOING A "SPECIAL CHRISTMAS BLEND" OR SOME-THING MIGHT NOT BE BAD.
mutter
UH-HUH...
WOW, THANKS FOR THE INSIGHT.
NNGH...
IT'S JUST... I DON'T REALLY KNOW MUCH ABOUT...
ALL THAT STUFF.
Ba-dmp
I KNOW.
SHFF

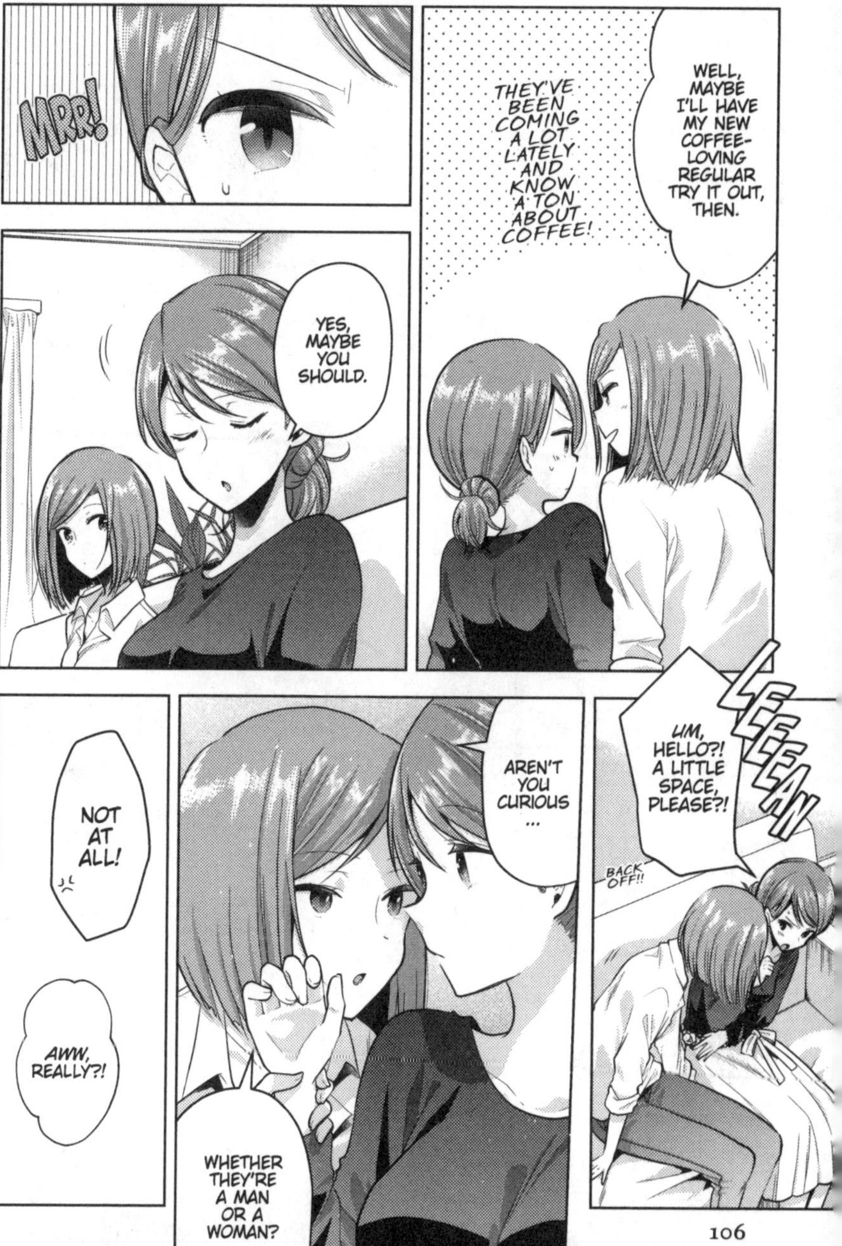
WELL, MAYBE I'LL HAVE MY NEW COFFEE-LOVING REGULAR TRY IT OUT, THEN.
THEY'VE BEEN COMING A LOT LATELY AND KNOW A TON ABOUT COFFEE!
MRR!
YES, MAYBE YOU SHOULD.
LEEEEAN
UM, HELLO?! A LITTLE SPACE, PLEASE?!
BACK OFF!!
AREN'T YOU CURIOUS ...
WHETHER THEY'RE A MAN OR A WOMAN?
NOT AT ALL!
AWW, REALLY?!

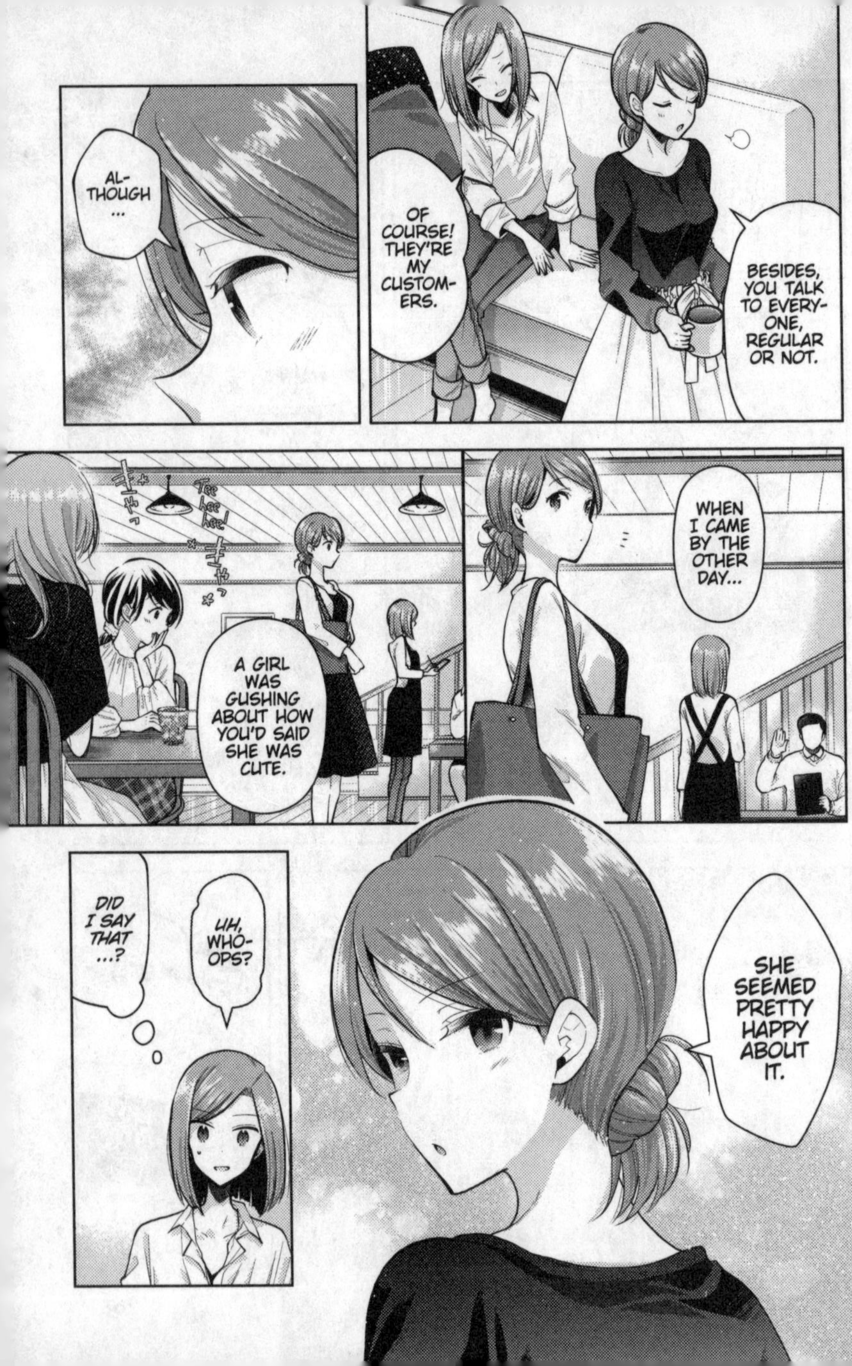
BESIDES, YOU TALK TO EVERYONE, REGULAR OR NOT.
OF COURSE! THEY'RE MY CUSTOMERS.
ALTHOUGH ...
WHEN I CAME BY THE OTHER DAY...
Tee hee hee!
A GIRL WAS GUSHING ABOUT HOW YOU'D SAID SHE WAS CUTE.
SHE SEEMED PRETTY HAPPY ABOUT IT.
UH, WHOOPS?
DID I SAY THAT ...?

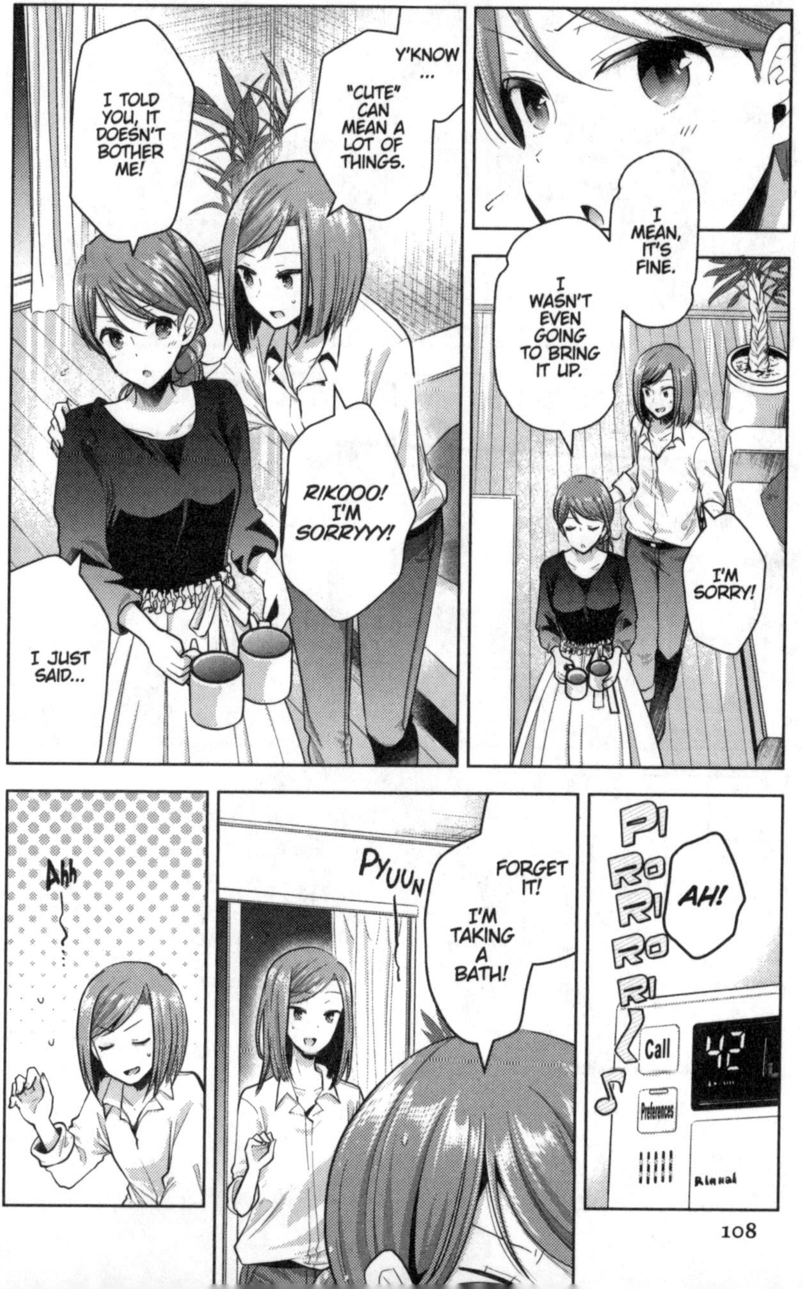
I MEAN, IT'S FINE.
I WASN'T EVEN GOING TO BRING IT UP.
I'M SORRY!
Y'KNOW ... "CUTE" CAN MEAN A LOT OF THINGS.
I TOLD YOU, IT DOESN'T BOTHER ME!
RIKOOO! I'M SORRYYY!
I JUST SAID...
PIRORIRORI
AH!
Call
42
Preferences
FORGET IT! I'M TAKING A BATH!
PYUUN
Ahh

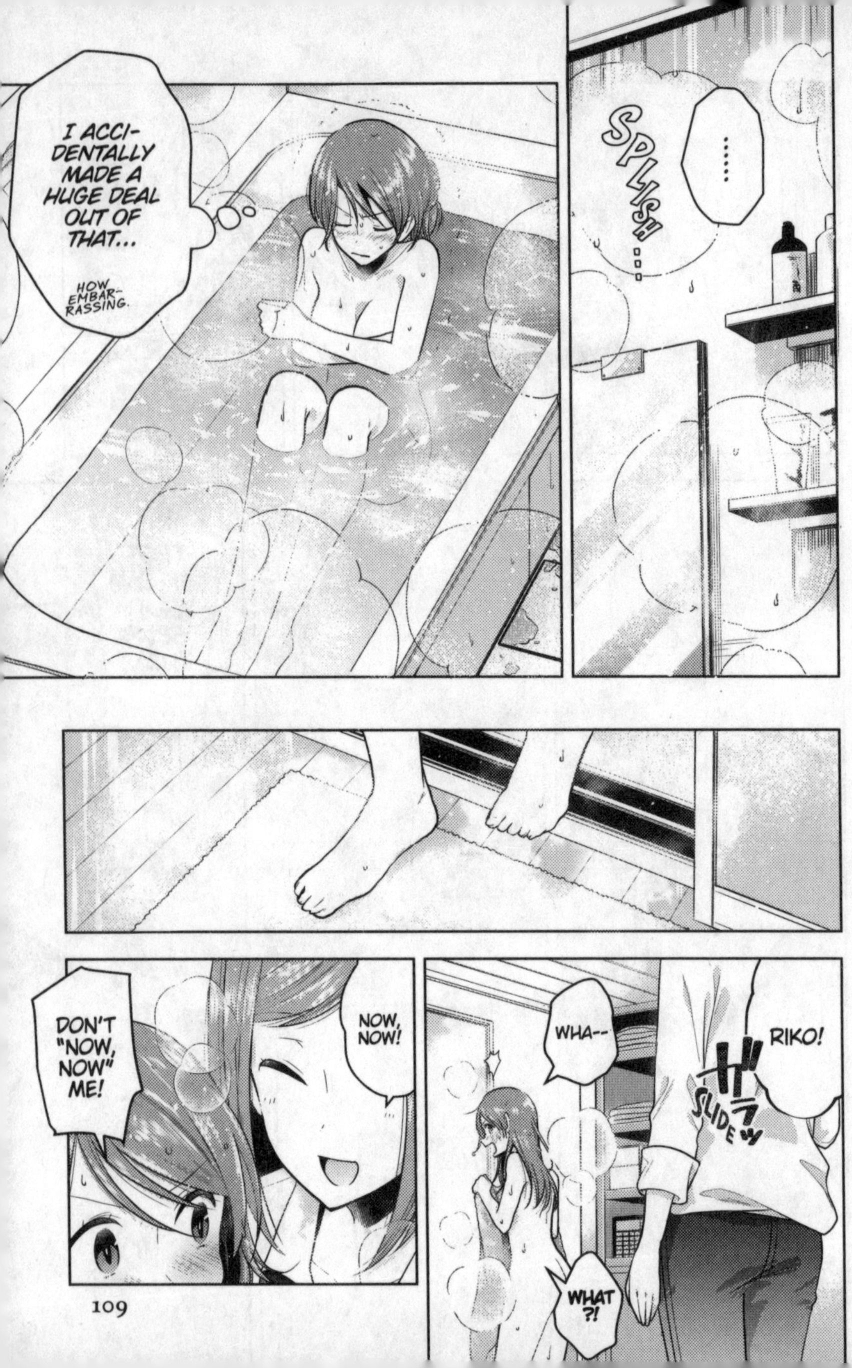
SPLISH...
......
I ACCIDENTALLY MADE A HUGE DEAL OUT OF THAT...
HOW EMBARRASSING.
RIKO!
SLIDE
WHA--
WHAT?!
NOW, NOW!
DON'T "NOW, NOW" ME!

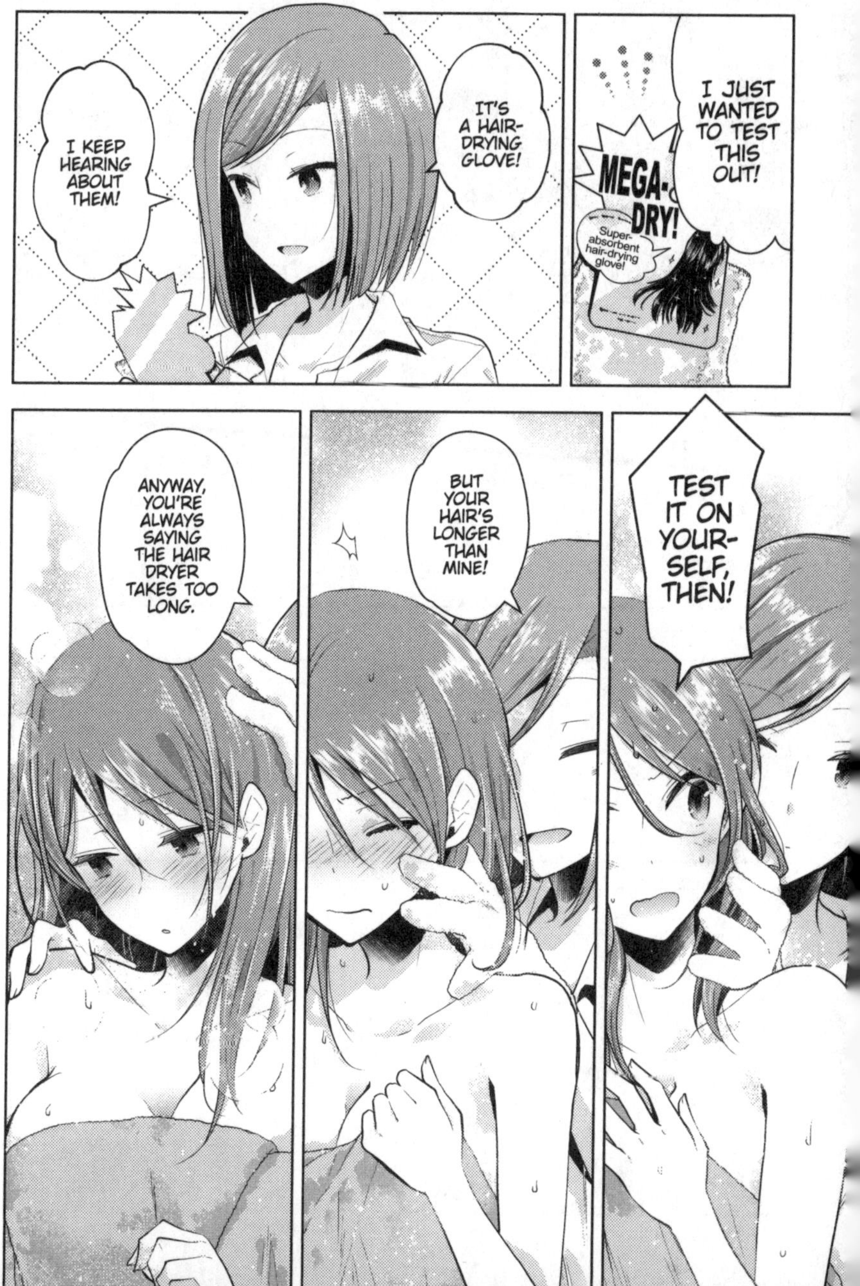
I JUST WANTED TO TEST THIS OUT!
MEGA-DRY!
Super-absorbent hair-drying glove!
IT'S A HAIR-DRYING GLOVE!
I KEEP HEARING ABOUT THEM!
TEST IT ON YOURSELF, THEN!
BUT YOUR HAIR'S LONGER THAN MINE!
ANYWAY, YOU'RE ALWAYS SAYING THE HAIR DRYER TAKES TOO LONG.

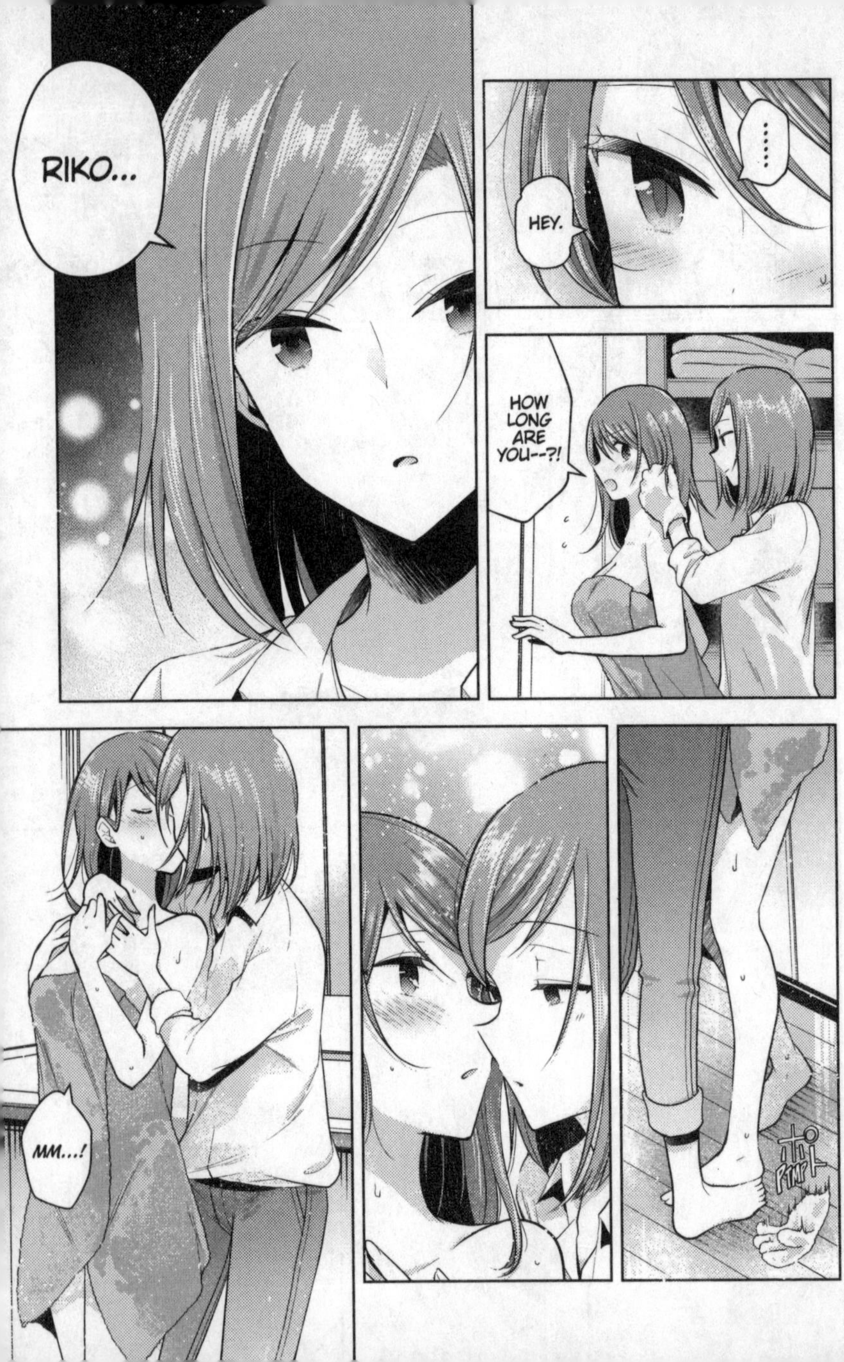

......
HEY.
HOW LONG ARE YOU--?!
RIKO...
PTMP
MM...!

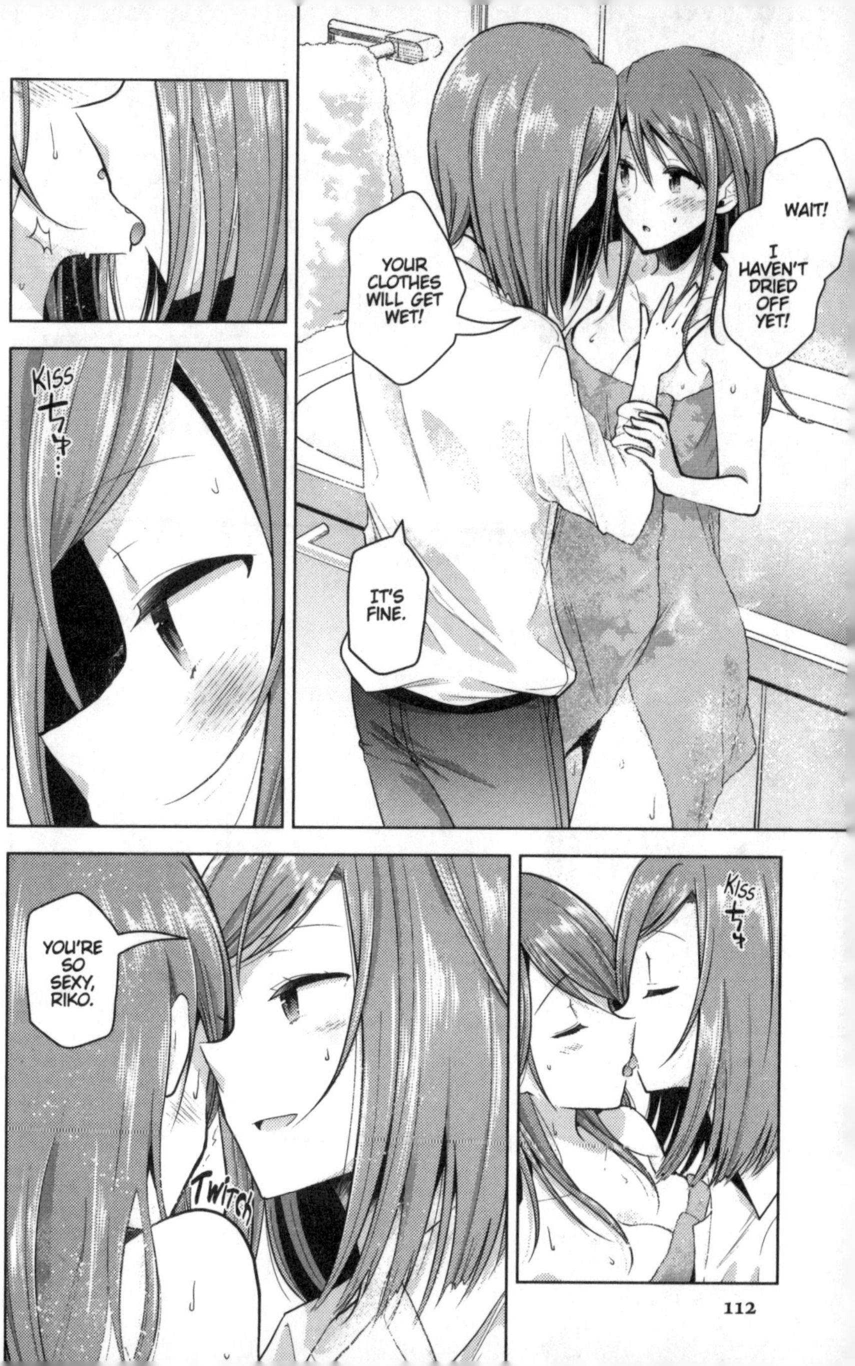
WAIT!
I HAVEN'T DRIED OFF YET!
YOUR CLOTHES WILL GET WET!
IT'S FINE.
KISS
ちゅ…
KISS
ちゅ
YOU'RE SO SEXY, RIKO.
Twitch

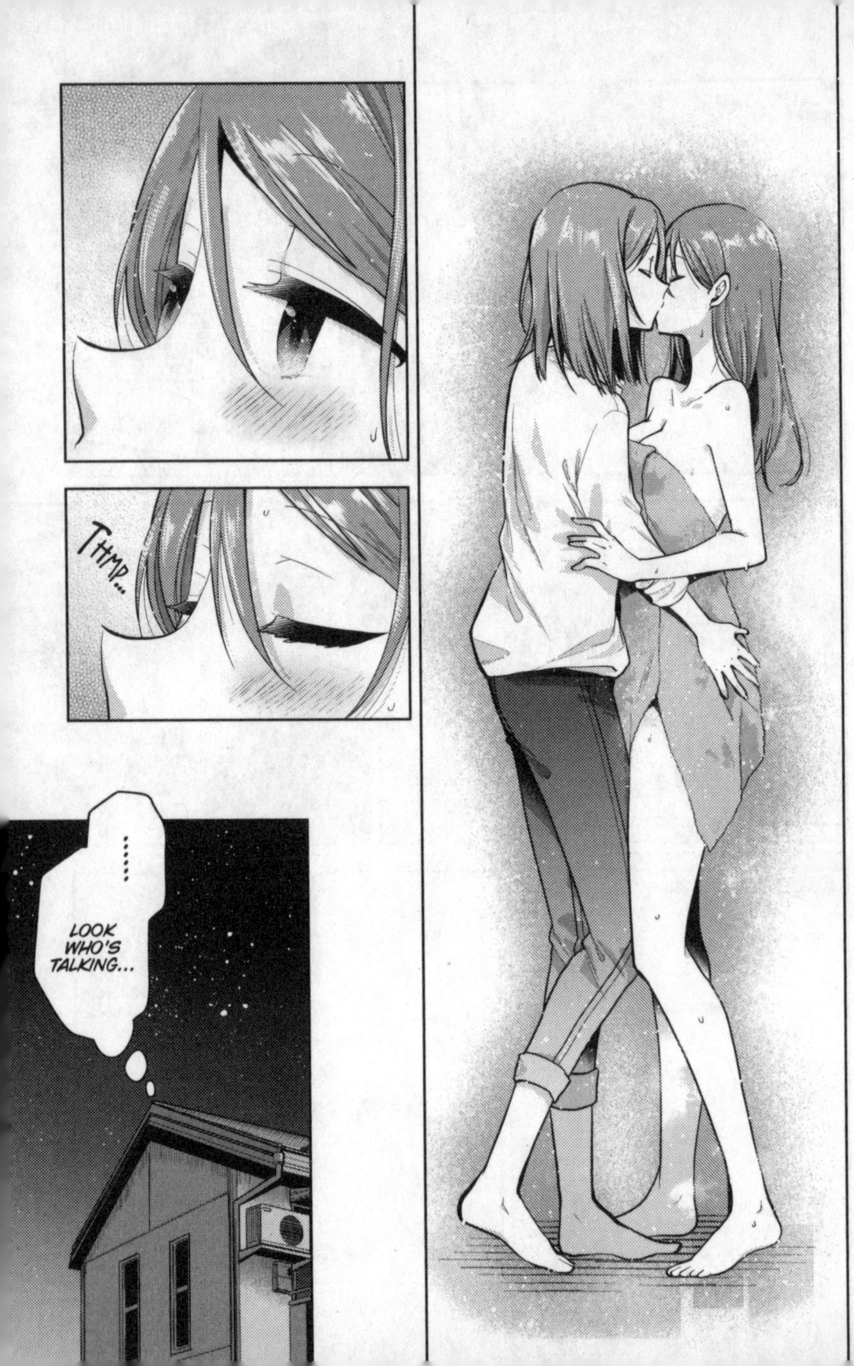
THMP...
......
LOOK WHO'S TALKING...

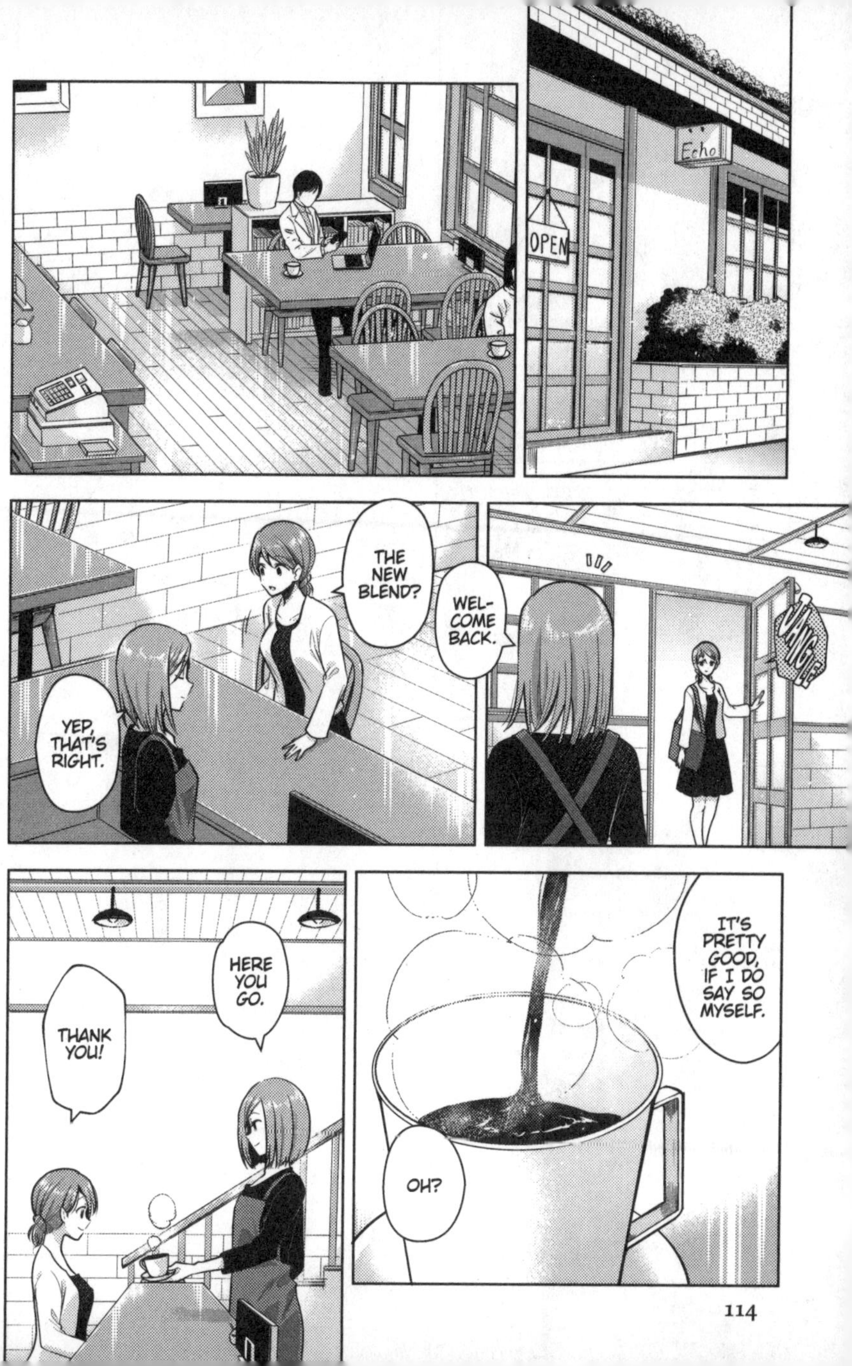
Echo
OPEN
JANGLE
WEL-COME BACK.
THE NEW BLEND?
YEP, THAT'S RIGHT.
IT'S PRETTY GOOD, IF I DO SAY SO MYSELF.
OH?
HERE YOU GO.
THANK YOU!

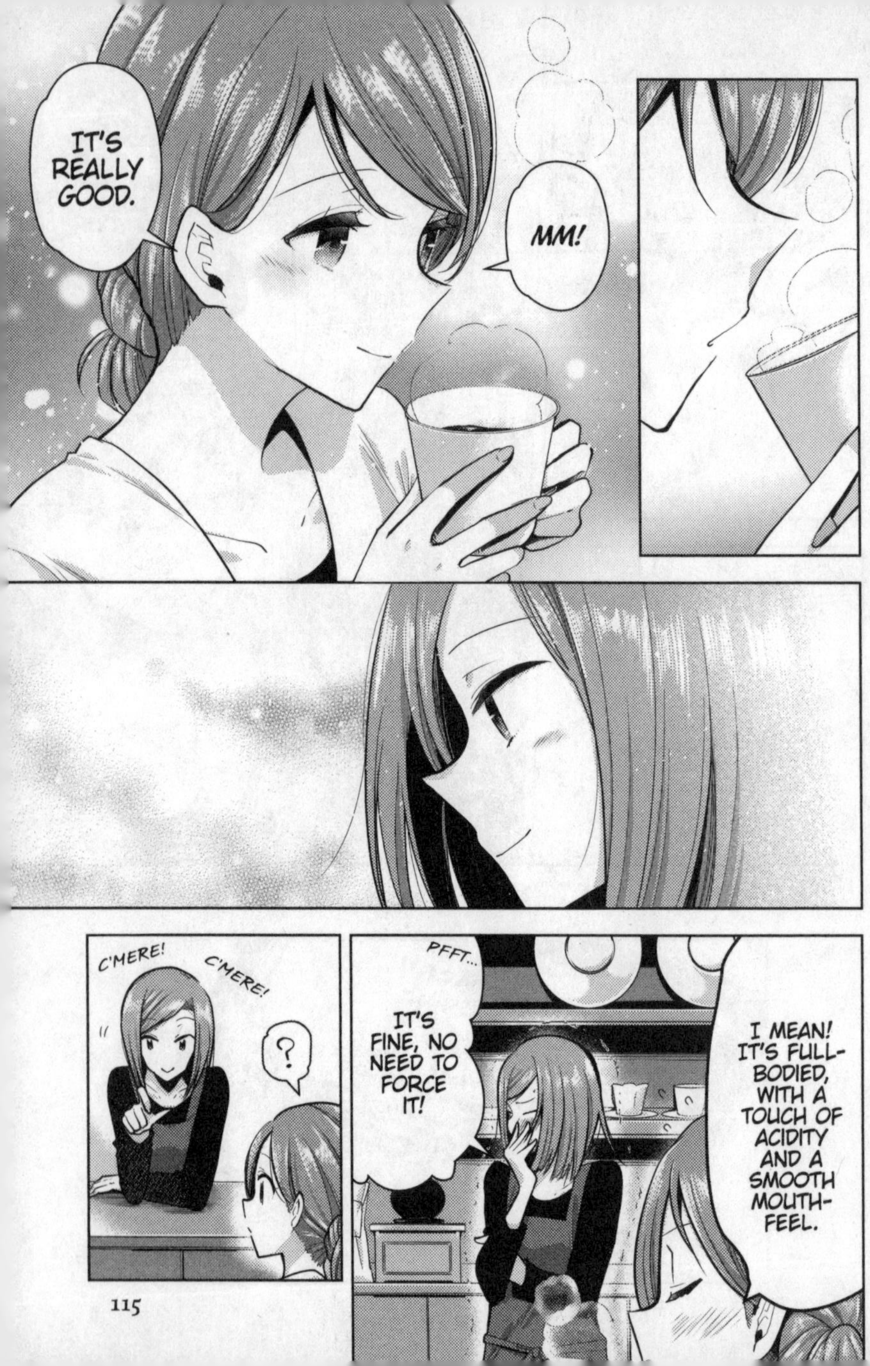
MM!
IT'S REALLY GOOD.
I MEAN! IT'S FULL-BODIED, WITH A TOUCH OF ACIDITY AND A SMOOTH MOUTH-FEEL.
PFFT...
IT'S FINE, NO NEED TO FORCE IT!
C'MERE!
C'MERE!
?

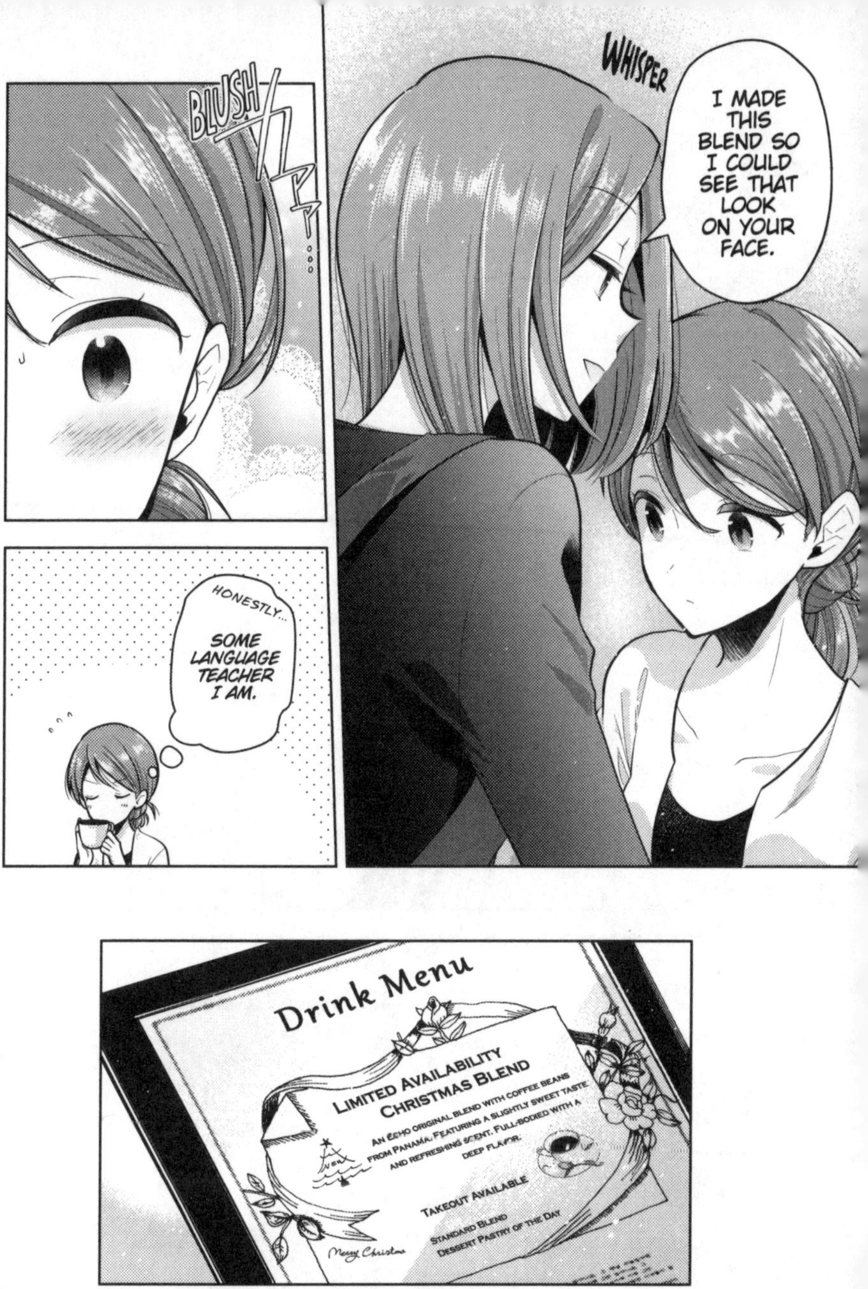
WHISPER
I MADE THIS BLEND SO I COULD SEE THAT LOOK ON YOUR FACE.
BLUSH
HONESTLY...
SOME LANGUAGE TEACHER I AM.
Drink Menu
Limited Availability
Christmas Blend
An Echo original blend with coffee beans from Panama. Featuring a slightly sweet taste and refreshing scent. Full-bodied with a deep flavor.
Takeout Available
Standard Blend
Dessert Pastry of the Day
Merry Christmas

The End

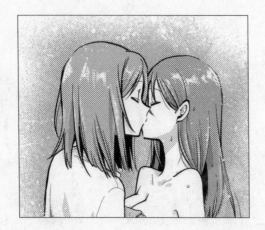

Hiroichi

(**Bloom Into You**)

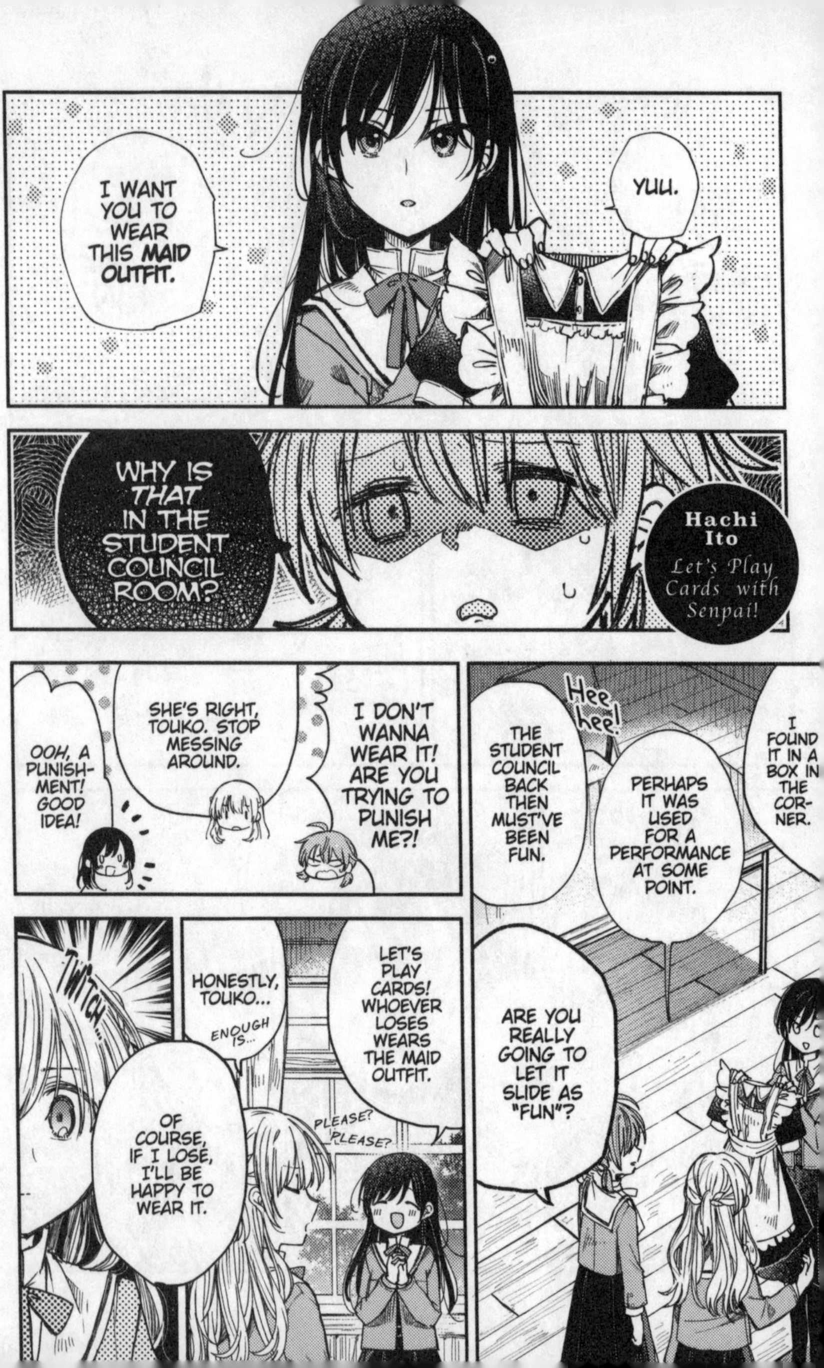
YUU.
I WANT YOU TO WEAR THIS MAID OUTFIT.
Hachi Ito
Let's Play Cards with Senpai!
WHY IS THAT IN THE STUDENT COUNCIL ROOM?
I FOUND IT IN A BOX IN THE CORNER.
PERHAPS IT WAS USED FOR A PERFORMANCE AT SOME POINT.
Hee hee!
THE STUDENT COUNCIL BACK THEN MUST'VE BEEN FUN.
ARE YOU REALLY GOING TO LET IT SLIDE AS "FUN"?
I DON'T WANNA WEAR IT! ARE YOU TRYING TO PUNISH ME?!
SHE'S RIGHT, TOUKO. STOP MESSING AROUND.
OOH, A PUNISHMENT! GOOD IDEA!
LET'S PLAY CARDS! WHOEVER LOSES WEARS THE MAID OUTFIT.
PLEASE? PLEASE?
HONESTLY, TOUKO...
ENOUGH IS...
OF COURSE, IF I LOSE, I'LL BE HAPPY TO WEAR IT.
TWITCH...

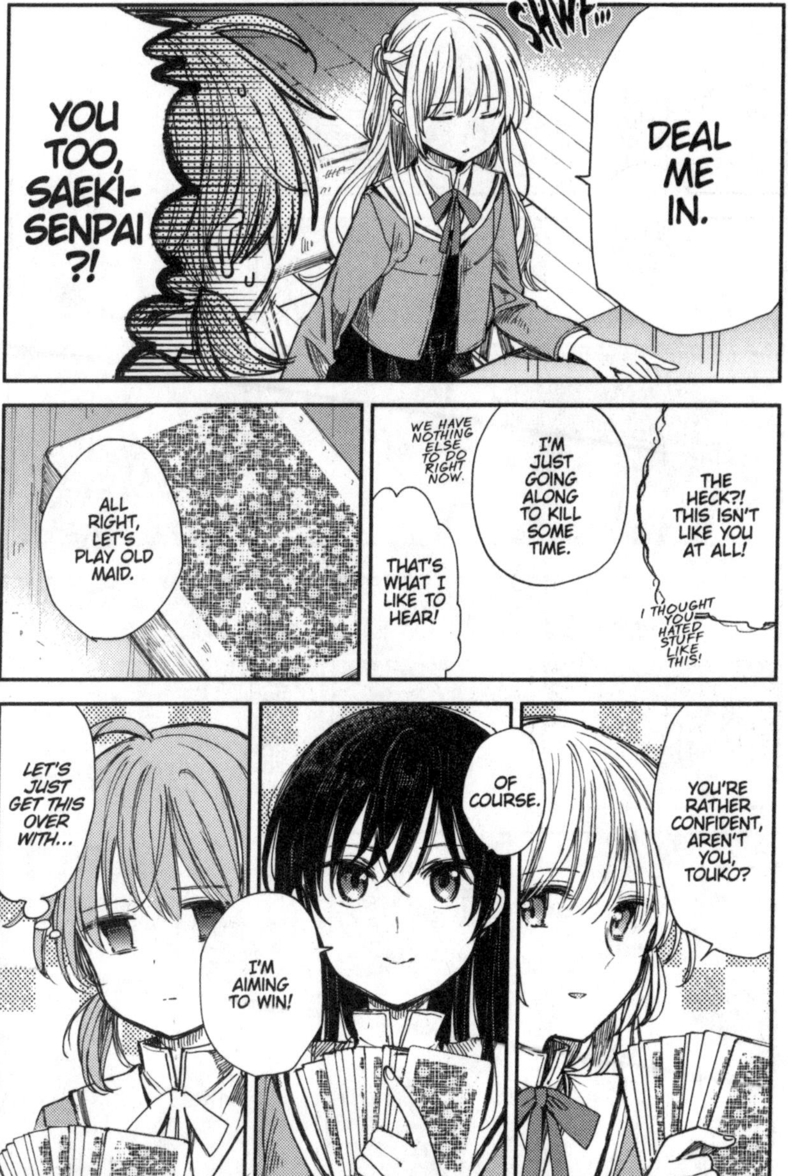
SHWF...
DEAL ME IN.
YOU TOO, SAEKI-SENPAI?!
THE HECK?! THIS ISN'T LIKE YOU AT ALL!
I THOUGHT YOU HATED STUFF LIKE THIS!
I'M JUST GOING ALONG TO KILL SOME TIME.
WE HAVE NOTHING ELSE TO DO RIGHT NOW.
THAT'S WHAT I LIKE TO HEAR!
ALL RIGHT, LET'S PLAY OLD MAID.
YOU'RE RATHER CONFIDENT, AREN'T YOU, TOUKO?
OF COURSE.
I'M AIMING TO WIN!
LET'S JUST GET THIS OVER WITH...

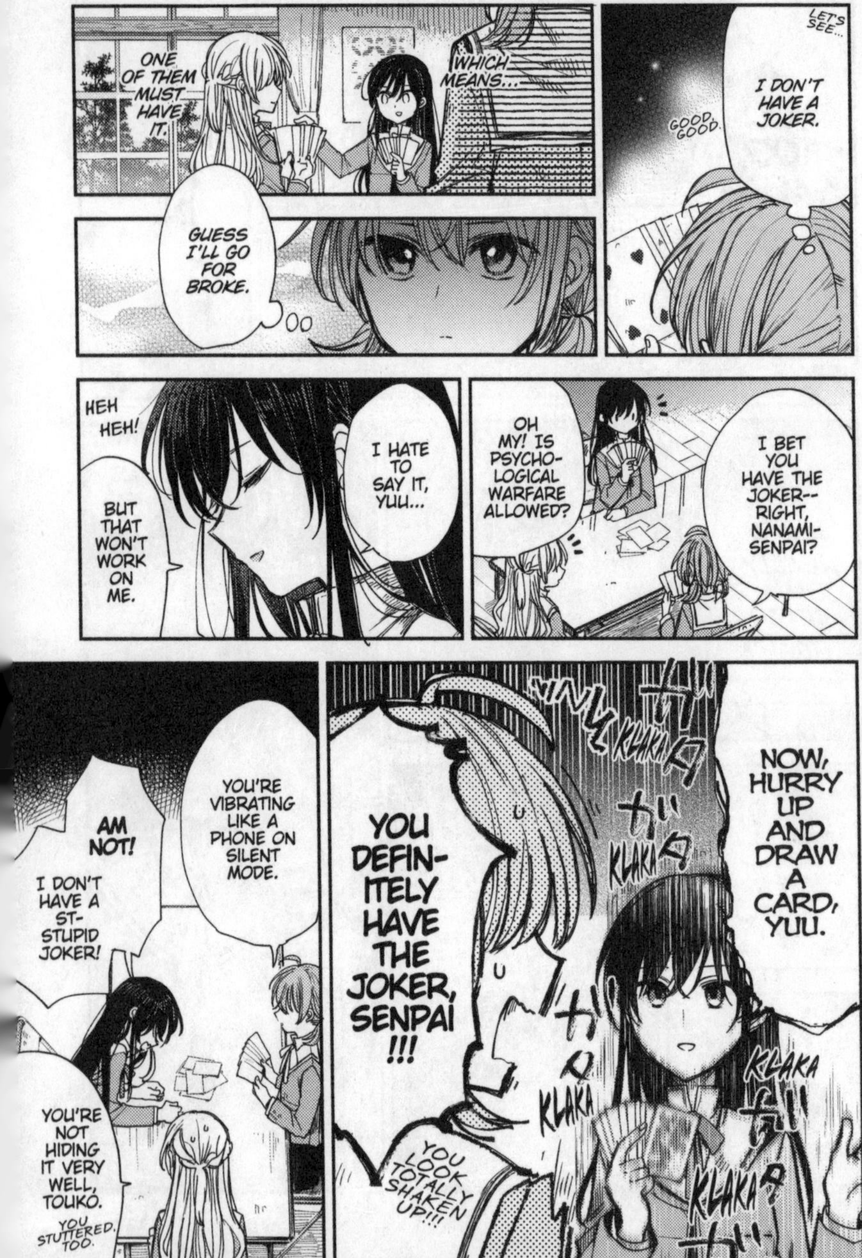
LET'S SEE...
I DON'T HAVE A JOKER.
GOOD, GOOD.
WHICH MEANS...
ONE OF THEM MUST HAVE IT.
GUESS I'LL GO FOR BROKE.
I BET YOU HAVE THE JOKER--RIGHT, NANAMI-SENPAI?
OH MY! IS PSYCHOLOGICAL WARFARE ALLOWED?
I HATE TO SAY IT, YUU...
HEH HEH!
BUT THAT WON'T WORK ON ME.
NOW, HURRY UP AND DRAW A CARD, YUU.
KLAKA
KLAKA
KLAKA
KLAKA
KLAKA
YOU DEFINITELY HAVE THE JOKER, SENPAI!!!
YOU LOOK TOTALLY SHAKEN UP!!!
YOU'RE VIBRATING LIKE A PHONE ON SILENT MODE.
AM NOT!
I DON'T HAVE A ST-STUPID JOKER!
YOU'RE NOT HIDING IT VERY WELL, TOUKO.
YOU STUTTERED, TOO.

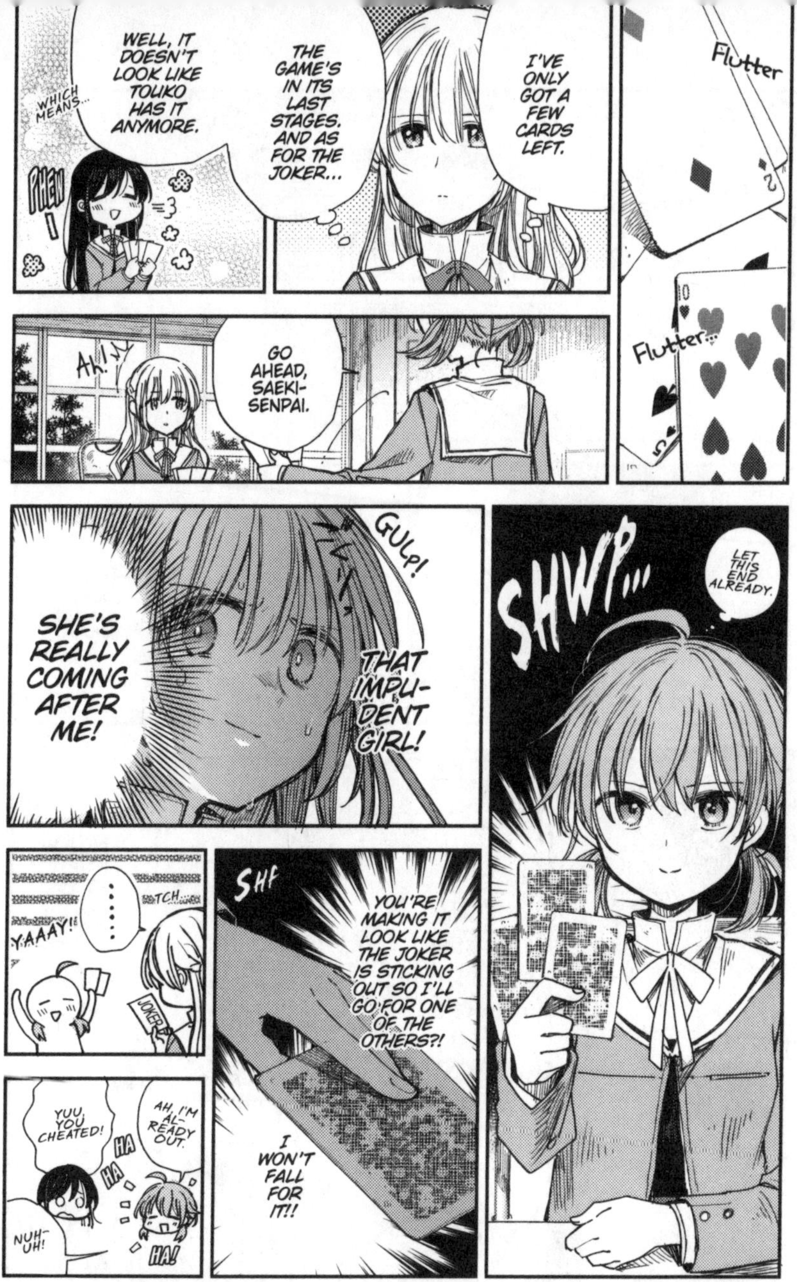

Flutter
Flutter...
I'VE ONLY GOT A FEW CARDS LEFT.
THE GAME'S IN ITS LAST STAGES. AND AS FOR THE JOKER...
WELL, IT DOESN'T LOOK LIKE TOUKO HAS IT ANYMORE.
WHICH MEANS...
PHEW!
GO AHEAD, SAEKI-SENPAI.
Ah!
SHWP...
LET THIS END ALREADY.
GULP!
THAT IMPUDENT GIRL!
SHE'S REALLY COMING AFTER ME!
SHF
YOU'RE MAKING IT LOOK LIKE THE JOKER IS STICKING OUT SO I'LL GO FOR ONE OF THE OTHERS?!
I WON'T FALL FOR IT!!
......
TCH...
Y-AAAY!
JOKER
YUU, YOU CHEATED!
AH, I'M AL-READY OUT.
HA
HA
HA!
NUH-UH!

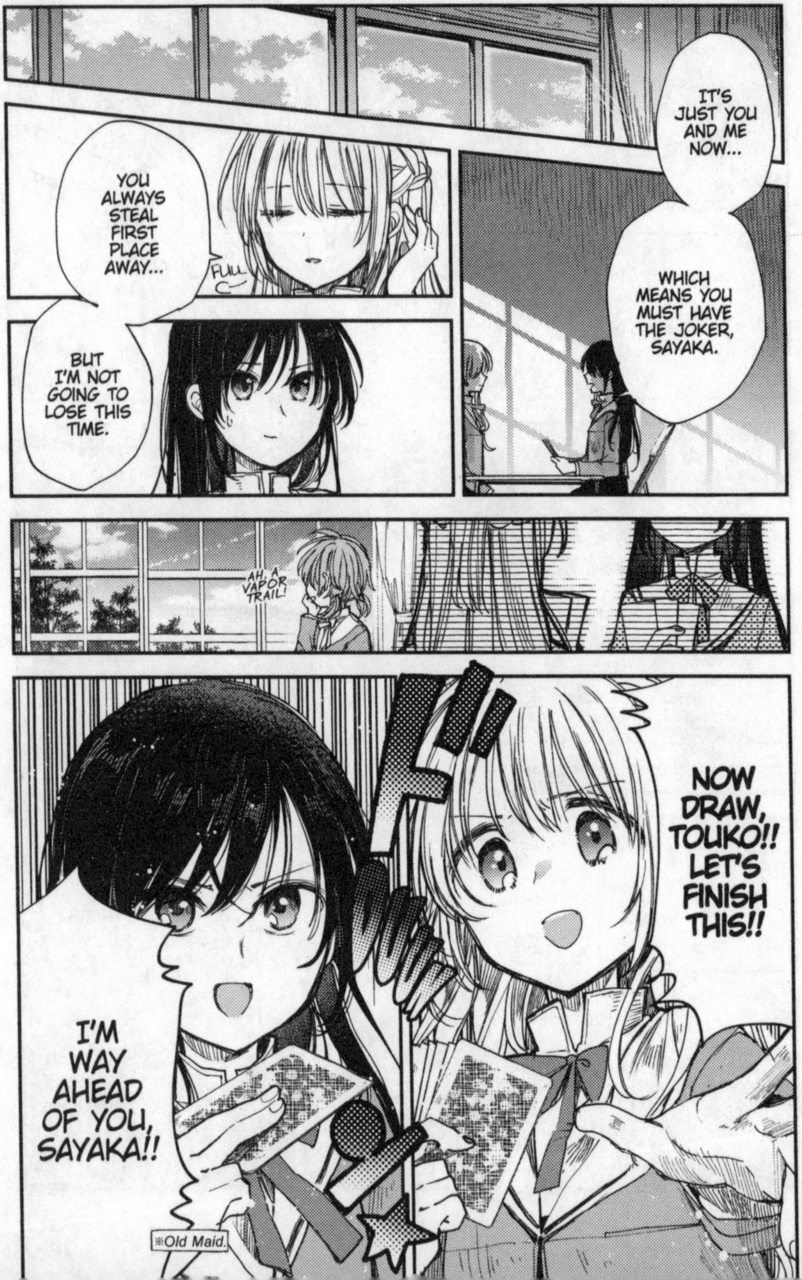
IT'S JUST YOU AND ME NOW...
WHICH MEANS YOU MUST HAVE THE JOKER, SAYAKA.
YOU ALWAYS STEAL FIRST PLACE AWAY...
FUU
BUT I'M NOT GOING TO LOSE THIS TIME.
AH, A VAPOR TRAIL!
NOW DRAW, TOUKO!! LET'S FINISH THIS!!
I'M WAY AHEAD OF YOU, SAYAKA!!
※Old Maid.

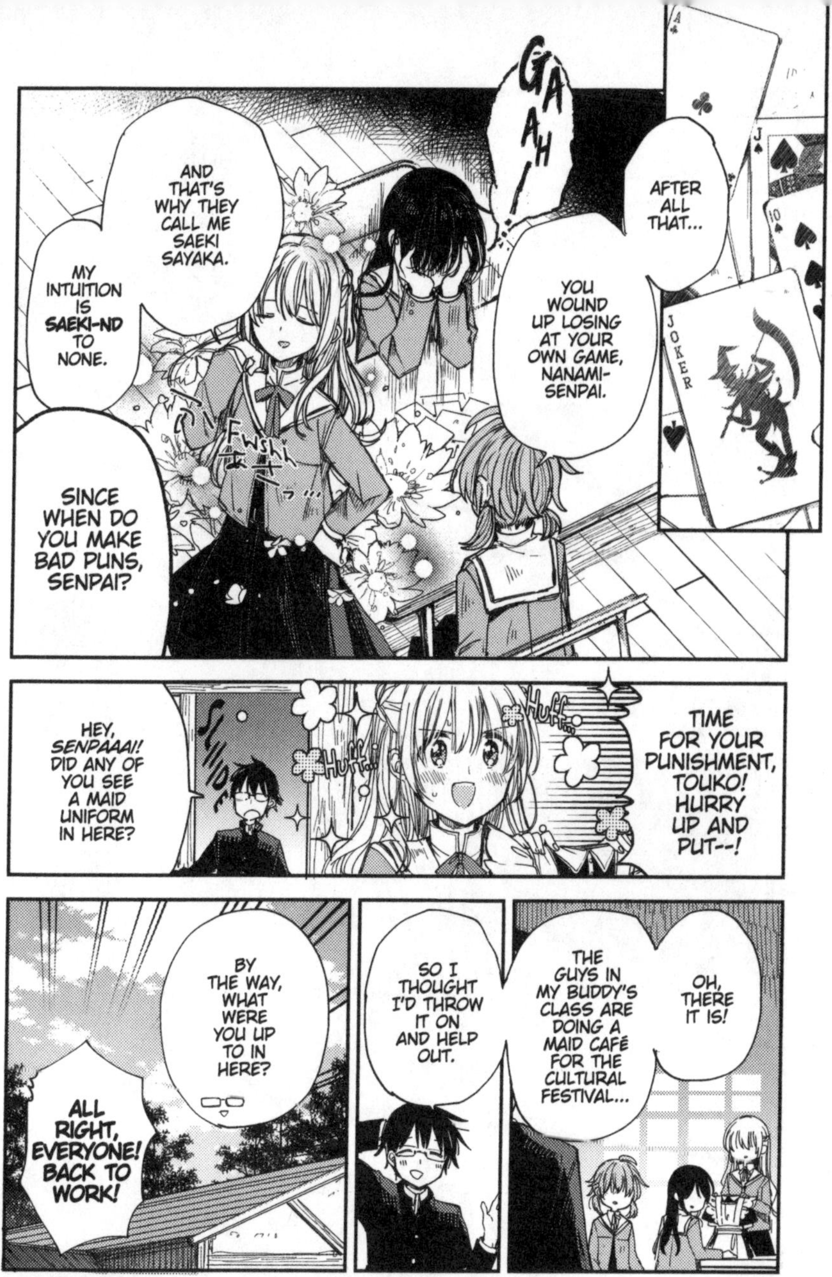
GAAAH!
AFTER ALL THAT...
YOU WOUND UP LOSING AT YOUR OWN GAME, NANAMI-SENPAI.
AND THAT'S WHY THEY CALL ME SAEKI SAYAKA.
MY INTUITION IS SAEKI-ND TO NONE.
Fwsh
SINCE WHEN DO YOU MAKE BAD PUNS, SENPAI?
TIME FOR YOUR PUNISHMENT, TOUKO! HURRY UP AND PUT--!
Huff...
Huff...
HEY, SENPAAAI! DID ANY OF YOU SEE A MAID UNIFORM IN HERE?
OH, THERE IT IS!
THE GUYS IN MY BUDDY'S CLASS ARE DOING A MAID CAFÉ FOR THE CULTURAL FESTIVAL...
SO I THOUGHT I'D THROW IT ON AND HELP OUT.
BY THE WAY, WHAT WERE YOU UP TO IN HERE?
ALL RIGHT, EVERYONE! BACK TO WORK!

The End

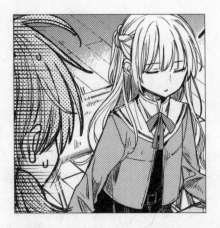

Hachi Ito

Best known for *Tsuki ga Kirei Desu Ne (Isn't the Moon Beautiful?)* (Ichijinsha).

(Bloom Into You)

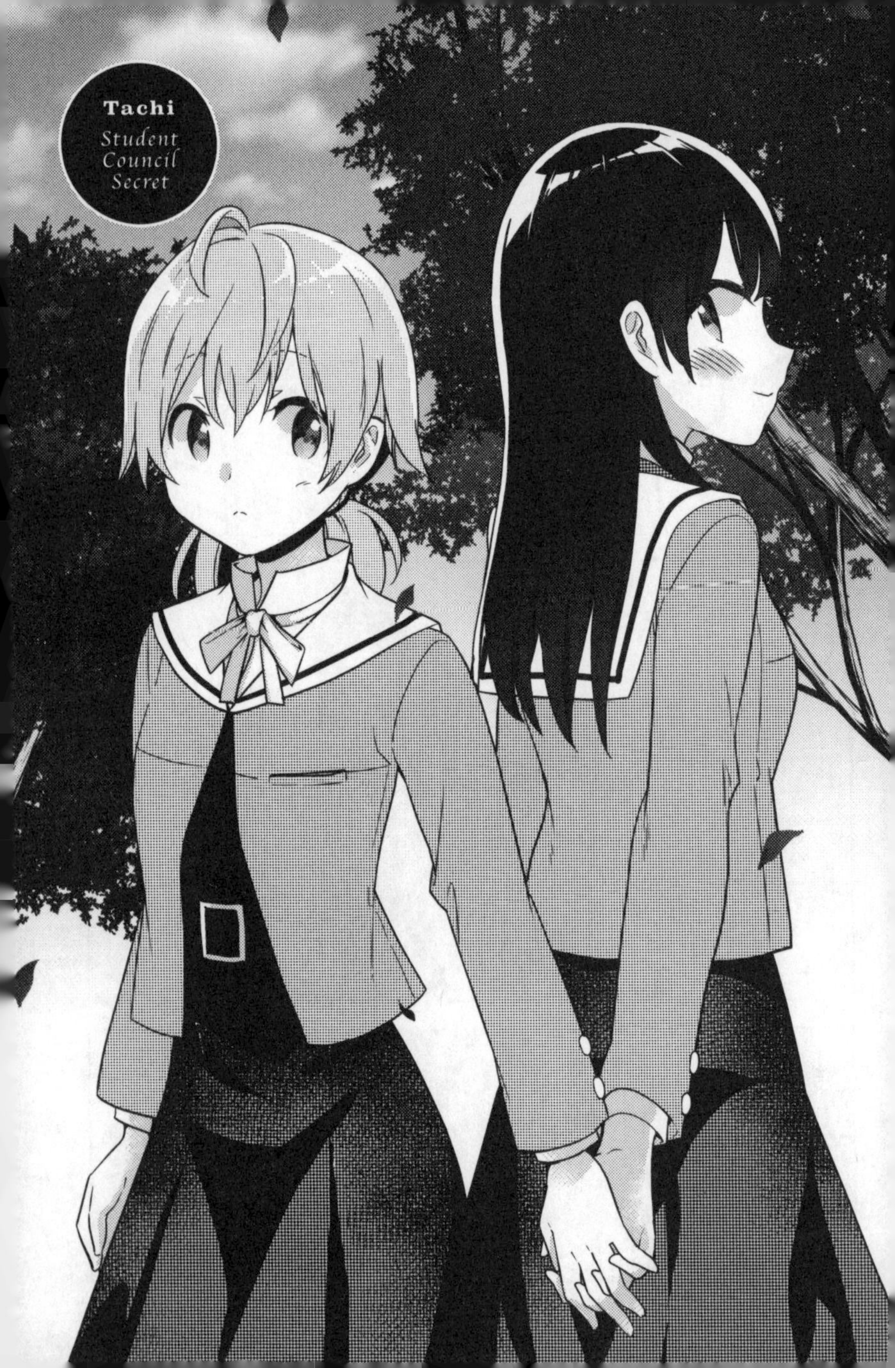
Tachi
Student Council Secret

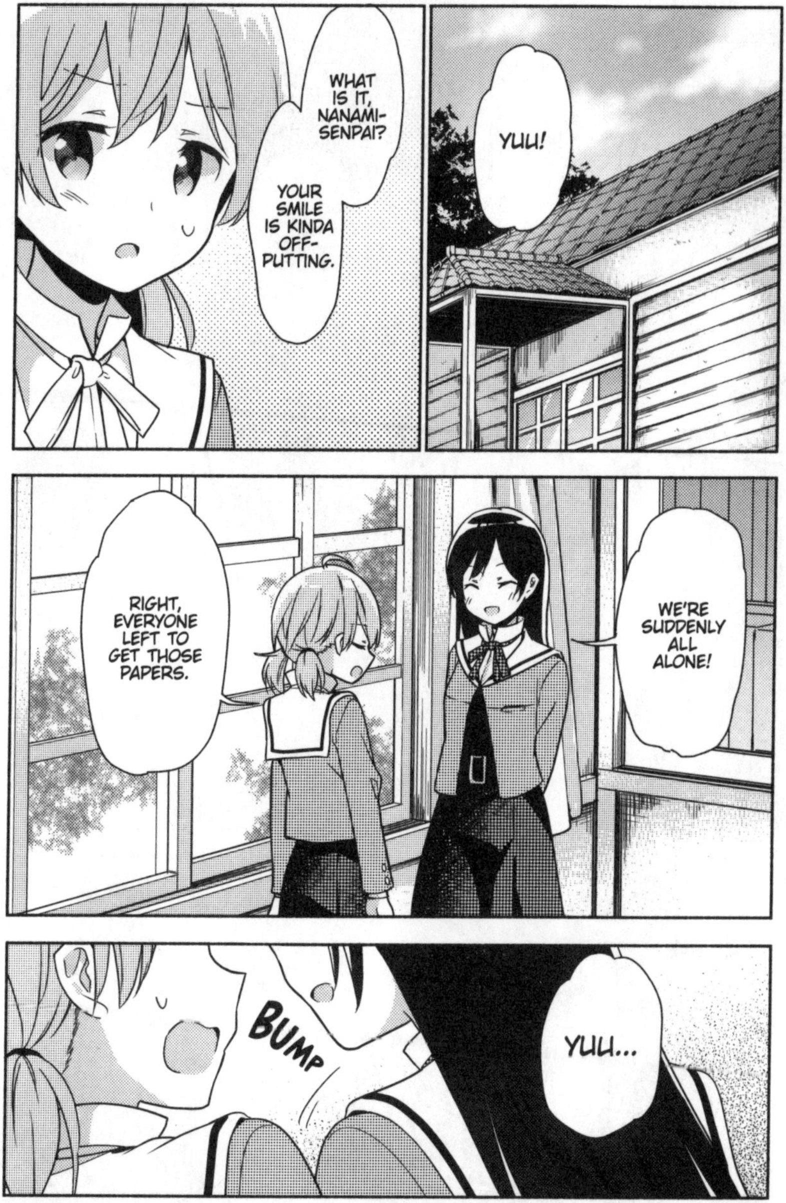
YUU!
WHAT IS IT, NANAMI-SENPAI?
YOUR SMILE IS KINDA OFF-PUTTING.
WE'RE SUDDENLY ALL ALONE!
RIGHT, EVERYONE LEFT TO GET THOSE PAPERS.
YUU...
BUMP

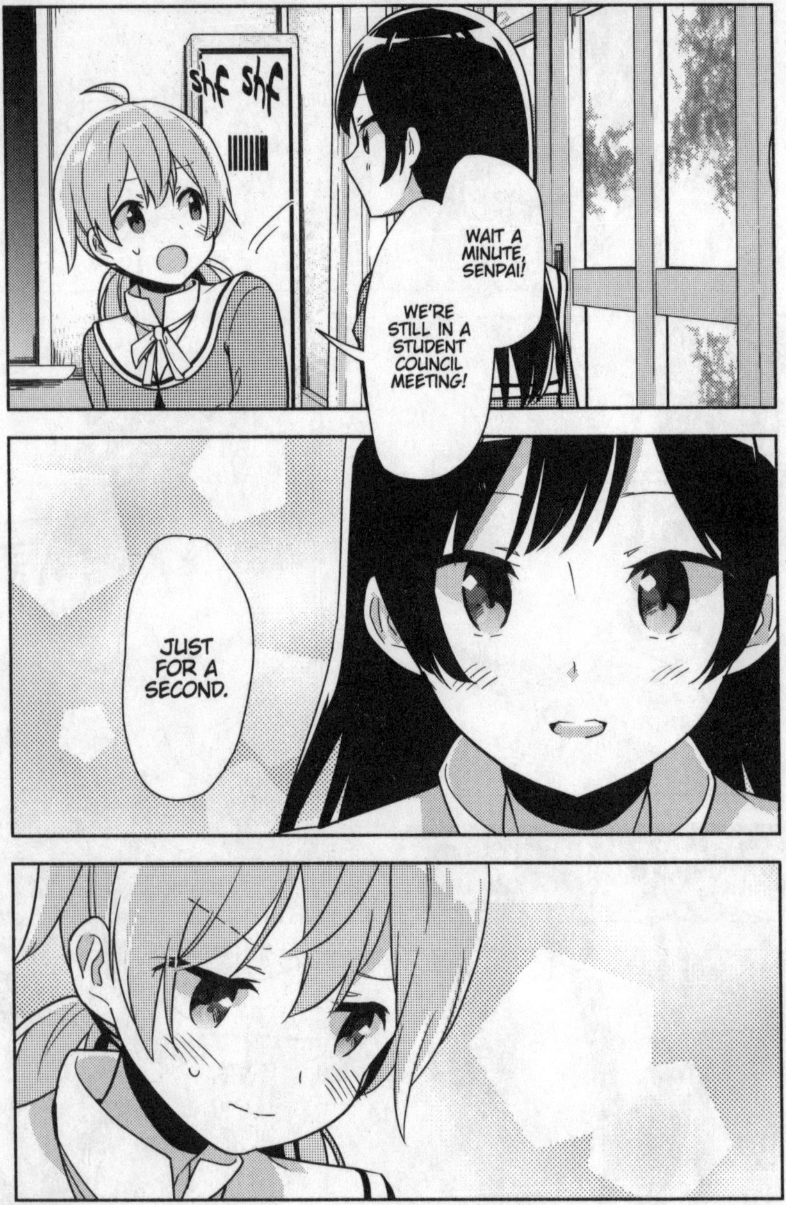
shf shf
WAIT A MINUTE, SENPAI!
WE'RE STILL IN A STUDENT COUNCIL MEETING!
JUST FOR A SECOND.

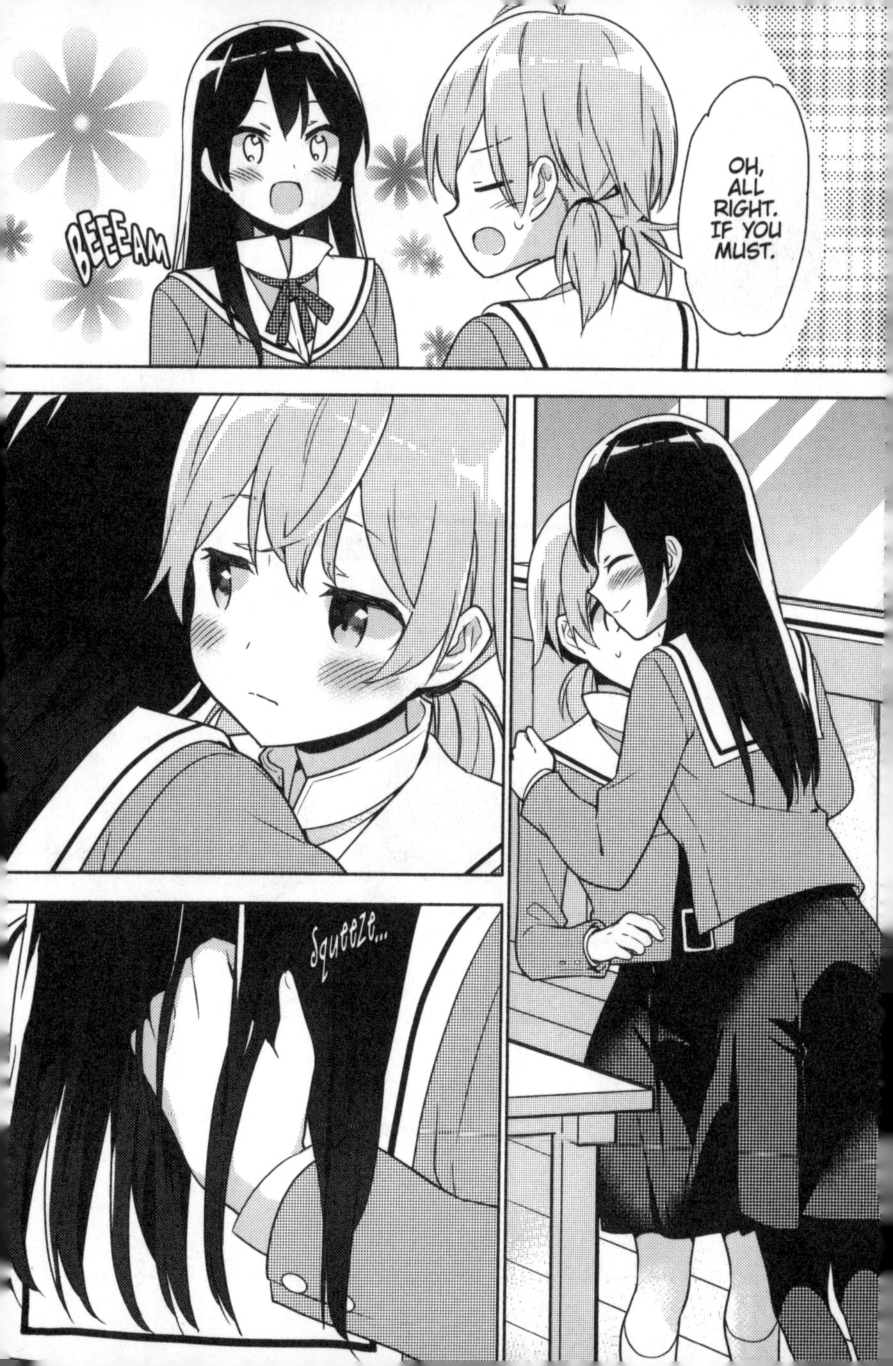
OH, ALL RIGHT. IF YOU MUST.
BEEEAM
Squeeze...

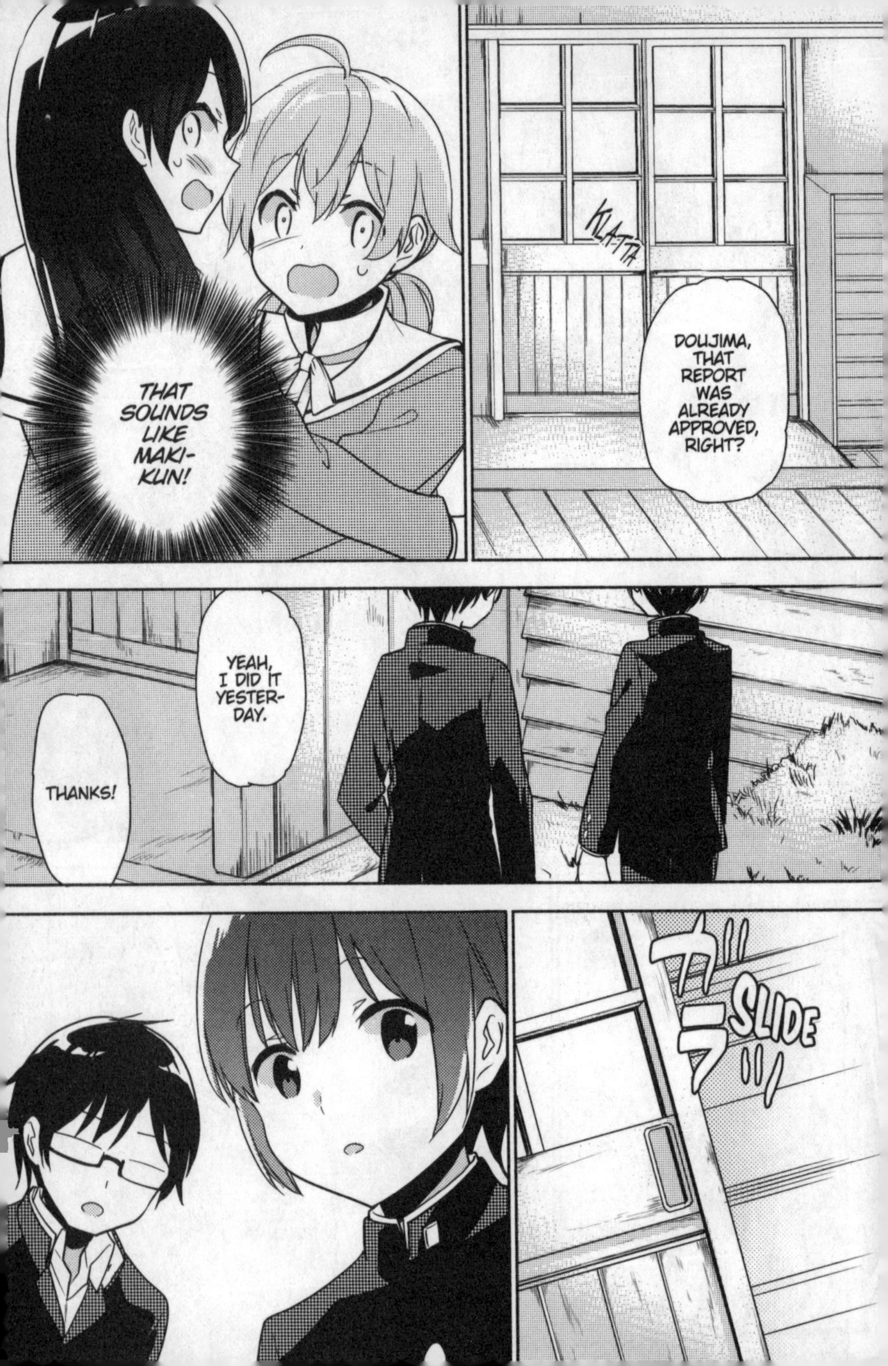
KLATTA
DOUJIMA, THAT REPORT WAS ALREADY APPROVED, RIGHT?
THAT SOUNDS LIKE MAKI-KUN!
YEAH, I DID IT YESTER-DAY.
THANKS!
ガラ
SLIDE

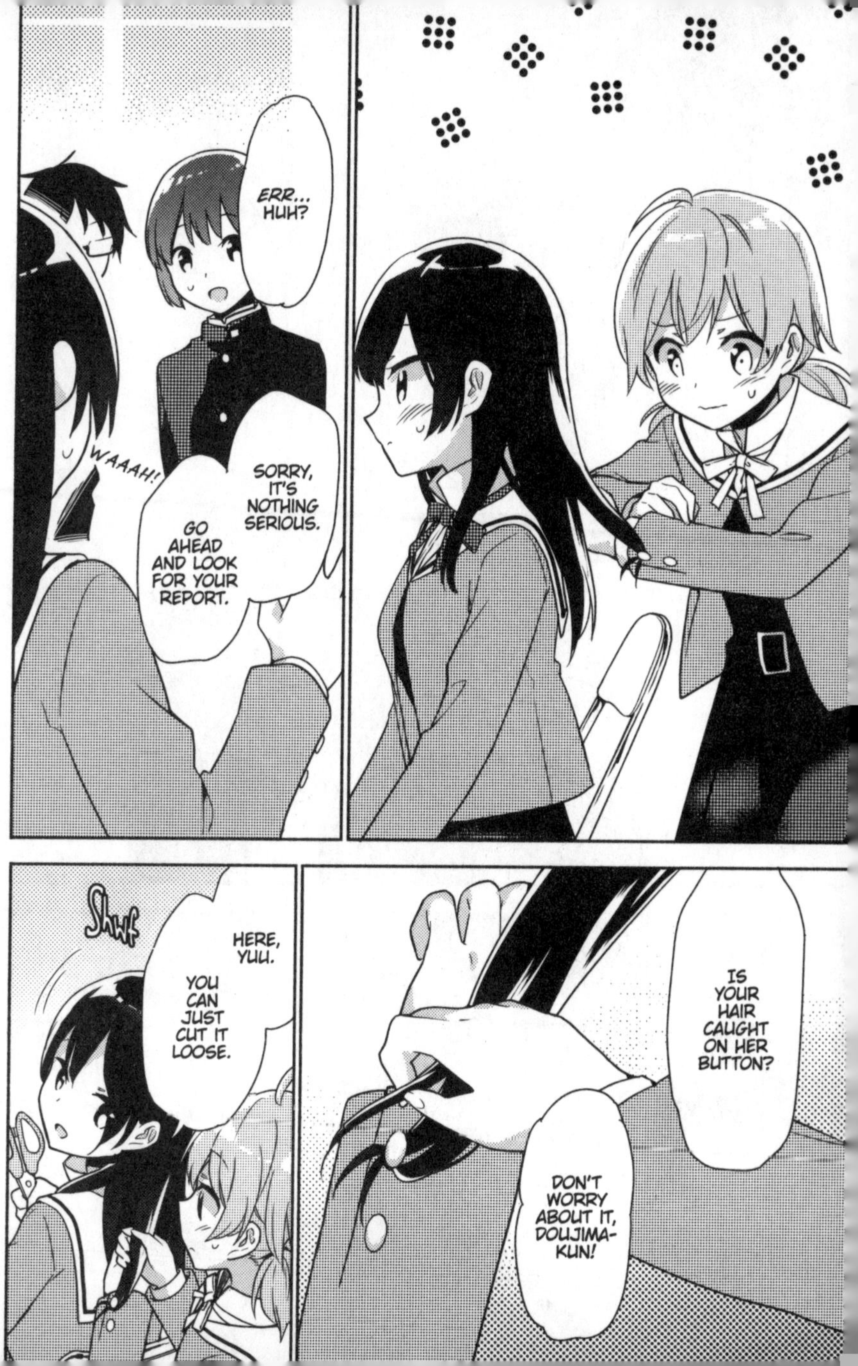
ERR... HUH?
SORRY, IT'S NOTHING SERIOUS.
GO AHEAD AND LOOK FOR YOUR REPORT.
WAAAH!
IS YOUR HAIR CAUGHT ON HER BUTTON?
DON'T WORRY ABOUT IT, DOUJIMA-KUN!
HERE, YUU.
YOU CAN JUST CUT IT LOOSE.
Shwf

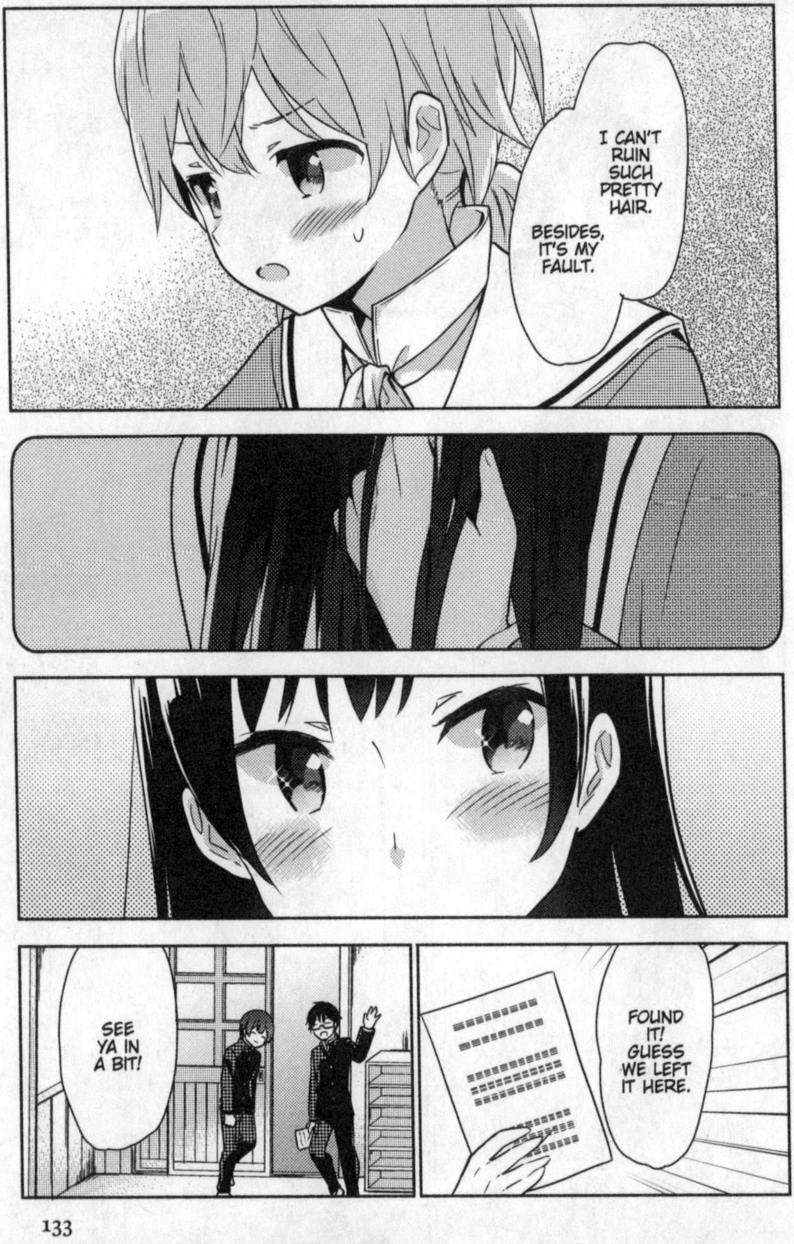
I CAN'T RUIN SUCH PRETTY HAIR.
BESIDES, IT'S MY FAULT.
FOUND IT! GUESS WE LEFT IT HERE.
SEE YA IN A BIT!

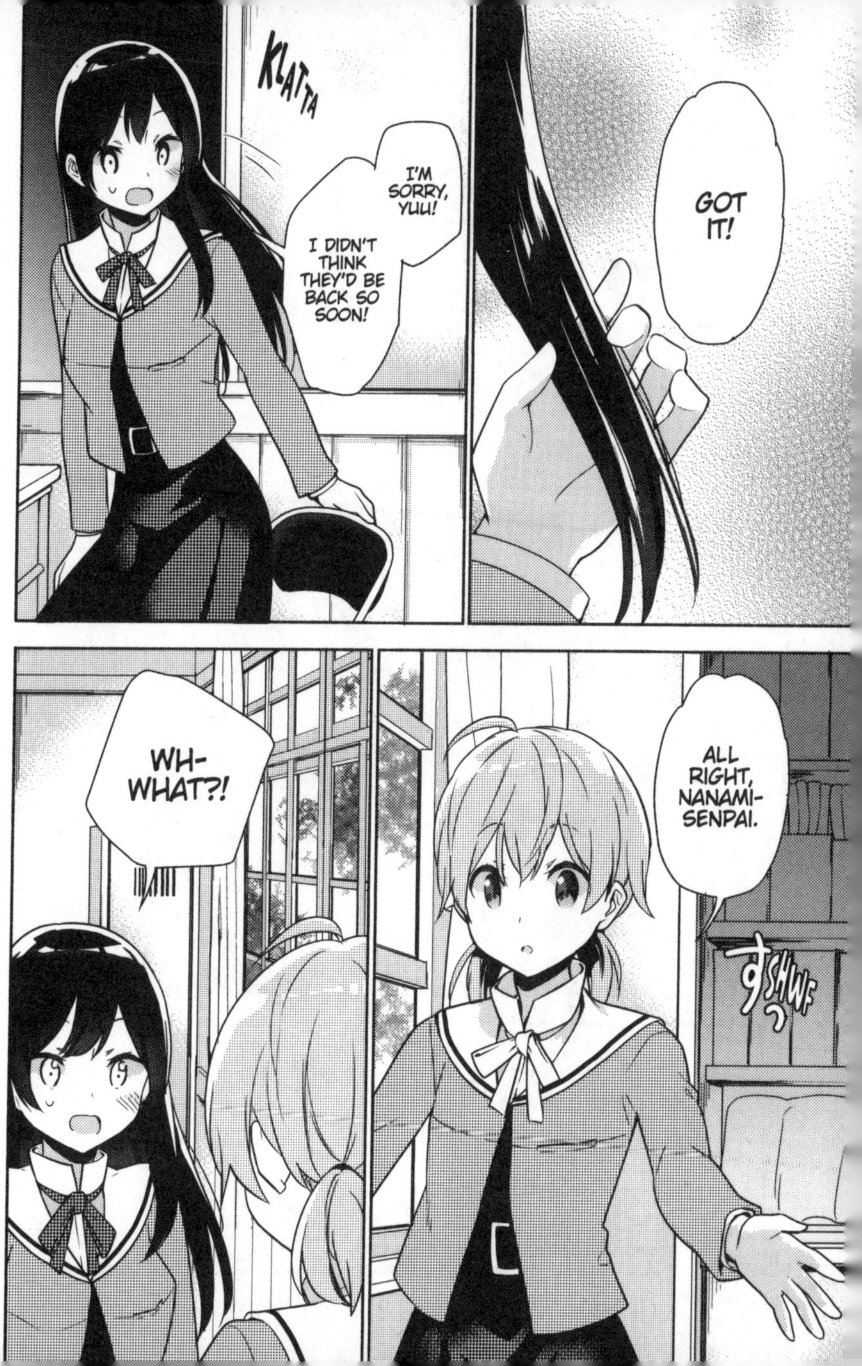
GOT IT!
KLATTA
I'M SORRY, YUU!
I DIDN'T THINK THEY'D BE BACK SO SOON!
ALL RIGHT, NANAMI-SENPAI.
すっ SHWF
WH-WHAT?!

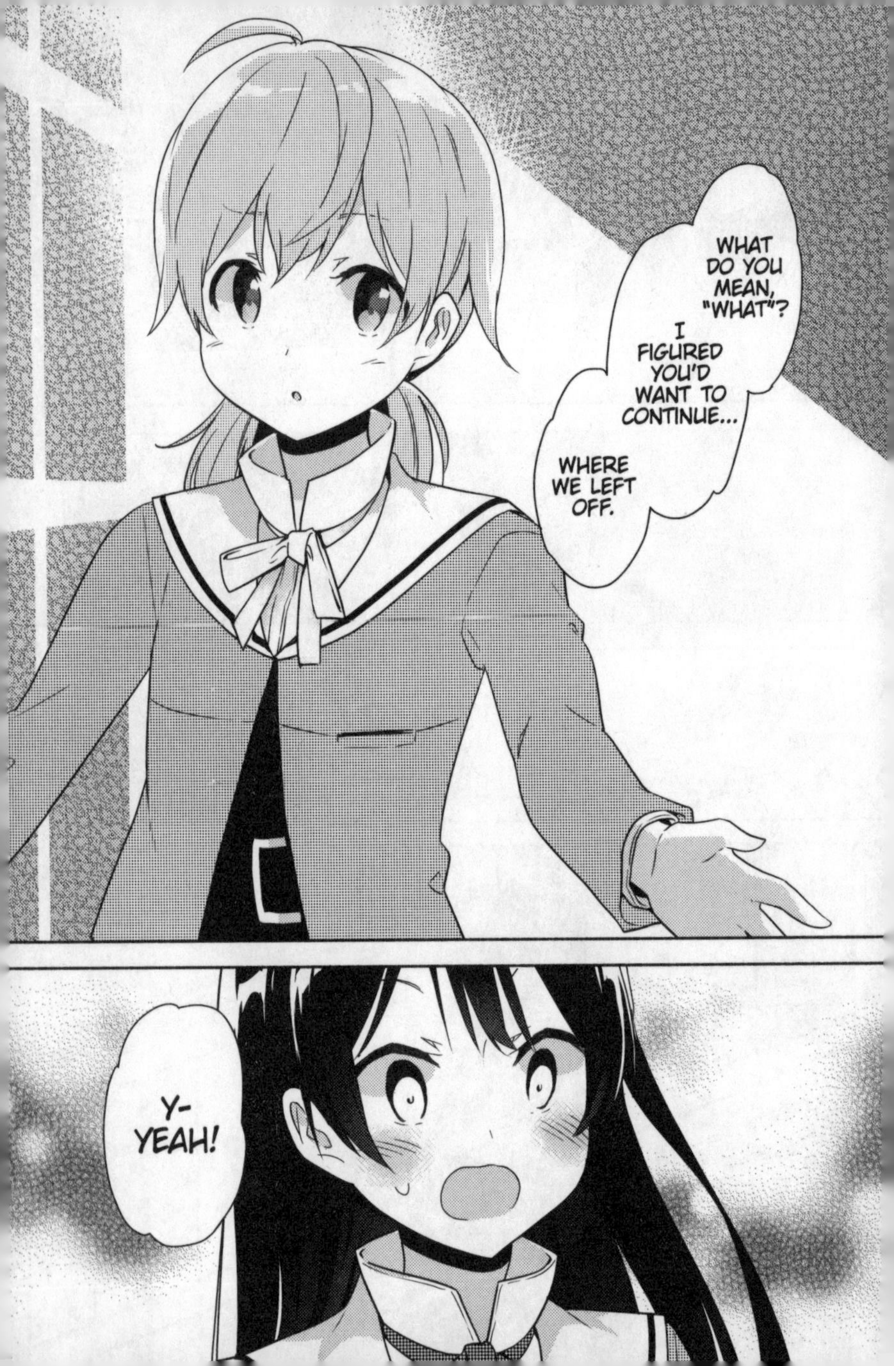
WHAT DO YOU MEAN, "WHAT"?
I FIGURED YOU'D WANT TO CONTINUE...
WHERE WE LEFT OFF.
Y-YEAH!

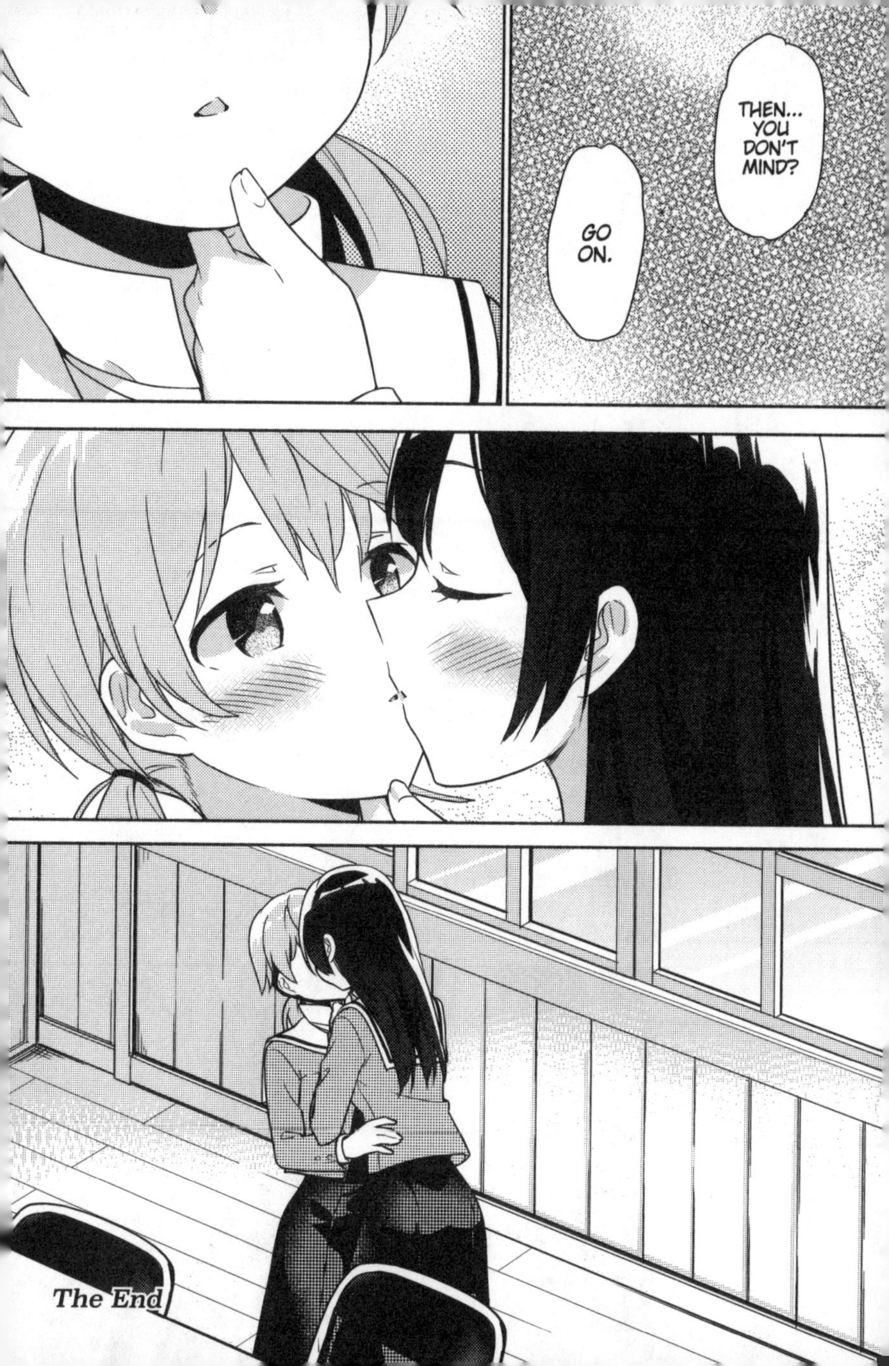
THEN... YOU DON'T MIND?
GO ON.
The End

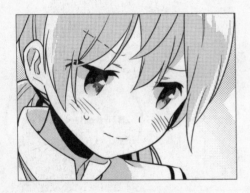

Tachi

Best known for *Sakura Trick* (Houbunsha).

(**Bloom Into You**)

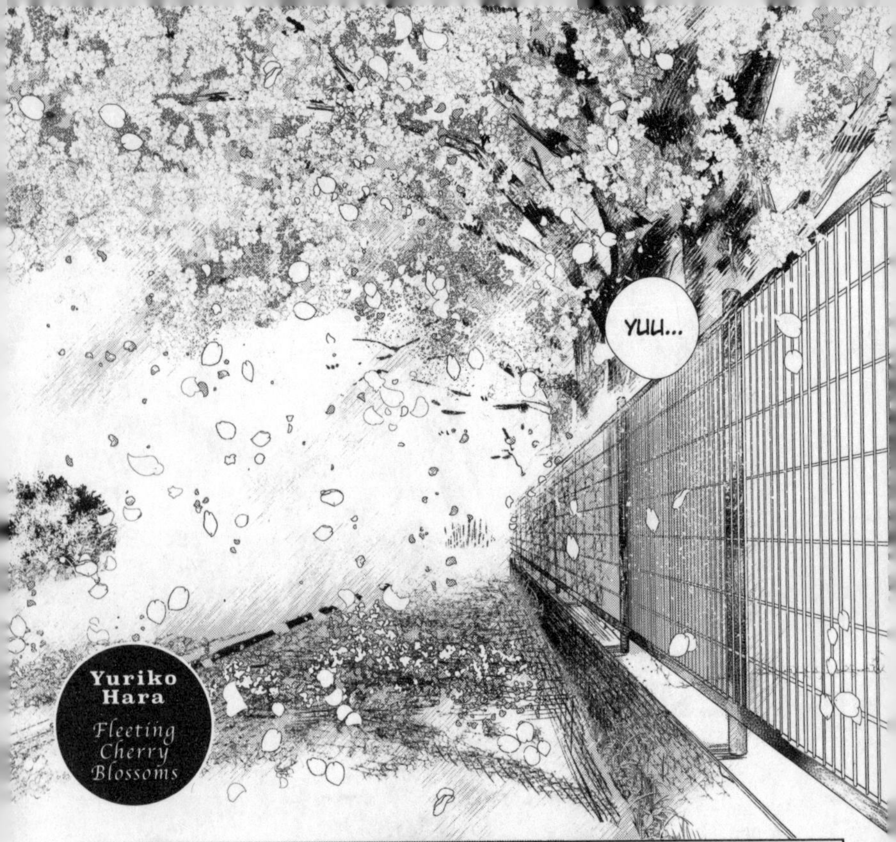
Yuriko Hara
Fleeting Cherry Blossoms
YUU...

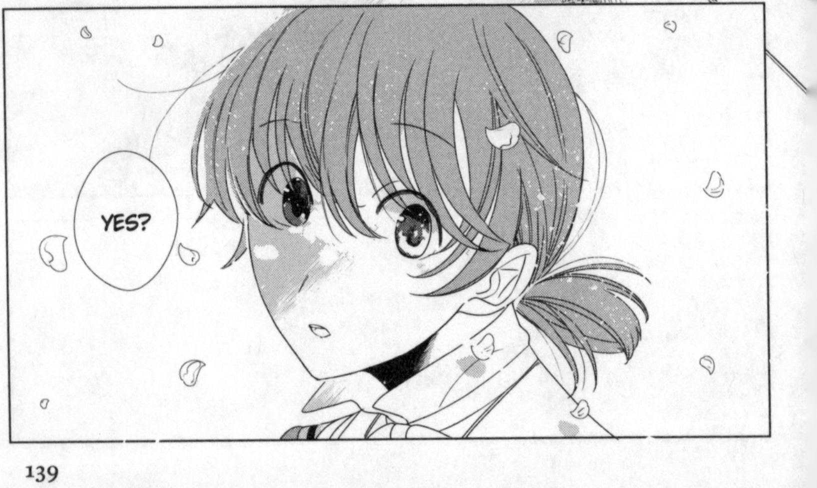
YES?

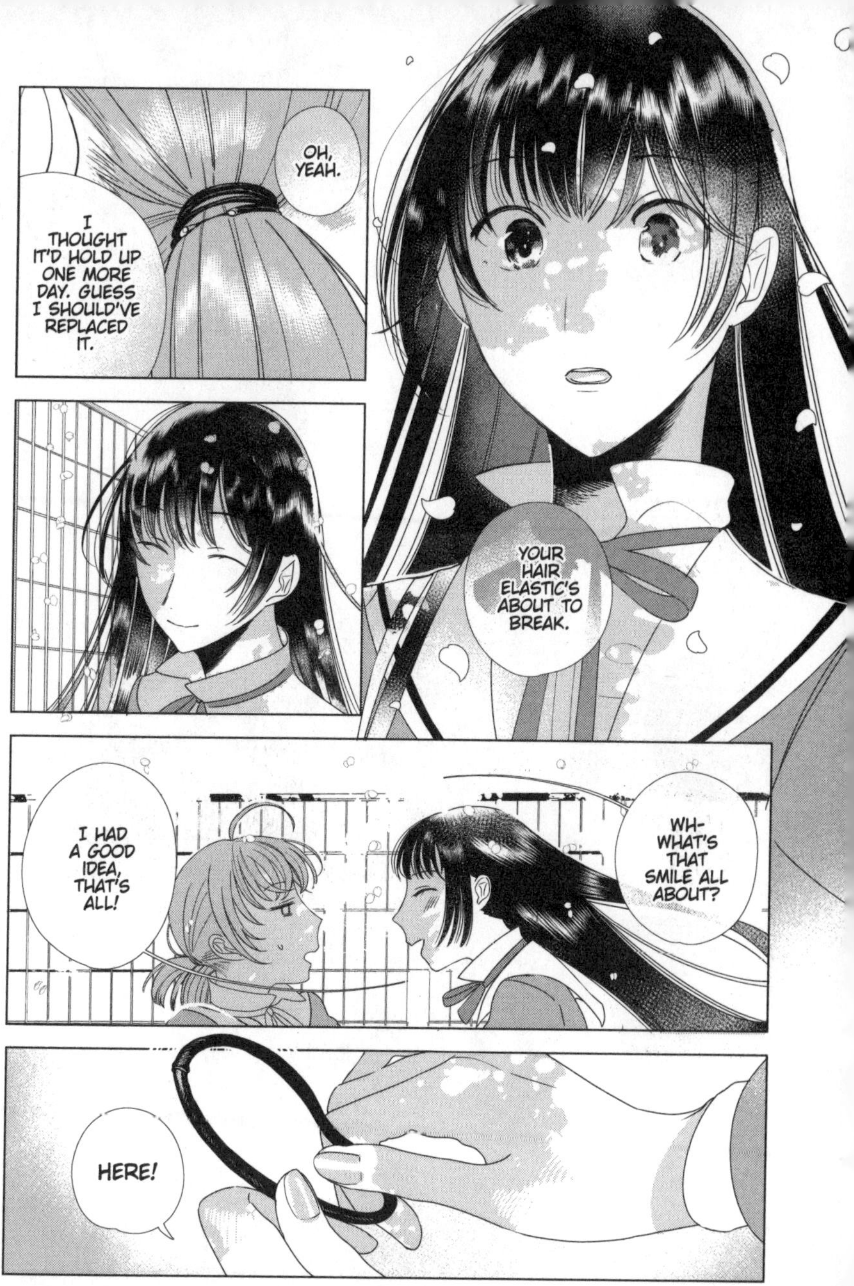
YOUR HAIR ELASTIC'S ABOUT TO BREAK.
OH, YEAH.
I THOUGHT IT'D HOLD UP ONE MORE DAY. GUESS I SHOULD'VE REPLACED IT.
WH-WHAT'S THAT SMILE ALL ABOUT?
I HAD A GOOD IDEA, THAT'S ALL!
HERE!

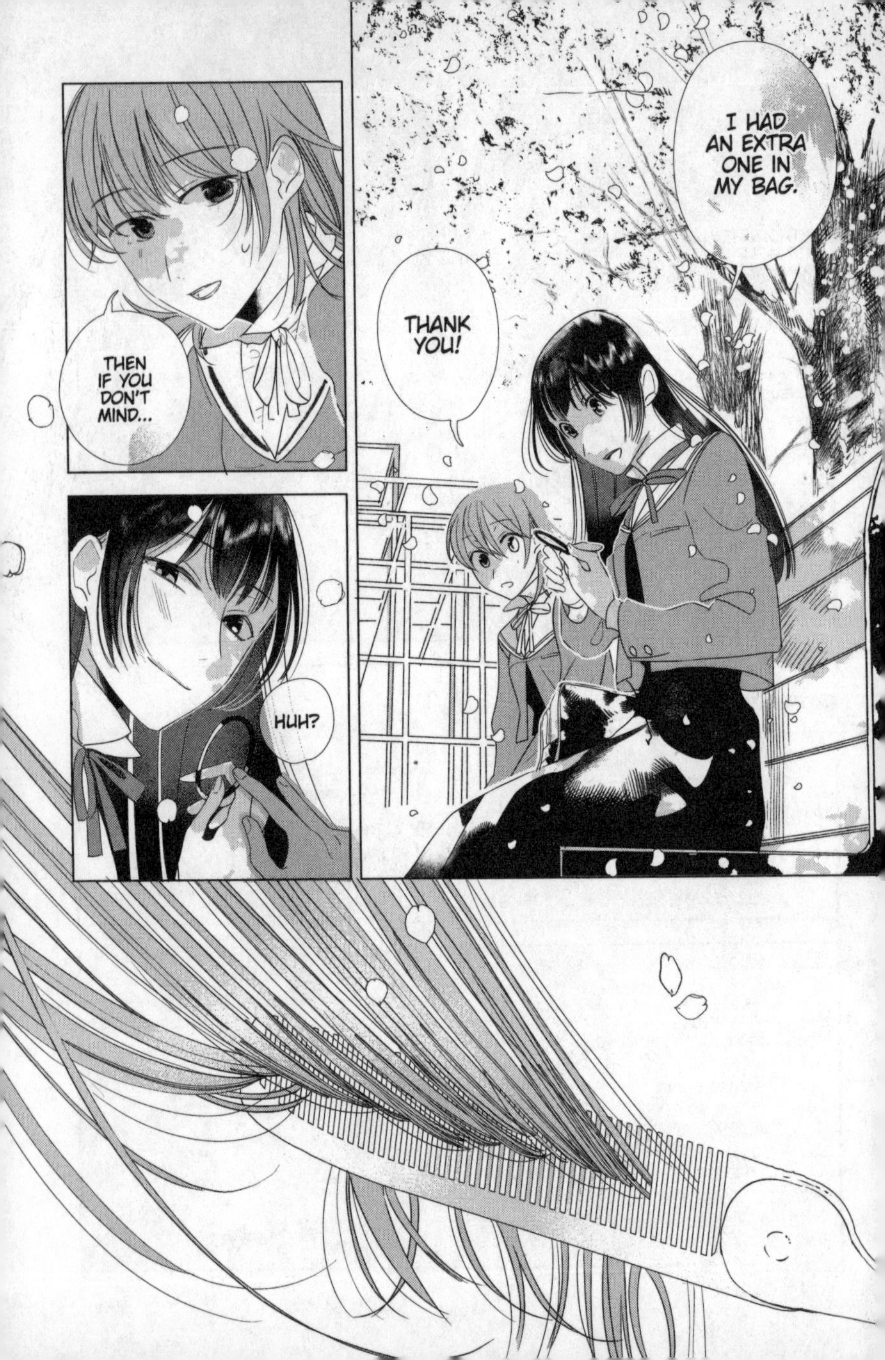
I HAD AN EXTRA ONE IN MY BAG.
THANK YOU!
THEN IF YOU DON'T MIND...
HUH?

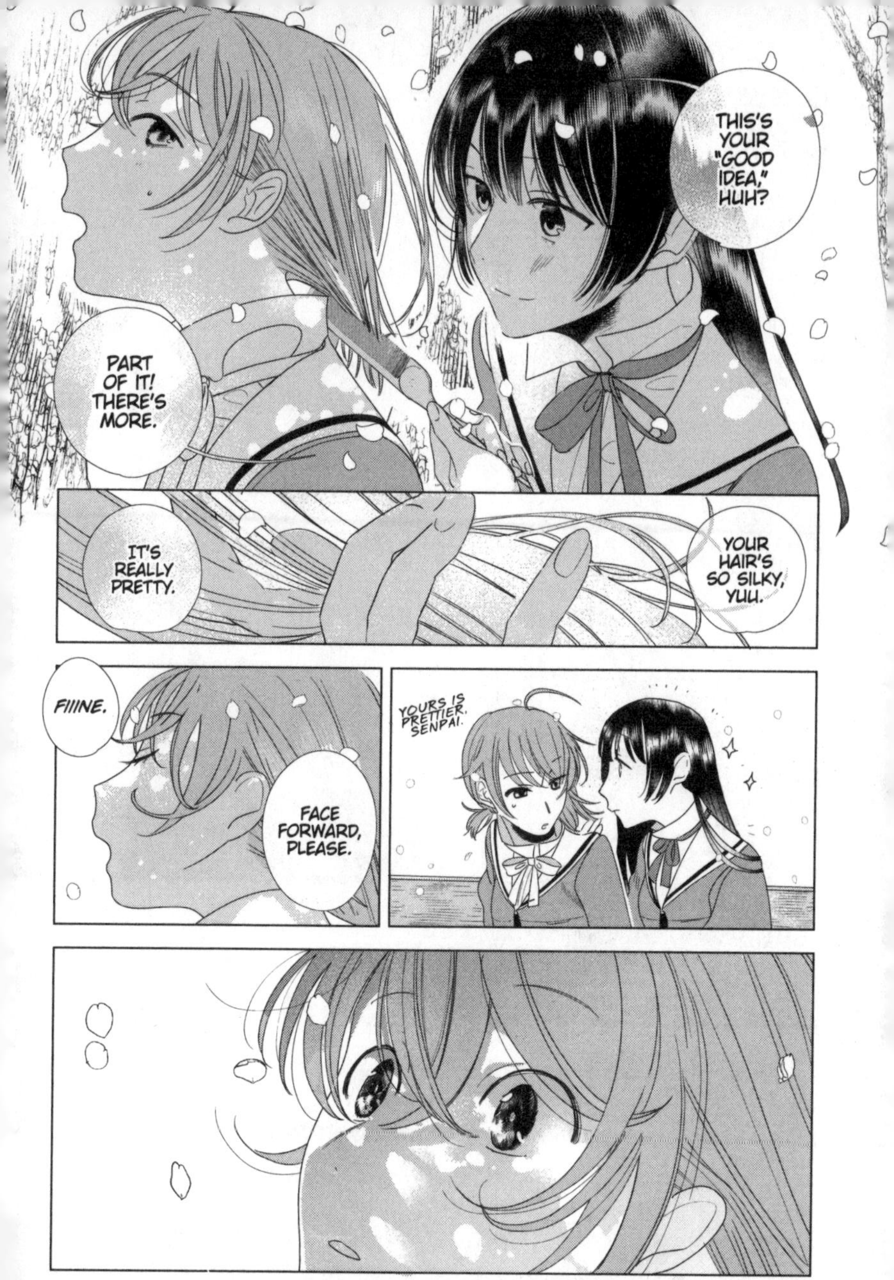
THIS'S YOUR "GOOD IDEA," HUH?
PART OF IT! THERE'S MORE.
YOUR HAIR'S SO SILKY, YUU.
IT'S REALLY PRETTY.
YOURS IS PRETTIER, SENPAI.
FACE FORWARD, PLEASE.
FIIINE.

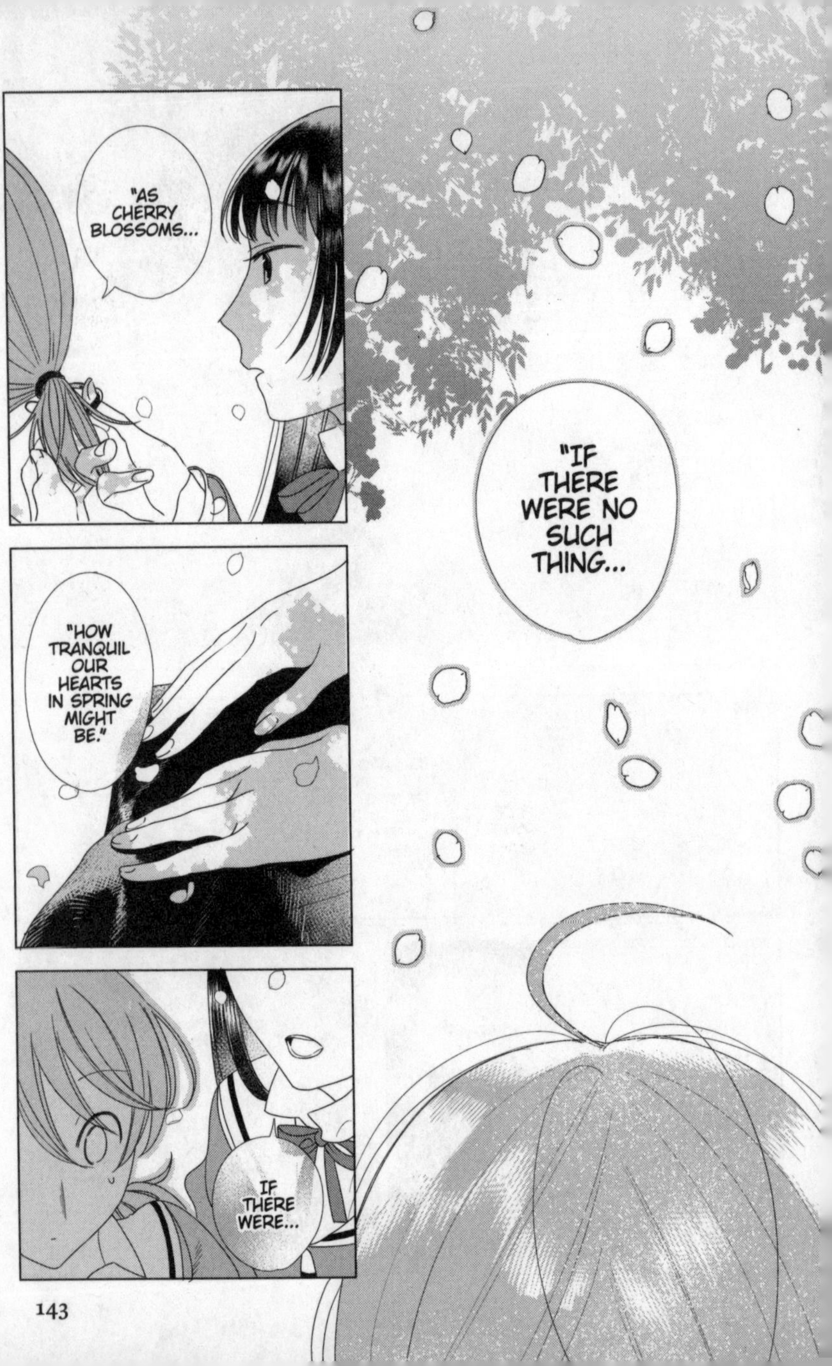
"IF THERE WERE NO SUCH THING...
"AS CHERRY BLOSSOMS...
"HOW TRANQUIL OUR HEARTS IN SPRING MIGHT BE."
IF THERE WERE...

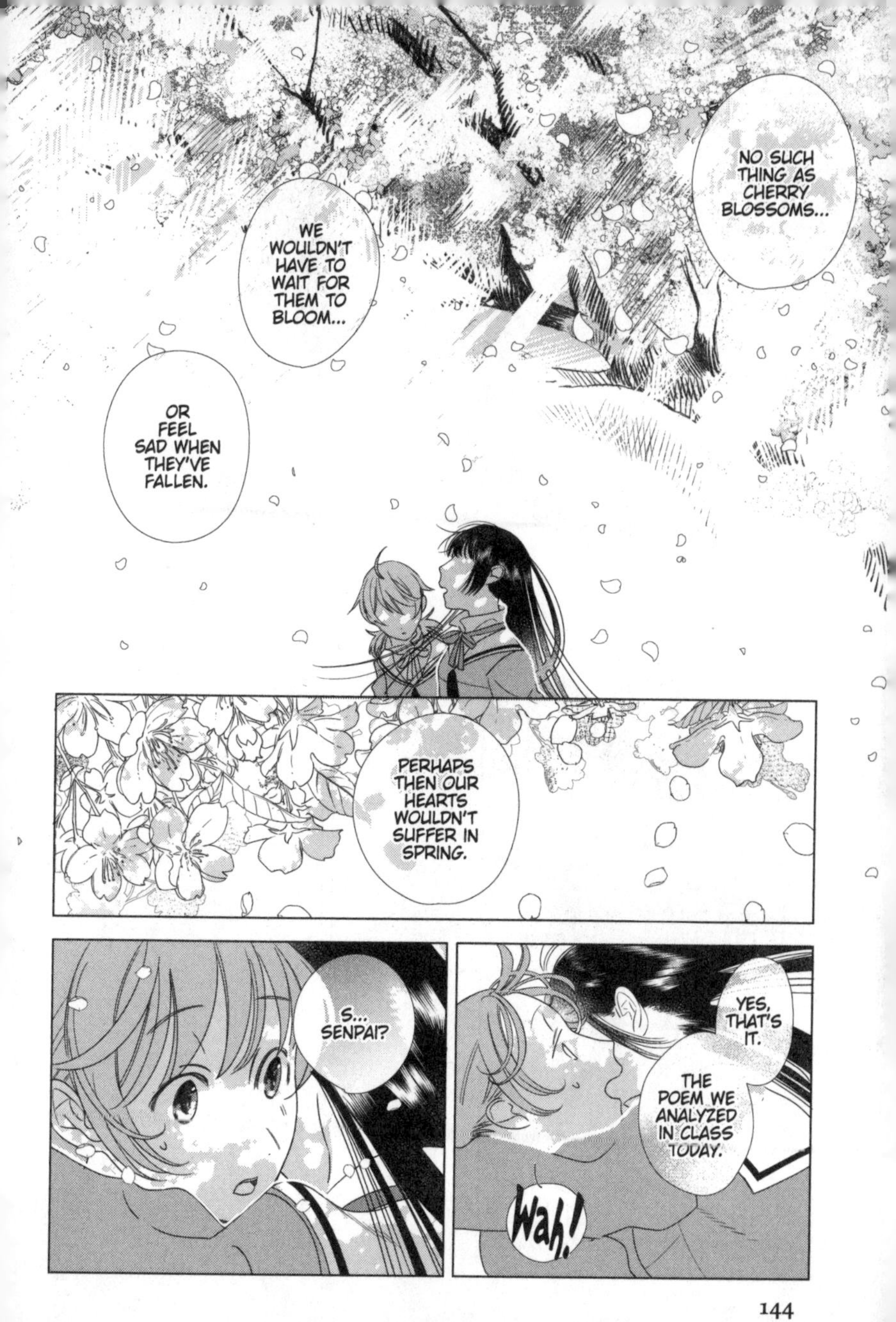
NO SUCH THING AS CHERRY BLOSSOMS...
WE WOULDN'T HAVE TO WAIT FOR THEM TO BLOOM...
OR FEEL SAD WHEN THEY'VE FALLEN.
PERHAPS THEN OUR HEARTS WOULDN'T SUFFER IN SPRING.
YES, THAT'S IT.
THE POEM WE ANALYZED IN CLASS TODAY.
Wah!
S... SENPAI?

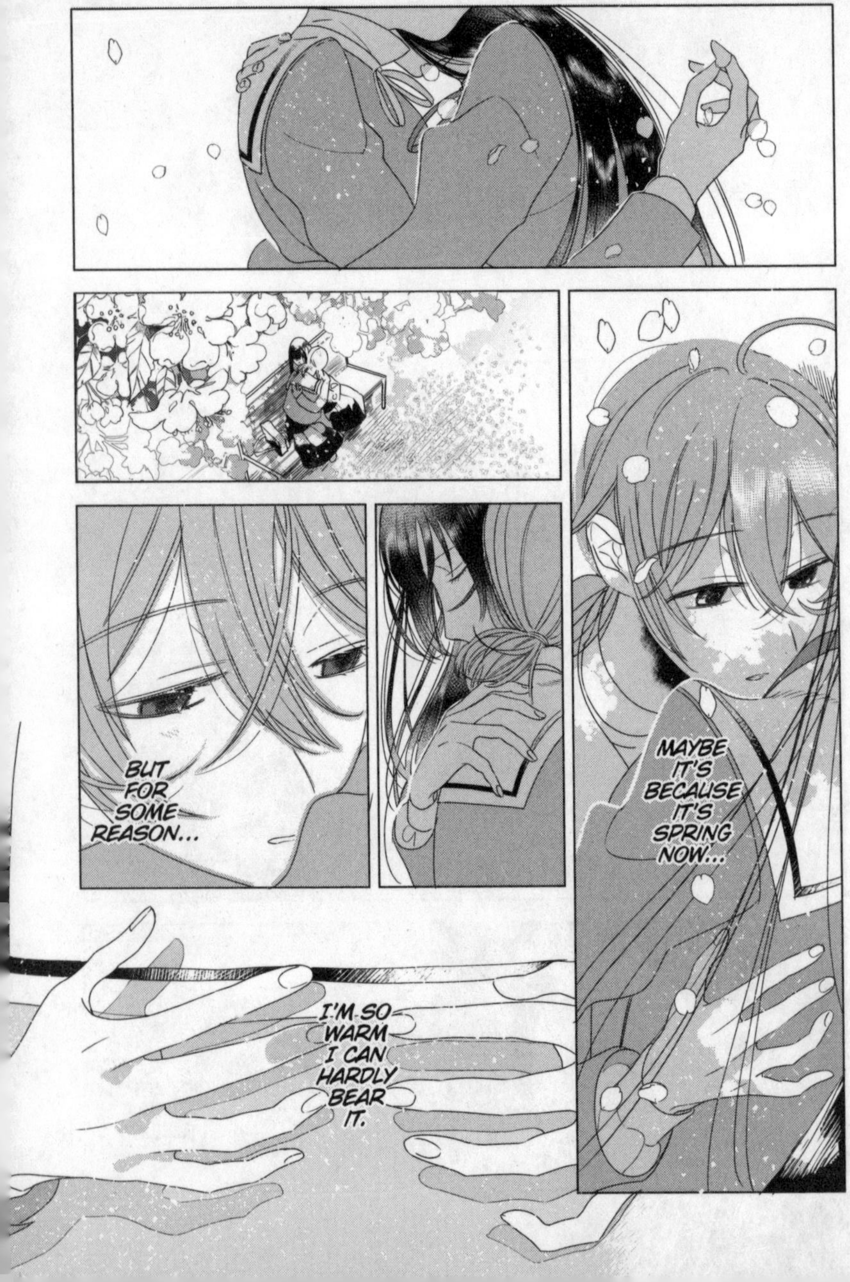
MAYBE IT'S BECAUSE IT'S SPRING NOW...
BUT FOR SOME REASON...
I'M SO WARM I CAN HARDLY BEAR IT.

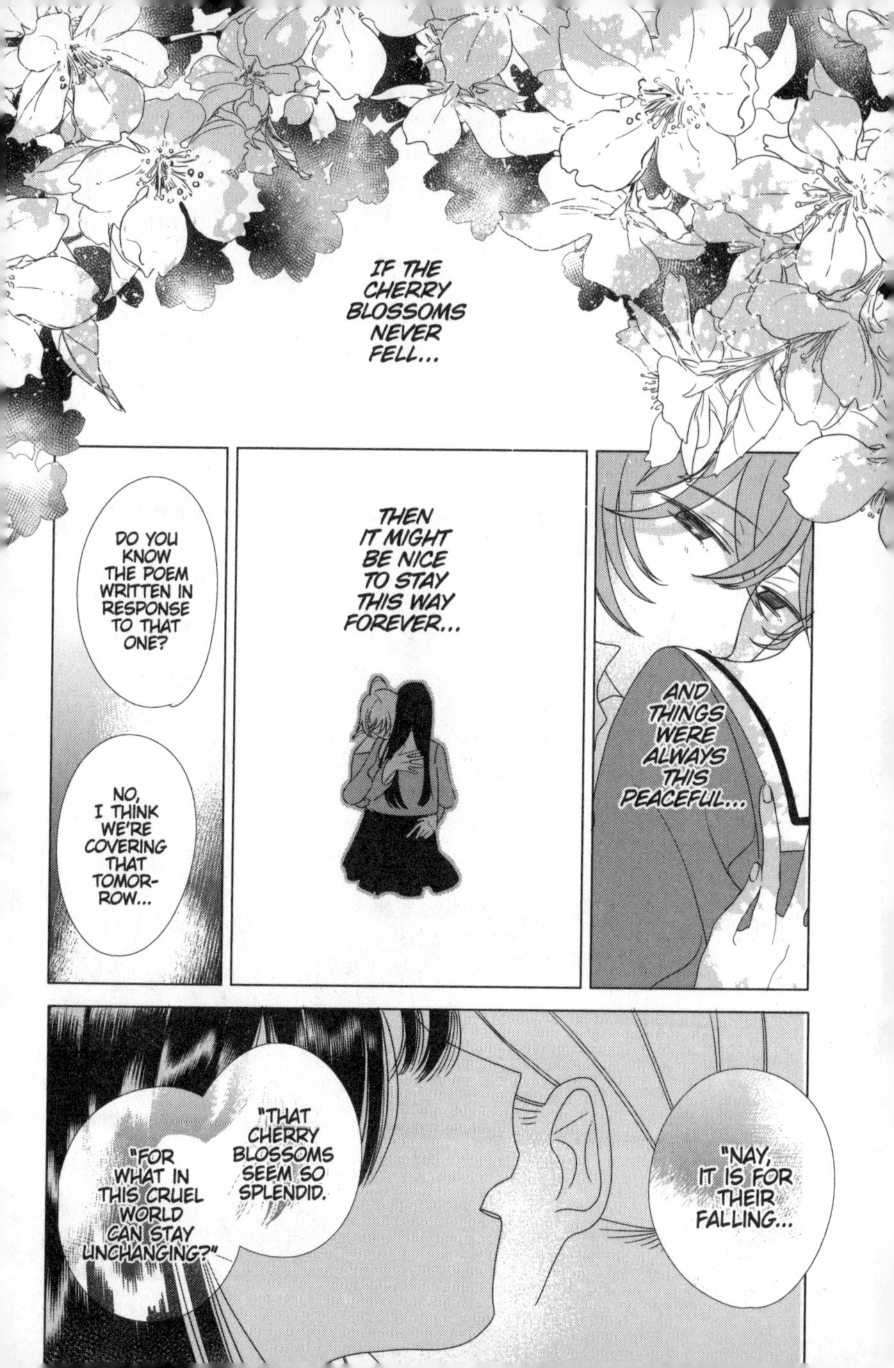
IF THE CHERRY BLOSSOMS NEVER FELL...
AND THINGS WERE ALWAYS THIS PEACEFUL...
THEN IT MIGHT BE NICE TO STAY THIS WAY FOREVER...
DO YOU KNOW THE POEM WRITTEN IN RESPONSE TO THAT ONE?
NO, I THINK WE'RE COVERING THAT TOMOR-ROW...
"NAY, IT IS FOR THEIR FALLING...
"THAT CHERRY BLOSSOMS SEEM SO SPLENDID.
"FOR WHAT IN THIS CRUEL WORLD CAN STAY UNCHANGING?"

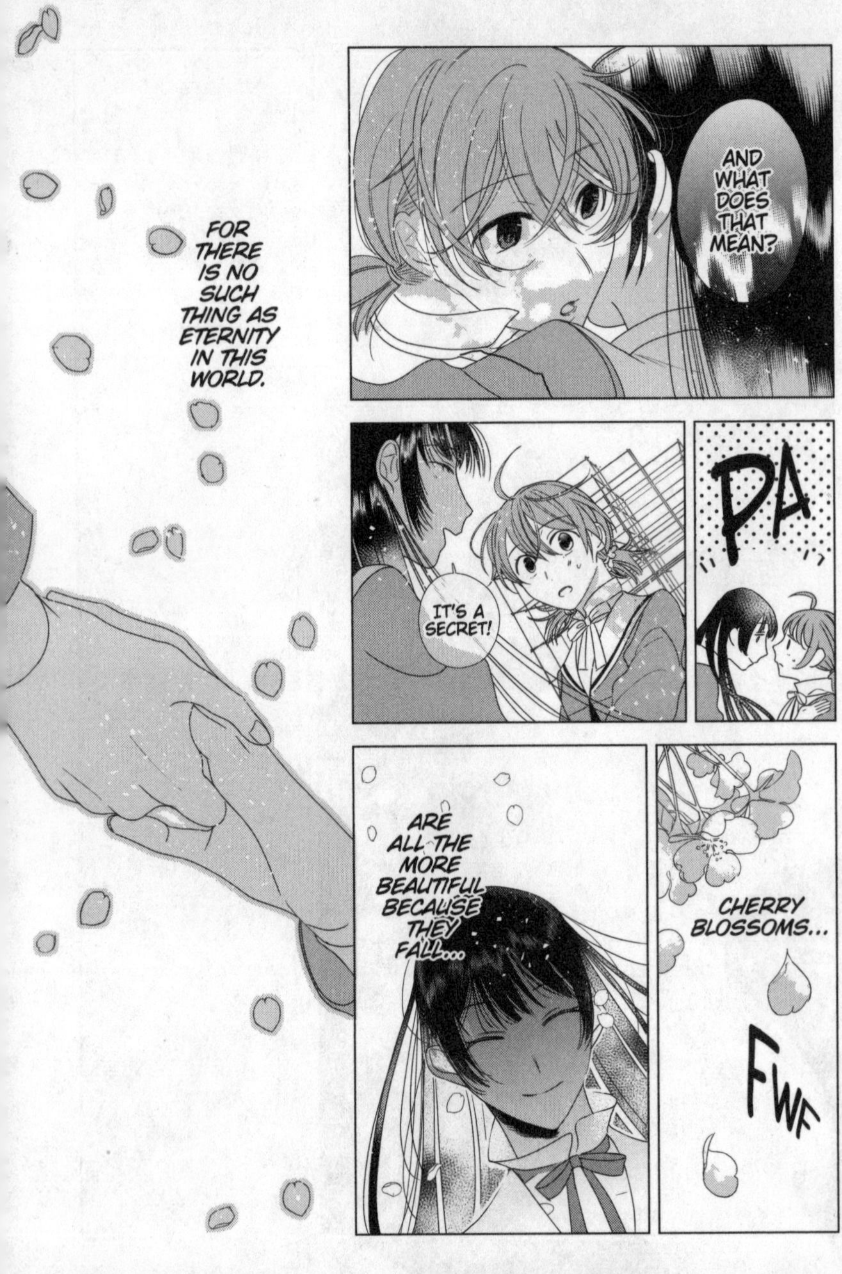
AND WHAT DOES THAT MEAN?
PA
IT'S A SECRET!
CHERRY BLOSSOMS...
FWF
ARE ALL THE MORE BEAUTIFUL BECAUSE THEY FALL...
FOR THERE IS NO SUCH THING AS ETERNITY IN THIS WORLD.

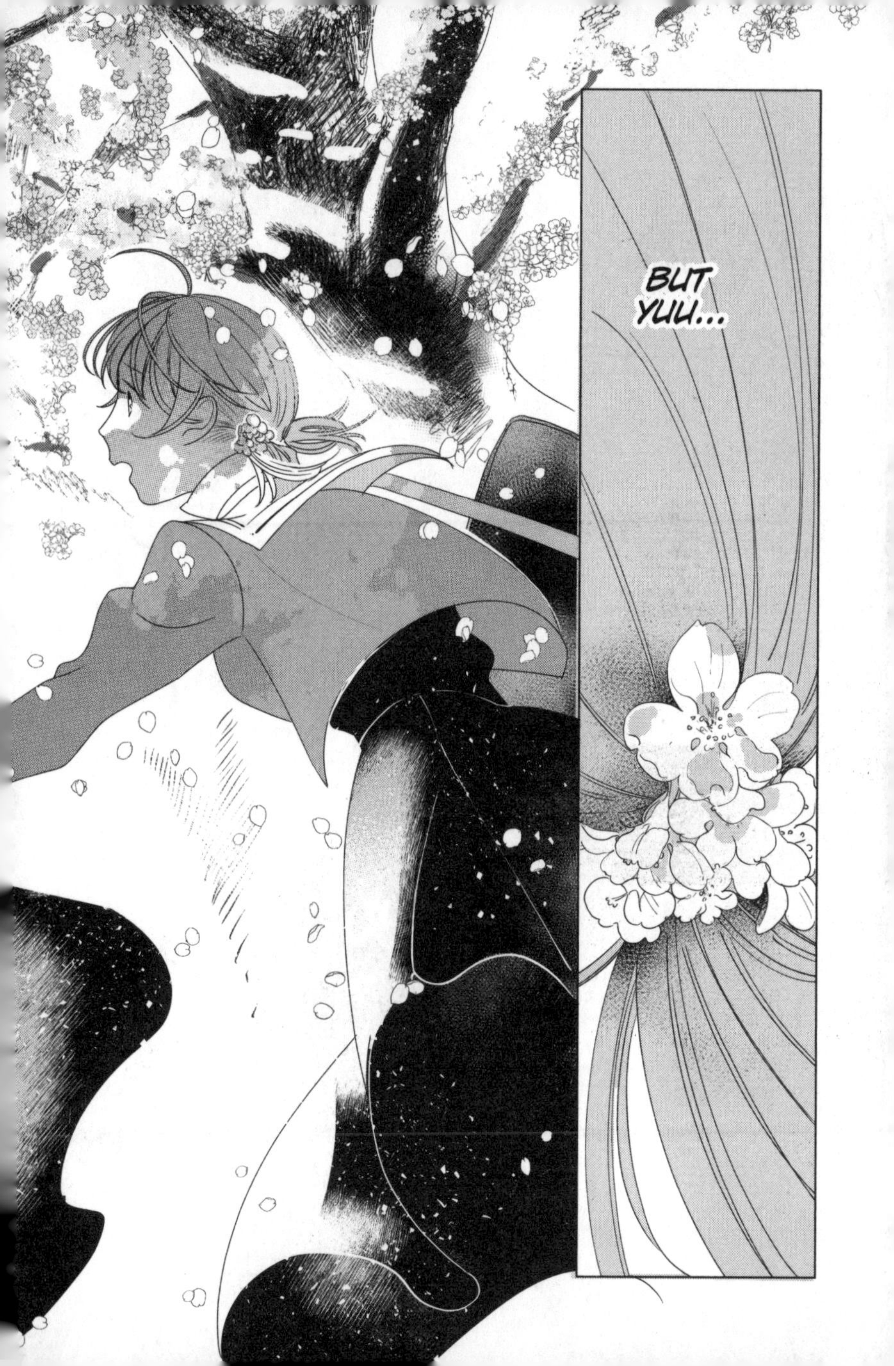
BUT YUU...

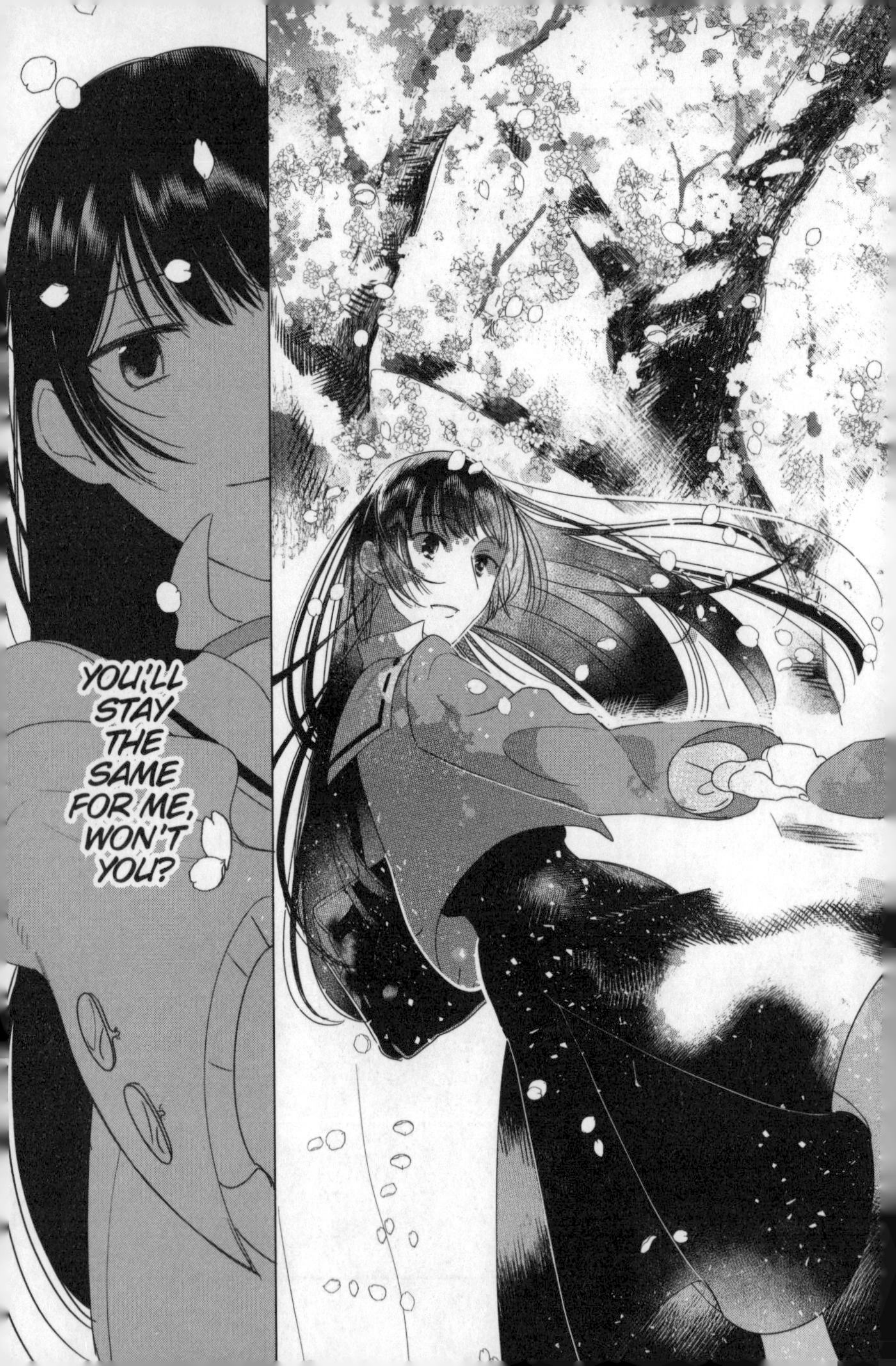
YOU'LL STAY THE SAME FOR ME, WON'T YOU?

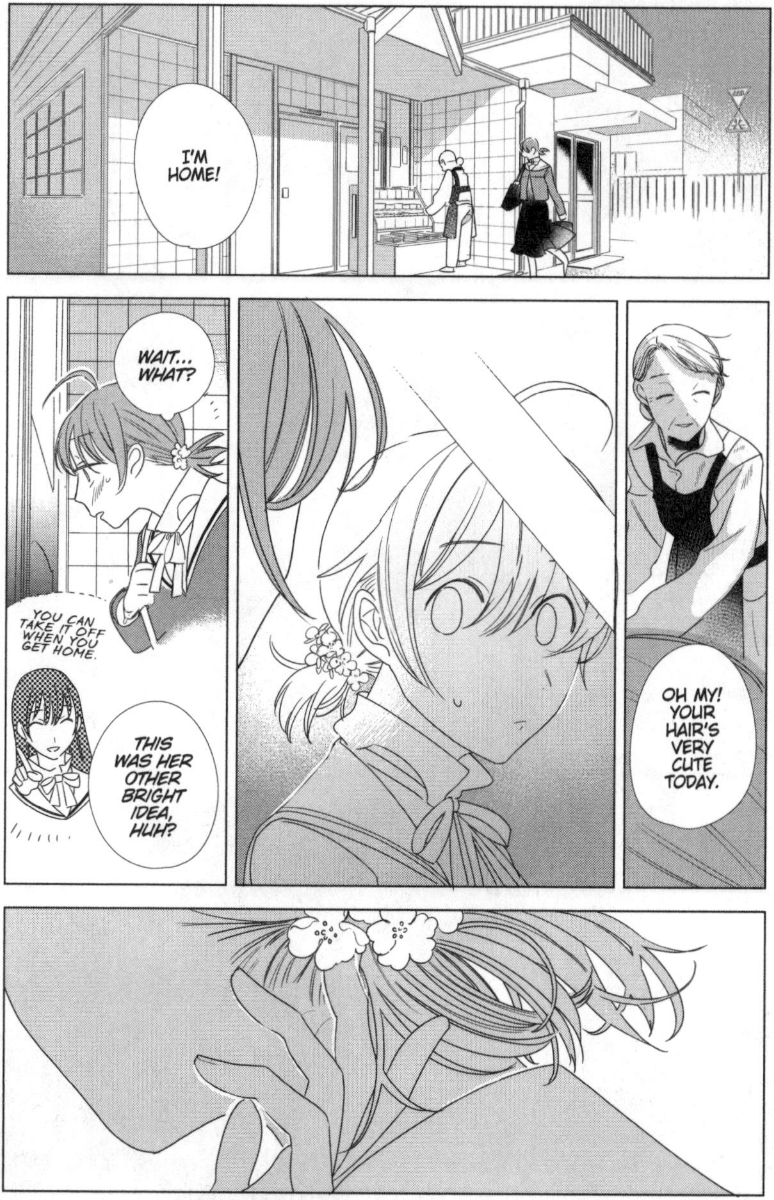
I'M HOME!
OH MY! YOUR HAIR'S VERY CUTE TODAY.
WAIT... WHAT?
YOU CAN TAKE IT OFF WHEN YOU GET HOME.
THIS WAS HER OTHER BRIGHT IDEA, HUH?

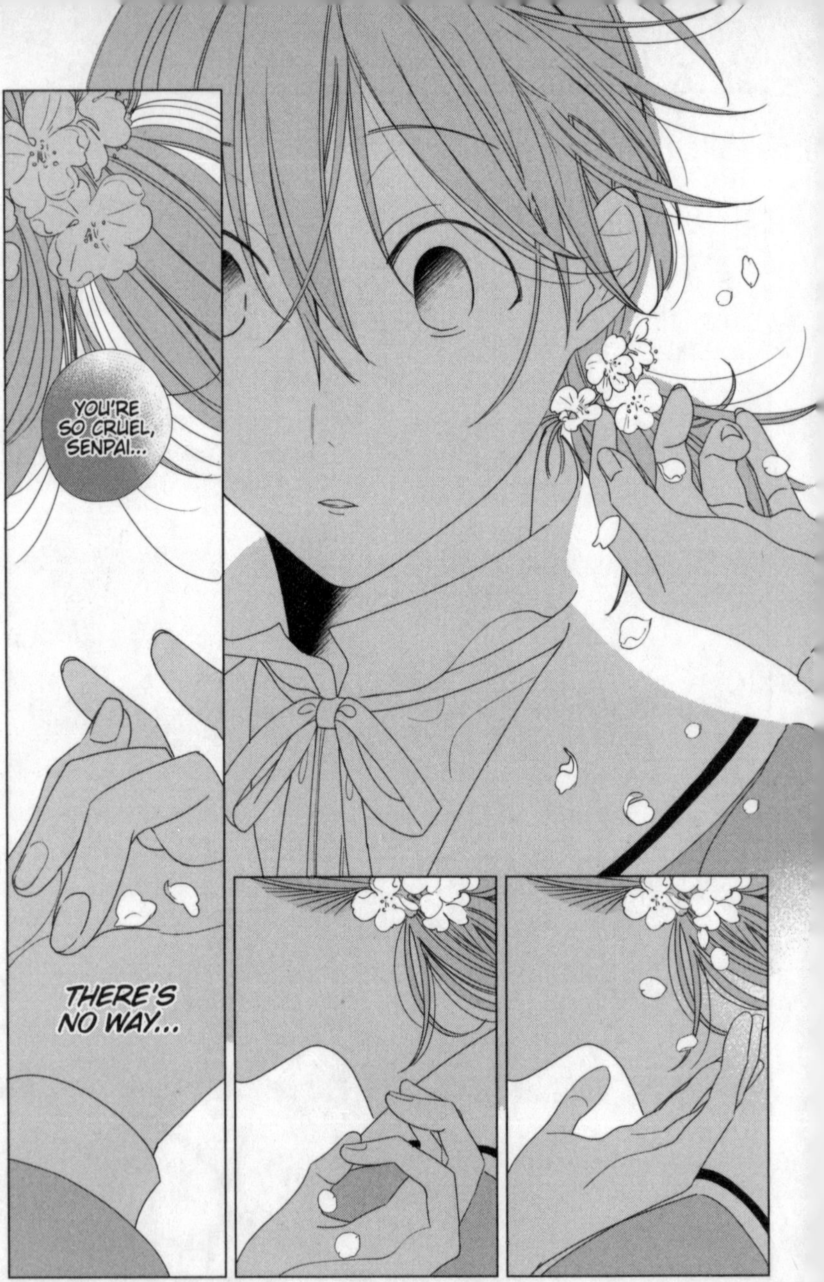
YOU'RE SO CRUEL, SENPAI...
THERE'S NO WAY...

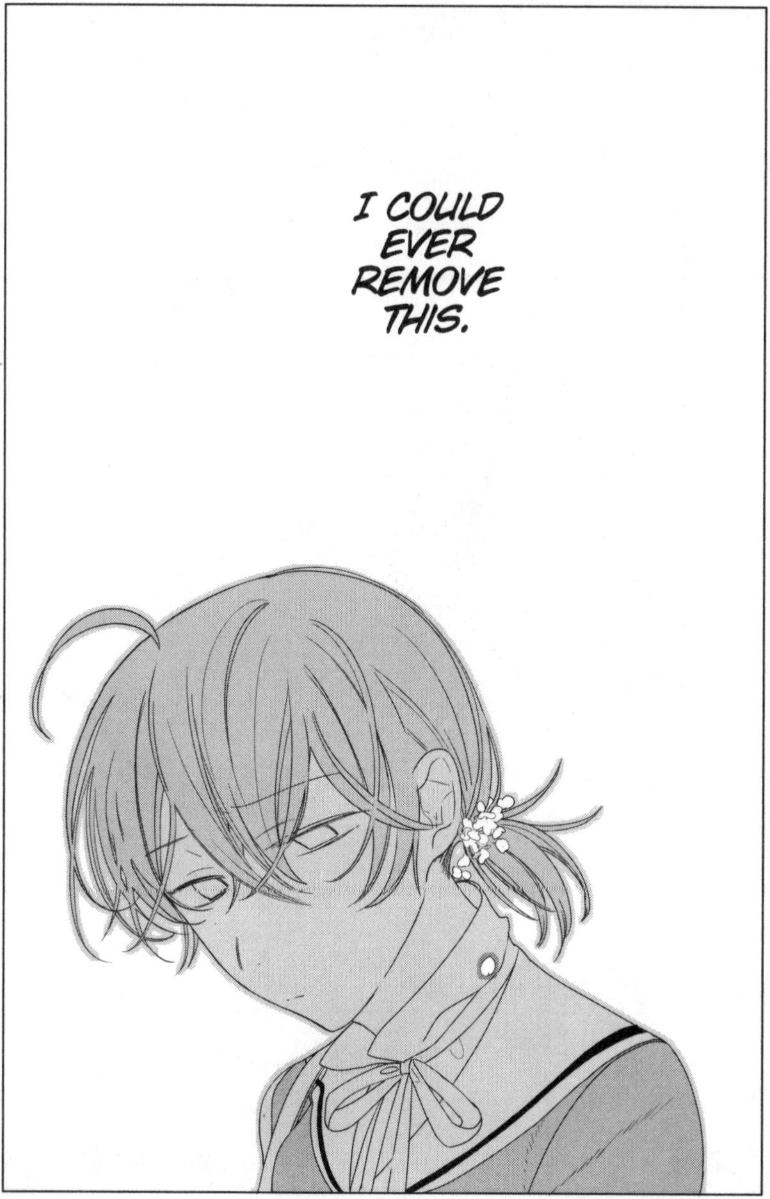
I COULD EVER REMOVE THIS.

The End

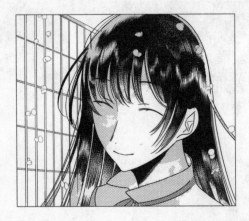

Yuriko Hara

Best known for *Cocoon Entwined* (KADOKAWA).

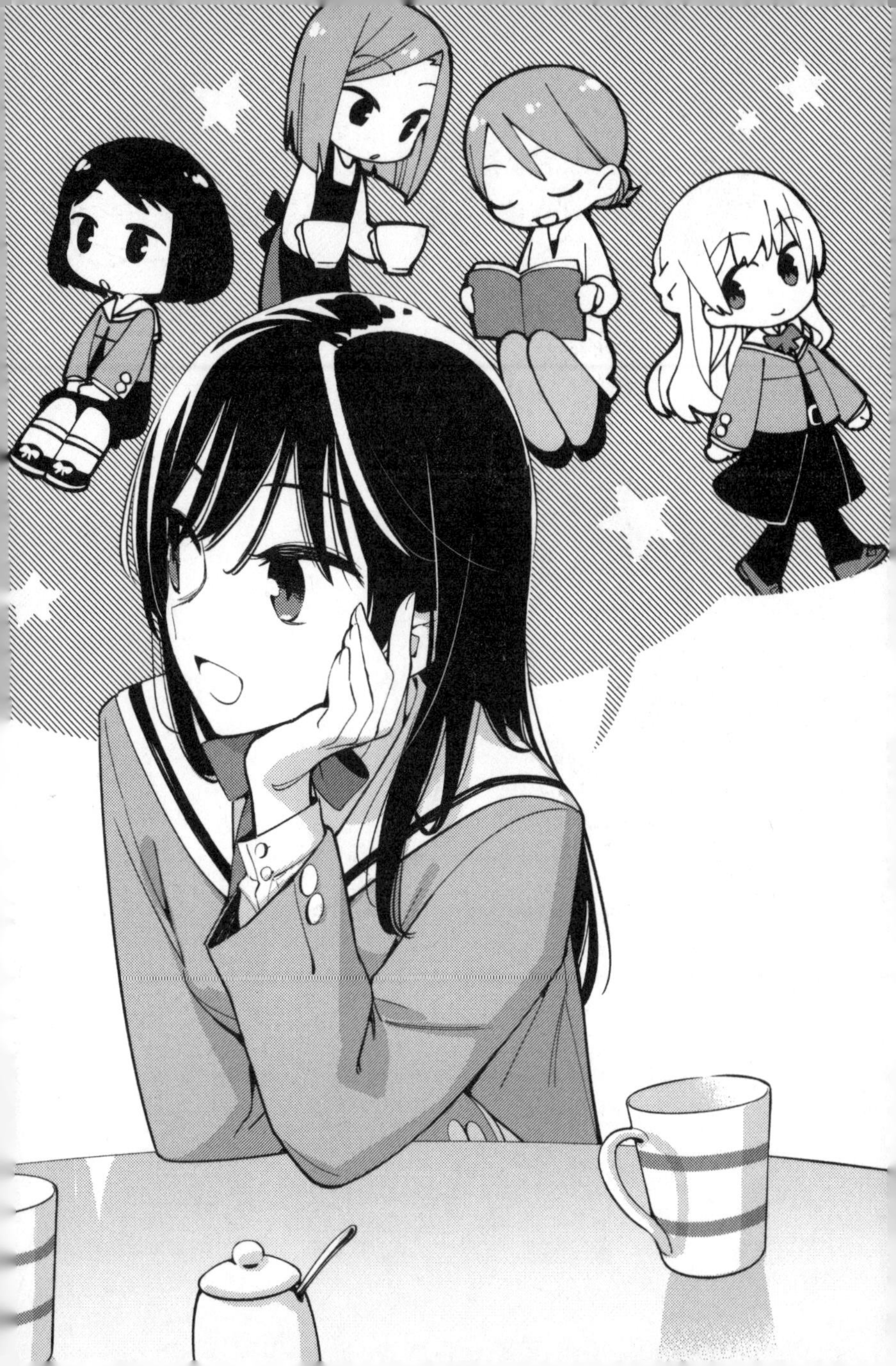

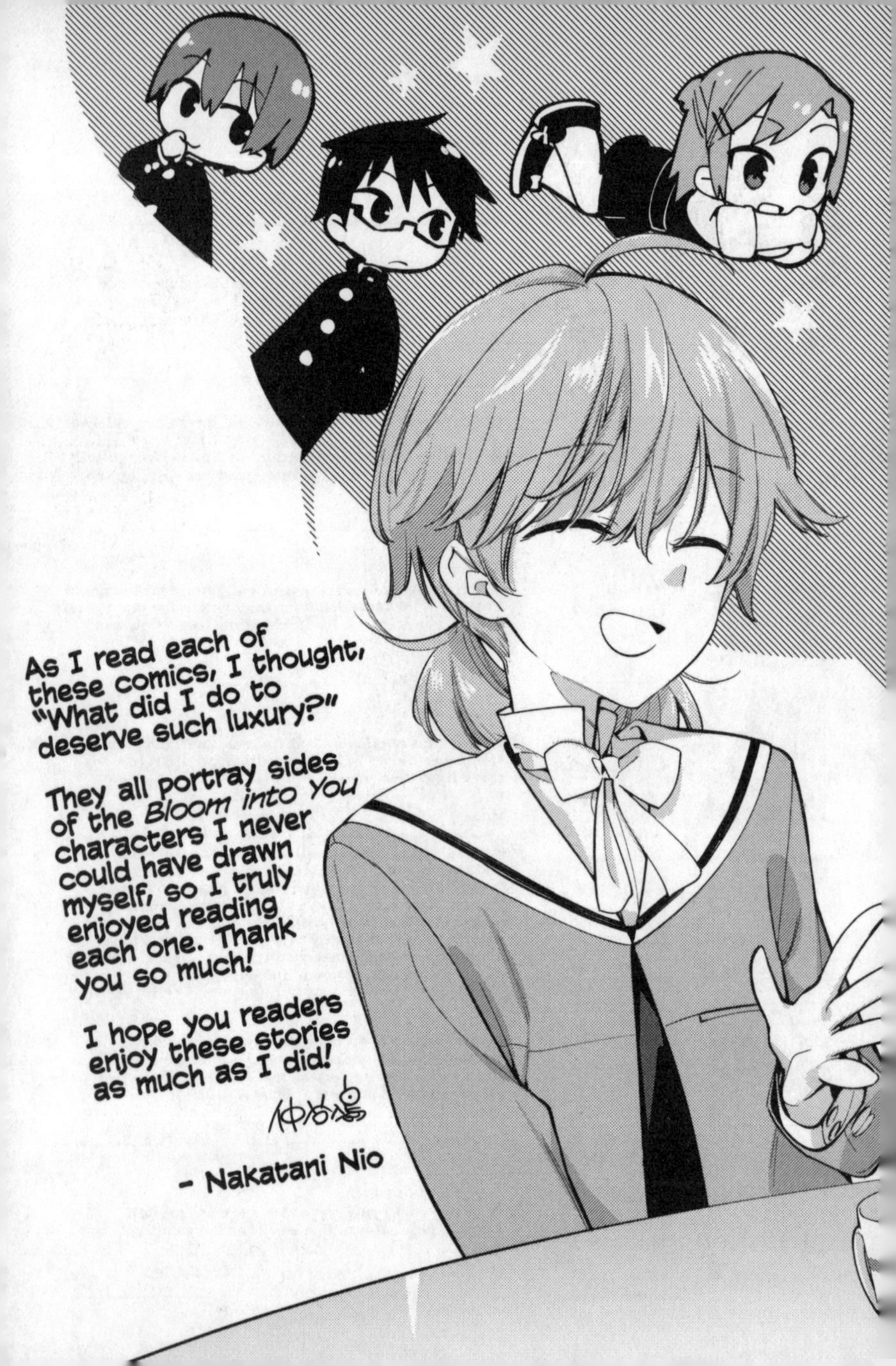
As I read each of these comics, I thought, "What did I do to deserve such luxury?"
They all portray sides of the *Bloom into You* characters I never could have drawn myself, so I truly enjoyed reading each one. Thank you so much!
I hope you readers enjoy these stories as much as I did!
- Nakatani Nio

Bloom Into You

Anthology

Afterwords

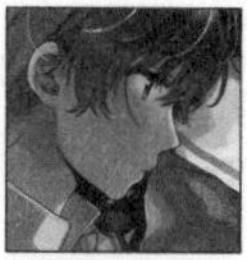

Name:
Fly

Congratulations on the anime and the publication of this anthology. I'm incredibly honored to have the chance to participate. Thank you very much.

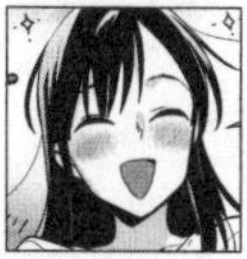

Name:
Yutaka Hiiragi

Congratulations on the anime and anthology release!

Every time I reread the manga, it fills my heart with joy. I look forward to finding out what will happen next!

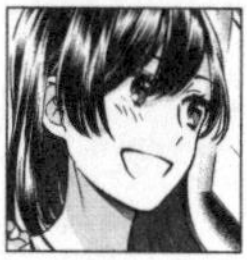

Name:
Canno

When I saw Saeki-senpai and Yuu-chan's birthdays in Volume 6, I was struck with inspiration for my piece! Thank you so much for inviting me to participate!

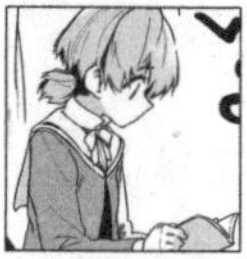

Name:
Chomoran

I loved that particular line (monologue?) in Chapter 1, so I was happy to be able to incorporate it into my story like this.

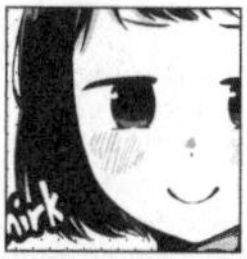

Name:
Okara Miyama

Congratulations on the *Bloom into You* anthology, and thank you for allowing me to create a story for it! I love the dynamic between Koyomi-chan and Yuu-chan, so it was really fun to draw them to my heart's content. When I read the recently released Volume 6, I cried quietly late into the night. I'm so happy to have encountered such a wonderful series. I'll keep supporting you to the end!

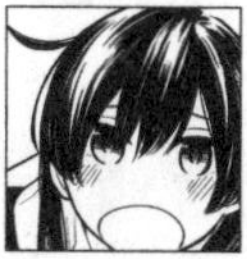

Name:
tMnR

Congratulations on publishing this anthology. My contribution ended up being a total fantasy story tailor-made to my own tastes, but I hope you all were able to enjoy it at least a little bit, too.

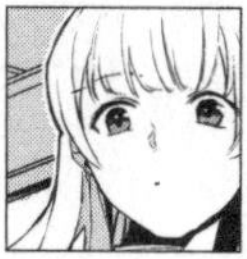

Name:
Kazuno Yuikawa

I'm a big Saeki-san supporter. I always mutter, "Touko, you... You're just so...!!" as I'm reading.

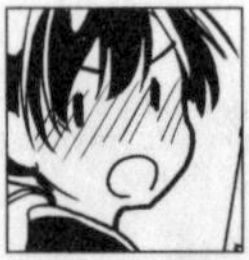

Name:
Mekimeki

Congratulations on the anime adaptation, and thank you for inviting me to join this wonderful project. It was a lot of fun drawing those two in yukata. I hope they'll find happiness wherever their slowly, carefully changing relationship leads.

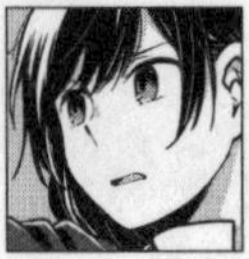

Name:
Aya Fumio

I love all the characters in *Bloom into You,* so I really enjoyed drawing them. I especially love Koyomi-chan!

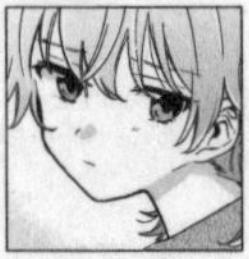

Name:
Moke

Congrats on the *Bloom into You* anthology! I love the series, so having a story appear in such a wonderful book was like a dream come true. I promise I won't take my eyes off Touko and Yuu!

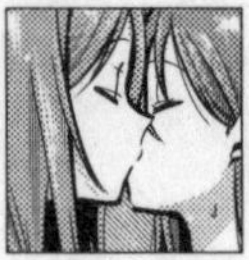

Name:
Hiroichi

When the working adult yuri couple first showed up, I was completely psyched!

I'm interested in the main story too, of course, but I'm equally interested in the developments between those two.

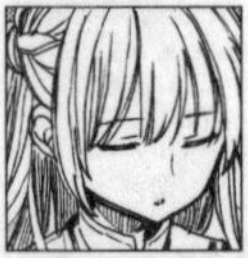

Name:
Hachi Ito

Congratulations on the release of this anthology. It was great to be able to draw these wonderful characters, so thank you very much for inviting me to participate.

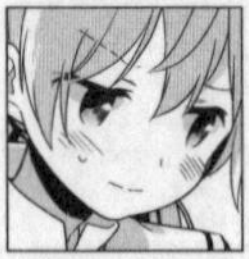

Name:
Tachi

Congratulations on the *Bloom into You* anthology! Sayaka-san was in the sketches for my story, but we decided to change it because she would never leave the student council room if she saw Touko-san's hair stuck like that. When the editor brought that up, I thought, "Aah, you're right!" In that moment, I really felt their love for the series. It was a pleasure to draw a story for the anthology! Thank you very much.

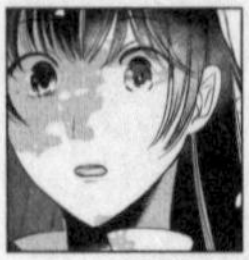

Name:
Yuriko Hara

I'm deeply grateful that I was invited to participate in this wonderful project. I drew the sketches for my story before I read Volume 6, but...Volume 6...! (*internal screaming*) As a huge fan, I'm dying to see what happens next!

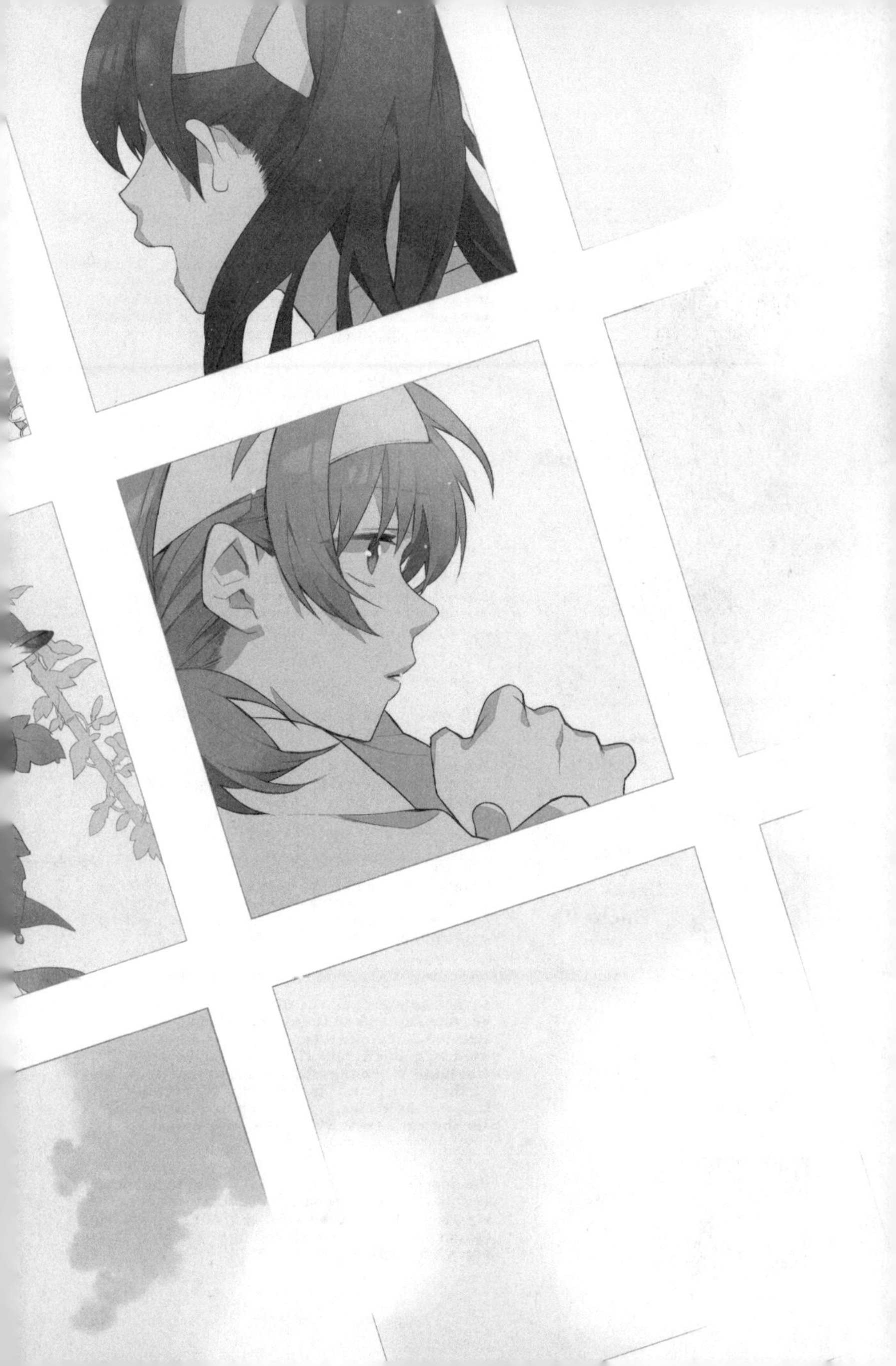

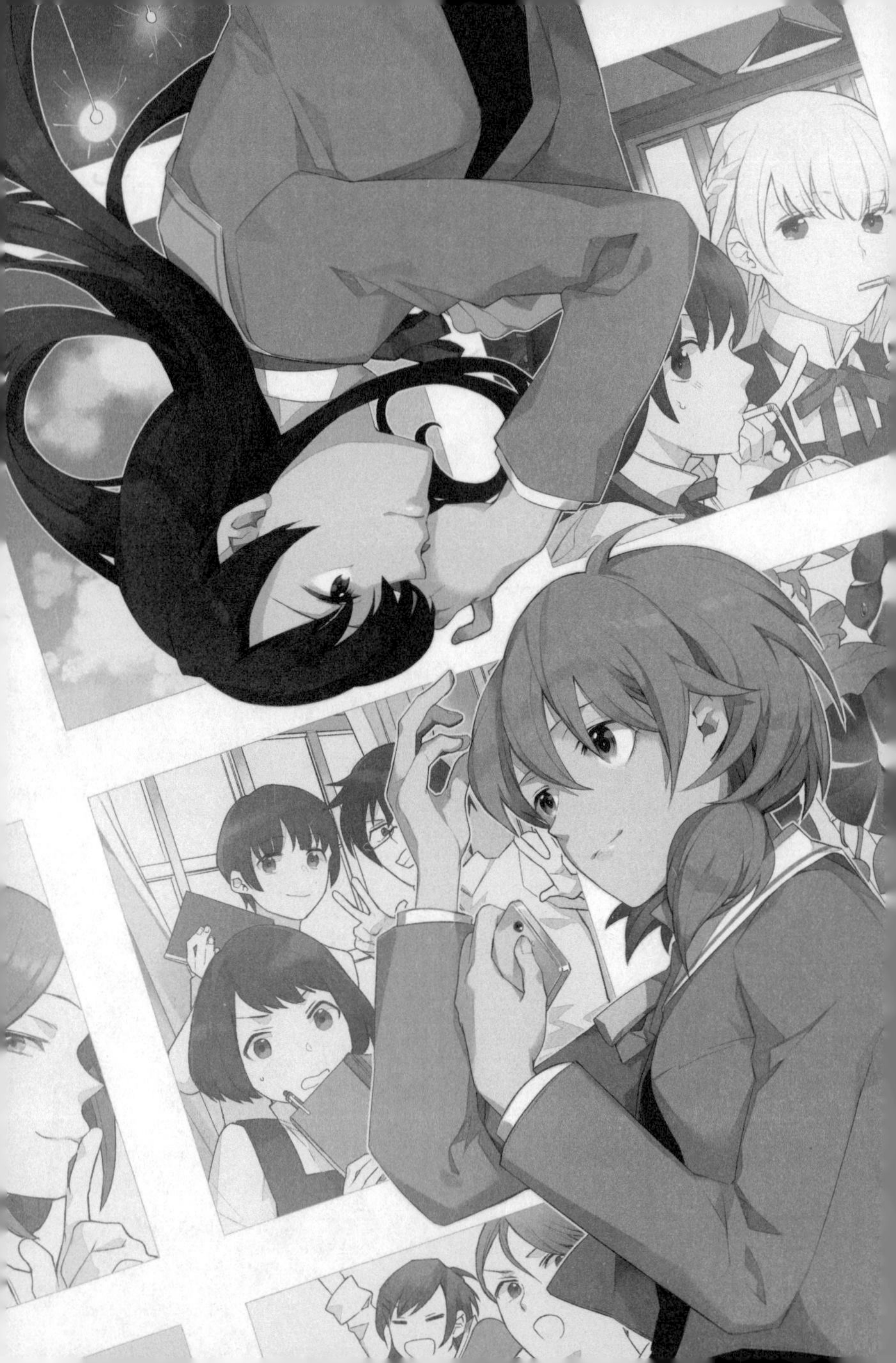

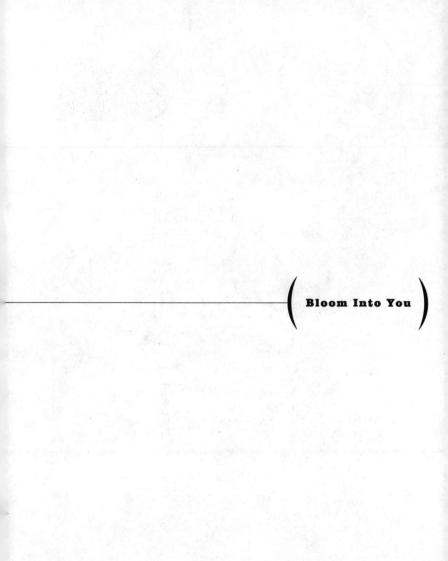

(Bloom Into You)

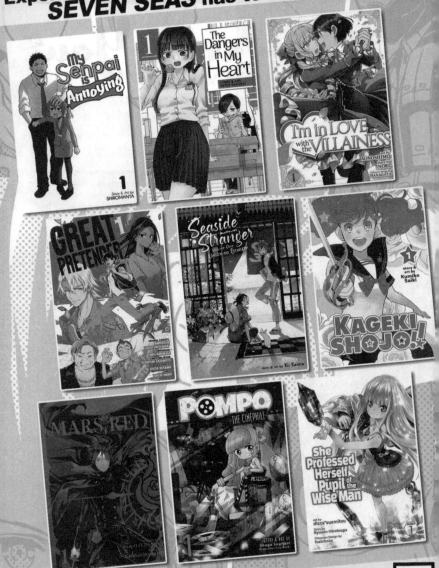

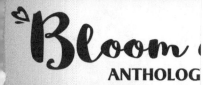

SEVEN SEAS ENTER...

Bloom
ANTHOLOG...

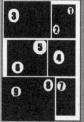

CW00566602

TRANSLATION
Jenny McKeon

LETTERING
CK Russell

COVER DESIGN
Nicky Lim

PROOFREADER
Danielle King

COPY EDITOR
Dawn Davis

EDITOR
Jenn Grunigen

PREPRESS TECHNICIAN
Rhiannon Rasmussen-Silverstein

PRODUCTION ASSOCIATE
Christa Miesner

PRODUCTION MANAGER
Lissa Pattillo

MANAGING EDITOR
Julie Davis

ASSOCIATE PUBLISHER
Adam Arnold

PUBLISHER
Jason DeAngelis

YAGATE KIMI NI NARU KOSHIKI COMIC ANTHOLOGY
©Nakatani Nio 2018
First published in Japan in 2018 by KADOKAWA CORPORATION, Tokyo.
English translation rights arranged with KADOKAWA CORPORATION, Tokyo.

Seven Seas press and purchase enquiries can be sent to Marketing Manager Lianne Sentar at press@gomanga.com. Information regarding the distribution and purchase of digital editions is available from Digital Manager CK Russell at digital@gomanga.com.

Seven Seas and the Seven Seas logo are trademarks of Seven Seas Entertainment. All rights reserved.

ISBN: 978-1-64827-788-7
Printed in Canada
First Printing: September 2021
10 9 8 7 6 5 4 3 2 1

READING DIRECTIONS

This book reads from *right to left*, Japanese style. If this is your first time reading manga, you start reading from the top right panel on each page and take it from there. If you get lost, just follow the numbered diagram here. It may seem backwards at first, but you'll get the hang of it! Have fun!!